India–Indonesia Bilateral Ties: An Introspection

India–Indonesia Bilateral Ties

Volume 1

An Introspection

Edited by

Gautam Kumar Jha

Son Kuswadi

Suryodaya Books

New Delhi

Cataloging in Publication Data — DK

[Courtesy: D.K. Agencies (P) Ltd. <docinfo@dkagencies.com>]

India-Indonesia Bilateral Ties (Conference) (2013 : Jawaharlal Nehru University)

India-Indonesia bilateral ties / edited by Gautam Kumar Jha, Son Kuswadi.

v. 1 cm.

Includes bibliographical references and index.

Contents: v. 1. An introspection.

ISBN 13: 9788192570235

1. India – Relations – Indonesia – Congresses. 2. Indonesia – Relations – India – Congresses. I. Jha, Gautam Kumar. II. Kuswadi, Son. III. Title.

DDC 327.540598 23

ISBN 13: 978-81-925702-3-5

First published in India in 2015

Printed and published by:

Suryodaya Books

"Suryodaya", D-36A/1, Mohan Garden

Najafgarh Road, New Delhi – 110 059

Phone: (011) 2535 3435

Distributed by:

D.K. Printworld (P) Ltd.

Regd. Office: "Vedaśrī", F-395, Sudarshan Park

(Metro Station: Ramesh Nagar), New Delhi – 110 015

Phones: (011) 2545 3975, 2546 6019; *Fax*: (011) 2546 5926

e-mail: indology@dkprintworld.com

Website: www.dkprintworld.com

Preface

This book is a culmination of our international conference on India–Indonesia Bilateral Ties (18-20 November 2013 at JNU, New Delhi), where a number of eminent scholars both from India and Indonesia spoke and presented their papers. The idea of having this conference was basically to bring the scholars from both the countries at one platform to have their deliberations as how we can take our bilateral ties to the next level, seeing a number of international issues arising in the region presently.

Indonesia being the largest country and one of the fastest growing economies in the South-East Asia is bestowed with abundant natural resources, and enjoys social, cultural and political stability compared to the other neighbouring countries. India, on the other hand, shares substantial cultural heritage with Indonesia and can collaborate in numerous areas for the welfare of mankind. As both the countries have strong democracy in governance, India and Indonesia are poised to make their presence felt internationally and here comes the strong need for overwhelming bilateral ties.

India and Indonesia have experienced very close historical and civilizational relations, which were actively fostered from the ancient times to sixteenth century CE. During the Indonesian freedom struggle, its leaders were very much inspired by the anti-colonial views of Rabindranath Tagore, Mahatma Gandhi, Jawaharlal Nehru, Vallabhbhai Patel and others.

The Indian National Congress had opposed British moves by expressing its resentment over the use of Indian resources, both human and material, against Indonesia and favoured the crusade for decolonization. Jawaharlal Nehru said:

> We must insist that no Indian troop is used against the Government of the Indonesian Republic and that no material of war is sent from India to help the Dutch government. We must help Indonesians wherever we can.

While expressing strong solidarity with Indonesians, he stated:

> I should like to convey to Dr Sukarno that if I can be of any service to the cause of Indonesian freedom, I shall gladly visit Java in spite of the urgent and important work in India.

During the post-colonial period, the bilateral relations passed through an incoherent phase coupled with confusion and misconceptions. None the less, well-wishers in both the countries worked hard to bring the derailed train back on the track. The Look East Policy (LEP) efforts initiated by the Indian government during the 1990s enabled her to participate actively in the South-East Asian affairs and happily Indonesia has proved itself as one of the greatest allies in realizing the overall objectives of LEP policy.

Indonesian economy has displayed growth and dynamism over the last few decades. Though problems remain, country's resilience in the wake of the current global economic crisis is commendable. There has been a remarkable improvement in the country's infrastructure.

Now, when both the countries are poised to fly high after having witnessed considerable economic reforms, they need to forge stronger ties in order to further expand bilateral trade and strategic relations.

In order to complete this great international conference we needed big manpower, financial and moral support and thankfully we received the same from the Embassy of Republic of Indonesia, New Delhi, ICSSR and JNU. As the conference was held in JNU we received overwhelming moral support from our Honourable Vice-Chancellor, Prof. Sudhir Kumar Sopory, Prof. Girijesh Pant, the Dean of School of International Studies, JNU, Prof. Aslam Islahi, the Dean of School of Language, Literature and Culture Studies, Prof. B.R. Deepak, the Chairperson, Centre for Chinese and Southeast Asian Studies, SLL & CS, JNU, Dr Girish Nath Jha, who presided over and spoke during the inauguration ceremony of the conference.

We are thankful to His Excellency Mr Rizali W. Indrakesuma, the Ambassador of Republic of Indonesia to India for his message, and Mrs Navrekha Sharma, the former Ambassador of India to Indonesia, and Prof. Baladas Ghoshal, the former Chairperson in School of International Studies, JNU, for giving keynote speech and participating the conference throughout.

We are thankful to Prof. Ganganath Jha and Prof. Manmohini Kaul, from the School of International Studies, who cared to encourage us by chairing the sessions. In this endeavour we would like to mention the names of our beloved students and scholars without whose support we would not have thought of success of this conference: Hammam, Rizki H. Attahiyat, Dodi Siregar, Dini Siregar, Budianto, Suhendri, Rehita Hasian Batubara, Dilyana Putrianza, Rahma Melina, Mustafa, Chaerul, Eko, Dosman Manalu, Kiki, Anurima Chanda, Raveesh Rajayanya, Mukesh Kumar, Siddharth Chakravarti, Azhar, Geeta and Bandana.

Gautam Kumar Jha
Son Kuswadi

Contents

Abbreviations

ADMM	ASEAN Defence Ministers Meeting
ADMM+	ASEAN Defence Ministers Meeting Plus
AICHR	ASEAN Inter-governmental Commission on Human Rights
APEC	Asia-Pacific Economic Cooperation
APSC	ASEAN Political and Security Community
APT	ASEAN Plus Three
ARF	ASEAN Regional Forum
ASEAN	Association of South East Asian Nations
ASEAN-ISIS	ASEAN Institutes of Strategic and International Studies
ASG	Abu Sayyaf Group
BIS	Bureau of Indian Standards
BJP	Bharatiya Janata Party
BKPM	Badan Kerjasama Penanaman Modal (Indonesia Investment Coordinating Board)
BRICS	Brazil, Russia, India, China, and South Africa
BSN	Indonesian National Standardization Agency
BTMF	Biennial Trade Ministers' Forum
CECA	Comprehensive Economic Cooperation Agreement
CII	Confederation of Indian Industry

COC	Code of Conduct
COMESA	Common Market of Eastern and Southern Africa
CORPATs	Coordinated Patrols
CPI–SEA	Convention of Pharmaceutical Ingredients – South East Asia
CSCAP	Council for Security Cooperation in the Asia Pacific
CTBT	Comprehensive Nuclear-Test-Ban Treaty
CVC	Central Vigilance Commission
D-8	Developing–Eight
DMK	Dravida Munnetra Kazhagam (DMK)
EAS	East Asia Summit
EEZ	Exclusive Economic Zone
EPG	Eminent Persons Group
FDI	Foreign Direct Investment
FHI	Freedom House Index
FICCI	Federation of Indian Chambers of Commerce and Industry
FMCG	Fast Moving Consumer Goods
FMD	Foot and Mouth Disease
FMF	Foreign Military Financing
FMS	Foreign Military Sales
FTAs	Free Trade Agreements
GAM	Gerakan Aceh Merdeka
GATS	General Agreement on Trade in Services
GDP	Gross Domestic Product
HADR	Humanitarian Assistance and Disaster Relief

HDI	Human Development Index
HMI	Himpunan Mahasiswa Islam
HUT	Hizb ut Tehrir
IAIN	State Academy of Islamic Sciences
IBF	India Business Forum
ICC	International Cricket Council
ICMI	Indonesian Association of Muslim Intellectuals
ICSSR	Indian Council for Social Science Research
IMET	International Military Education and Training
IMF	International Monetary Fund
IONS	Indian Ocean Naval Symposium
IORA	Indian Ocean Rim Association
IOR-ARC	Indian Ocean Rim Association for Regional Co-operation
IOR	Indian Ocean Rim
ISO	Islamic Students Organization
JDCC	Joint Defence Co-operation Committee
JMM	Jharkhand Mukti Morcha
JNU	Jawaharlal Nehru University
JWG	Joint Working Groups
KADIN	Indonesian Chamber of Commerce
KMM	Kumputan Militant Malaysia
KPK	Komisi Pemberantasan Korupsi
LEP	Look East Policy
MERCOSUR	Southern Common Market
MMTC	Metals and Minerals Trading Corporation of India
MoU	Memorandum of Understanding

MRAs	Mutual Recognition Arrangements
NAFTA	North American Free Trade Agreement
NAM	Non-Aligned Movement
NTBs	Non-tariff Barriers
NU	Nahdtlaul Ulama
OFDI	Outward Foreign Direct Investment
OIC	Organisation of Islamic Conference
OIC	Organization of Islamic Countries
OLI	Ownership Location and Internalization
PKI	Indonesian Communist Party
PPP	Partai Persatuan Pembangunan (PPP)
RCEP	Regional Comprehensive Economic Partnership
RJD	Rashtriya Janata Dal
R&D	Research and Development
SAARC	South Asian Association for Regional Cooperation
SCS	South China Sea
SEANWFZ	Southeast Asian Nuclear Weapons Free Zone
SEATO	Southeast Asia Treaty Organization
SEEPZ	Santacruz Electronic Export Processing Zone
SEZs	Special Economic Zones
SLOCs	Sea Lines of Communication
STC	Society for Technical Communication
TIFA	Trade and Investment Framework Agreement
TNC	Trade Negotiations Committee
TOR	Terms of Reference
TPP	Trans-Pacific Partnership
UDP	United Development Party

UN	United Nations
UNCTAD	United Nations Conference on Trade and Development
UNDP	United National Development Programme
UNSC	United Nations Security Council
WTO	World Trade Organization
ZOPFAN	Zone of Peace, Freedom and Neutrality

AMBASSADOR
REPUBLIC OF INDONESIA

NEW DELHI

MESSAGE

The present book *India–Indonesia Bilateral Ties: An Introspection* is a culmination of the International Conference on India–Indonesia Bilateral Ties, held during 18-20 November 2013, where a constellation of scholars from both the countries presented papers and indulged in academic discourses to converge our efforts to forge stronger bilateral ties between the two nations. At the three-day international conference, the course of discussions happened over a range of topics: politics, strategy, social, religion, art and culture.

I think the present work is significant as it could serve as a guideline for both the governments to respond to the needs of the people and realize the same by bringing various policies in order to understand each other better and bring both the countries as close as possible.

Indonesia is the most populous and largest economy in Southeast Asia, aspiring to fly high amid numerous challenges. I think it is the same with India. Thus it is easier for us to identify such challenges and work to resolve the roadblocks for the welfare of the common people.

I congratulate Prof. S.K. Sopory, the Honourable Vice Chancellor of Jawaharlal Nehru University (JNU); Prof. Aslam Islahi, the Dean School of Languages, Literature & Culture Studies, JNU; Prof. B.R. Deepak, Chairperson; Dr Gautam Kumar Jha, Centre for Chinese & Southeast Asian Studies, School of Languages, Literature & Culture Studies, JNU; Dr Son Kuswadi, the Education Attaché of the Indonesian Embassy, New Delhi; and Mr Hammam, the President of the Association of Indonesian Overseas Students, New Delhi for the success of this conference. I would also like to thank and congratulate all the participants for their enthusiasm and interest which contributed to its success.

New Delhi
16 April 2014

Rizali W. Indrakesuma

KEYNOTE ADDRESS

1

India–Indonesia : Natural Partners?

Navrekha Sharma

WHEN Indonesia's President Susilo Bambang Yudhoyono (popularly known as SBY) came to India three years ago as the chief guest of the Republic Day celebrations, the *Deccan Herald* (23 February 2011) welcomed the development and described India and Indonesia as "natural partners". Others too picked up the theme and used it in their commentaries. One is drawn therefore to explore it a little more deeply. What does "natural partnership" mean exactly? Is it about being similar or is it about being different? Perhaps it is about being complementary?

If it is true that Indonesia and India are indeed "natural partners" we should welcome the fact wholeheartedly but not otherwise. In international relations in general and diplomacy in particular, it is important to avoid harsh language, but even more important not to allow sentimentality to cloud ones judgement. At a time of celebration of India's growing relations with Indonesia this note of caution may sound provocative or even perverse! However, it springs from a genuine concern of India–Indonesia "natural partners". By using extravagant words we may become complacent and fail to perform the hard work which is required to build a strong relationship between two countries. Indonesia is too important to India that is cannot treat the former lightly.

We have to recollect that the strong links that existed between India and Indonesia for over a millennia, were broken 300 years ago when our countries came under the sway of two equally ruthless (but also very different) colonial powers. The break continued until the early twentieth century when, with the growing spirit of nationalism in Asia, both the countries produced visionary leaders who started the struggle against the colonizers. Nehru and Hatta who first met in Brussels in the 1930s, took inspiration from one another but, because of critical differences between British colonization and Dutch colonization, their chosen forms of resistance were not identical. India resorted to persuasion and non-violence for the most part, while Indonesia was forced to wage an armed revolution for four years before the Dutch conceded to indonesia's demand for independence. During these four years, India gave Indonesia unstinting and critical support, both in material and diplomatic means. In January 1950, Indonesia's President Soekarno came to New Delhi to grace India's first Republic Day celebrations in response to an invitation from Nehru. But his purpose of calling was also to thank the Indian government for supporting Indonesia's *Revolusi*. Three months later, Nehru reciprocated Soekarno's call with a ten-day visit to Indonesia which he has very movingly described in his *Memoirs*. For several years thereafter, earnest attempts by both leaders to build a "Brave New World" based on ideals of multilateralism and faith in the United Nations kept them together but gradually, ego issues intervened and inter-personal relations turned sour.

Externally, the Cold War began to sink into both countries' consciousness and the euphoria of Asian relations and Bandung was replaced by a harsher sense of reality. Had a strong economic underpinning been built into the relationship, perhaps these setbacks would have been overcome, but unfortunately this was not done. Indeed the most important take away from the first twenty years of independent India's history with Indonesia is this: even between the best of friends, it is important not to rely on friendship alone. A solid economic base to bilateral relations could have given our relations a second line of defence and the disaster which followed might have been avoided.

After President Soeharto took power in 1967, normalcy was restored but not the euphoria. Both countries came to terms with a world in which power, not principle, was the primary fuel of international relations. National interests located them on opposite sides of the Cold War fence and they started to pay lip service to the Non-Aligned Movement (NAM) (the Indonesians call it Free and Active Foreign Policy) which they had themselves founded. Indeed, Soeharto often skipped NAM Summit Meetings. For three decades, relations between India and Indonesia continued in this vein, i.e. civil but indifferent. It was only after the Cold War had ended (1989), after India had started to Look East (1992) and after the Soeharto dictatorship fell (1998), that external conditions changed and the partnership once again started to warm up.

Today, the two countries are meeting after a long period of virtual stagnation and it is not surprising that they are cautious about opening up too many fronts of engagement too soon. Trade is growing well but shows very little diversification; there is little or no Indonesian investment in India and while there has been phenomenal growth of air traffic between India and the ASEAN countries, there is as yet no direct airline plying between India and Indonesia. Indeed eight years ago Air India closed its limited service of three flights a week to Jakarta! Fortunately, the leaders of both countries are fully aware of the contextual nuances and are doing their best to bring relations to their fullest creative potential by combining a forward-looking approach with patience and sensitivity. To build confidence between countries is hard work; however, doing so after overcoming historical baggage is still harder! Governments alone cannot do the job; academics, media, cultural personalities, youth, ordinary people and of course traders, businessmen and industrialists, will have to get involved.

To return now to the question what constitutes a "natural partnership", Is it similarities, differences or complementarities? The distinctions are important. Indians love to dwell upon cultural similarities with Indonesia, but this should not be a one-sided exercise as it has tended to be in the past. Besides, India's experience in dealing with her immediate neighbours in South Asia shows that similarities are interesting but not always useful. Indeed they can even be counter-productive if they make countries mistrustful of those they think they know too well! Differences, on the other hand, can provide traction to a relationship and help take it forward but if countries are too different they may not establish common ground for dialogue at all! Complementarity is a sounder basis of friendship. However, to discover the areas where useful complementarities lie, diplomats in both countries need to make a huge effort. Engaging diligently, exploring unfamiliar ground, learning new languages, etc. and more are needed if the many complementarities between India and Indonesia are to be used to mutual advantage. Above all, one needs a clear vision about what one wants from the relationship. If the vision is unclear all the efforts will be futile.

A healthy partnership in other words, even a so-called "natural" one, demands identification of common interests. This is a self-evident truism but it needs to be emphasized over and over again! For nothing grows "naturally" in international relations. Clarity of vision, calibration of approach and hard work alone can produce results.

What are then the main common interests of India and Indonesia?

In international relations size matters. Indians, especially from the continental north, do not always realize this, but Indonesia with 17,000 islands covering an area of 3 million sq. miles (inclusive of Exclusive Economic Zone) is the world's largest archipelagic state and as world's fourth largest population. She is abundantly rich in mineral resources. Her geographical location is crucial too for it being located along the world's most important sea lane, the Malacca Strait (which she controls together with Malaysia and Singapore). She also has the Sunda and Lombok straits under her exclusive control. These factors in combination make Indonesia one of the world's most important countries.

As a naval power India would like to maintain peace and tranquillity in the Indian Ocean for which she needs friends along the littoral. Unsurprisingly, therefore, one of India's primary interests in a friendly Indonesia is to promote maritime security. But with her economy expanding rapidly, India has legitimate needs to secure internationally recognized rights to peaceful passage even beyond the Indian Ocean in East Asia and the Pacific. India presently gets her energy from West Asia and not through the Malacca Straits, but she has a strong potential interest in energy (oil and gas) and other valuable resource materials both in Indonesia and beyond. Her investments in Indonesian coal are already extensive while Indonesia is India's biggest source of palm oil.

But India's interests in Indonesia go beyond the material links. Remember that the world's largest concentration of Muslims lives in Indonesia, but Indonesia is not a theocratic state. Traditionally Indonesians are under *sufi* influence and hence broadminded and eclectic. These qualities are reflected in their secular, pluralist and (now) democratic, constitutional framework which is much like India's (the main difference is that the Indian Constitution permits atheism while the Indonesian "Pancasila" Constitution does not). But India's own muslim population is second in size only to Indonesia's and, therefore, at the minimum, India would be concerned if anything were to happen to disturb the region's finely balanced, socio-political structures. Maximally of course (in a post-9/11 world) India and Indonesia, who's voice is hardly heard on the role and future of Islam in the world, could make a significant impact if they were to combine forces and join the discourse. For all these reasons and more, a friendly Indonesia is vital for Indian interests.

What are Indonesia's interests in India? From Indonesia's point of view, it is no secret that historical and present-day concerns regarding China made her reach out to India initially. Indonesia was India's most vocal and consistent supporter in ASEAN, having influenced the development of regional political and economic institutions favourable to India from ASEAN Regional Forum (ARF) in 1996 to EAst Asia Summit (EAS) in 2004. Today, India with her expanding technical and economic clout and investments in Indonesia is in her own right a valuable friend and partner for Indonesia. Many Indians have brought technology and employment opportunities to Indonesia (while enriching themselves too). Second, Indonesia's growing economic and political strength and her success with democracy particularly in contrast with West Asia (with whom Indonesia is often compared) have given her recognition in the world beyond ASEAN. With her large agricultural potential and mineral wealth, Indonesia is today heard with respect in multilateral fora such as World Trade Organization (WTO). On global issues such as environment, Indonesia (host to the world's largest forest reserves after Brazil), holds a commanding voice. International recognition is feeding legitimate ambitions to secure a place on the high tables of the world along with India, Russia and others for which Indonesia needs Indian support. She was pleased to receive the invitation to join G-20 but expressed (informally and at an individual level) dismay at not being in BRICS, an invitation she well deserves. Defence and space technology, English language, IT and agriculture are some of the areas which Indonesia has herself identified for co-operation with India. With more dialogue and increasing confidence, other areas of co-operation could be considered.

The dialogue between India and Indonesia has picked up well in recent years. The calendar of high level visits between the two countries is revealing: eight heads of state/government level visits have taken place to and fro since 2000, which is quite a change from the Soeharto era when, in thirty-two years, not even half as many took place! All elected presidents after Soeharto have made it a point to prioritize an early visit to India and, helped by the regional and multi-lateral occasions where they meet as well, comfort levels between our leaders have risen considerably in the last few years. Meetings at ministerial level or between business delegations now take place regularly.

In 2005 during a state visit by President SBY to India, a strategic partnership between India and Indonesia was established which opened the field for development of ties in the political, security, defence, commercial and cultural fields. In 2011 when SBY again came to India as chief guest on India's Republic Day, eighteen business deals for a total value of $ 15 billion were signed. Although the action upon them subsequently has not been as rapid as hoped (perhaps because of the slowdown in the world's economy), another goal, to raise bilateral trade to US $ 25 billion by 2015 from the present US $ 18/20 billion is considered achievable. Since 2007 a regular defence secretary level dialogue has been taking place (under an agreement signed in 2001) to which was joined a defence minister level dialogue in October 2012. Cultural exchanges too are frequent which was not the case even a few years ago. Film festivals, dance performances, photography and painting exhibitions, etc. rare just six years ago, are a daily feature of bilateral relations today. In September 2013 the Government of Indonesia organized an International Ramayana festival at the Prambanam Temple Complex in Jogyakarta under the aegis of ICCR. In this festival, a joint production of the *Ramayana* was performed by Indonesians together with artists from India's Sri Ram Bharatiya Kala Kendra. It received an overwhelming response and travelled to several towns in east Java and Bali also, later.

Where should relations go in the future? India and Indonesia are large Asian countries who also happen to be direct maritime neighbours. Over millennia of trading across the Indian Ocean, important commercial links were forged between them which are still visible in peoples' food, cloths, languages, etc. India may have started recently to Look East, but Indonesia for over 1,000 years has looked with awe to the West. The Bahasa Indonesian word for West is Barat (from the Sanskrit Bharat)! Javanese muslims of high lineage still carry Sanskrit names together with a Muslim/Malay name, e.g. Indonesia's president who's name is Susilo Bambang Yudhoyono or our dear friend Indonesia's Ambassador to India Rizali Indrakusuma! Bahasa Indonesian language, which was created to promote Nationalism in the 1920s, abandoned many Sanskrit words and incorporated words from Malay, Dutch, English, Arabic, etc. instead (words which were commonly used in Indonesia's port towns) but it retains many words of Sanskrit origin still. Also from India came the art of writing, three major religions Hinduism, Buddhism and much later, Islam; kingship and statecraft, courtly manners and customs, symbolism and ceremonial. Architecture, mythology (*Ramayana* and *Mahabharata*) and dance came from India to Indonesia although sometimes local innovation is so rich that only traces of the original can be made out. Most of these cultural transfers occurred in Java, where 60 per cent of

Indonesia's people live and from where, thanks to the presence of the capital city Jakarta, Indonesia continues to be governed. Sumatra received influences from India such as Buddhism in the early stages and later, Islam from Gujarat. People of Kalimantan, Sulawesi and Papua by and large are tribal and/or converts to Christianity. Modern India and Indonesia are thus similar in sharing an ancient heritage of multiple cultures, languages and ethnicities who reside side by side. In both countries the followers of a single religious majority (Hindus in India, Muslims in Indonesia) live amidst smaller minorities of other faiths.

This makes Indonesia a virtual "mirror" of India. In a closer partnership, inter-community best practices in one could have a ripple effect on the other and help to keep both on their toes. Javanese Islam has many Hindu and Buddhist practices woven into it which makes Indonesians eclectic and, with only occasional aberrations, moderate. Like the practice of Hinduism in India, Islam in Indonesia has cultural nuances and varies from place to place. Demographically youthful, creative, energetic and capable of high levels of productivity under the right conditions, Indians and Indonesians get along well with one another at the inter-personal level. Indonesians love watching Indian films and sway to Bollywood tunes even if they do not understand the words! In both the countries it is not religious extremism but corruption and nepotism, inflation, pollution and rising inequality which are the day-to-day concerns. Indonesia globalized earlier than India under Soeharto, who made the term "crony capitalism" known to the world but India is fast catching up, alas!

One institution which intrigues Indonesians is India's Federalism. Federalism allowed India to carve out linguistic states and yet maintain the nation's integrity. In Indonesia, thanks mainly to her fragmented geography, a single language was felt to be necessary in the early years of Indonesia's national movement but today some Indonesians are beginning to miss the creative energy which was lost when Indonesia officially abandoned her multiplicity of languages. Adoption of Shariah laws in various districts of Indonesia today is a poor substitute for Federalism and in the long run could even prove harmful. India's loosely-structured Federal polity helped promote curiosity, flexibility and resourcefulness in people and lent itself to building higher human resource capabilities. But conversely, Indonesia's strongly centralized state did better in addressing mass poverty, illiteracy, gender and health care. While literacy in Indonesia is close to 100 per cent, many Indians lack primary education for which until now there was no state compulsion. The UNDP's Human Development Index (HDI) for 2013 shows India's overall HDI to be below Indonesia's (136 against Indonesia's 121). Given their complementarities, important lessons can be learned by both from one another.

Yuwono Sudarsono, one of Indonesia's formost intellectuals, former diplomat and formerly also Indonesia's minister of defence, says:[1]

> . . . both India and Indonesia must come to terms in rebuilding a more equitable political and economic system. The notion of India as the largest and Indonesia as the third largest democracy must be substantiated by seriously addressing existing critical micro and macro socio-economic disparities, iniquities and abject poverty. . . .

and further,

> the leadership commitment and effective capacity to deliver robust and distributive political and socio-economic goods

---

[1] Yuwono Sudarsono," India and Indonesia, the Performance Commitment", *Decades of Dynamic Diplomatic Relations*, a publication of Indonesia's Ministry of Foreign Affairs to mark six decades of Diplomatic Relations.

> in both countries seems to be hampered by a system that largely serves the interests of vested groups.

The fight against poverty and for redistributive justice in both India and Indonesia is far from over. In the years to come one would hope to see both countries tackle these issues through sustained and focused partnership. No common interest is more important than this fight which concerns directly the peoples' economic prosperity, physical state of health and well-being, and the overall intellectual growth and happiness.

Terimah Kasih

KEYNOTE ADDRESS

2

India–Indonesia
Economic and Foreign Policy

Baladas Ghoshal

THERE is a lot of scope in India–Indonesia bilateral co-operation, be it cultural, economic, industrial or trade. In addition to these common factors what comes to my mind is our mutual co-operation in state building and state formation. What makes it possible is the similarity between India and Indonesia. If I say, there are no two other countries in Asia as similar as India and Indonesia. Both are multicultural, multilingual and multi-religious societies or diverse societies, or what we call plural societies. And all plural societies face certain challenges in nation building. Both India and Indonesia experience the same kind of challenges in terms of integrating the various communities, groups and so on. Sometimes, sharing of experiences can also enhance co-operation between two countries, especially in foreign policies.

India has a federal structure and was quite successful in integrating the various regions, having a structure of central and state governments. Indonesia is a multi-racial, multicultural archipelago, and thus has a multi-racial or multicultural society. It is trying to build up a strong nation having governance only at the central level. This paves the way for both the nations to understand and imbibe useful experiences for the welfare of their people and better governance. Each can provide the other certain experiences. For example, in spite of the talks about separation here and there, India has been able to evolve a kind of a bargain federalism, and has been able to bring about some equation between the centre and the states. And even for the distribution of revenues and other resources, there are institutional mechanisms which have been able to create a durable system by which the centre and state relations are instituted and well maintained. Indonesia today is one of the most decentralized nations in the world. In fact, practically many of the functions which were dealt by the centre once are now being managed by the provinces and the districts. In Indonesia due to the absence of strong institutional mechanisms, some of the administrative functions have not really worked well. And sometimes people do talk about the need to decentralize powers to curb corruption and to make the administration more efficient. What I would like to envisage in the relationship between India and Indonesia is an exchange of their experiences of how they have addressed some of these issues in terms of developing centre–state relations and also their experiences in terms of nation building.

To my mind, the nation-building process has not yet been completed in either of these countries although it might sound a little bit strange to talk about it. I think there are lots of issues which need to be addressed in integrating the different regions of the country and in completing the democratization process of the entire society. And in the democratization process, I firmly believe that India and Indonesia can learn from each other's experiences.

Another major issue that comes to my mind is again related to nation building. Since the federal states are not properly integrated both the countries face many a challenge. One of the challenges is religious fundamentalism or terrorism, and both India and Indonesia have been victims of this development in the last few years. And this is one area where there is also some institutional arrangement between India and Indonesia is required to co-operate with each other. Indonesia has a wider experience in handling many of the issues related to terrorism — in the last couple of years Indonesia has been able to develop an institutional mechanism by which it could reduce the terrorist challenges to a large extent. Still those challenges are there, but I think Indonesia could do a lot in terms of reducing the menace of terrorism to a manageable level. And India can take a cue from Indonesia in this regard in arresting terrorism within its soil. I am confident that this will pave the way for broadening the co-operation between the two countries on this particular front — in facing the challenges of international and domestic terrorism. Having said so, one should not come to the conclusion that no other areas are not pertinent as that of terrorism. There are other areas as well, like climate change and environmental issues. India, Indonesia and many of the other countries in Asia face similar environmental challenges. So, this is another area where we can build up co-operation. This coming together of Asian countries will enable them to jointly put up a strong stand against the Western pressures that some of these countries face today in climate change talks.

Now having said that, one of the most important aspects of the relationship between any two countries also depends to a large extent on how one perceives the other — as inimical, friendly or without having any strategic content. If one looks back and audits the relationship between India and Indonesia from the time of their Independence movements, one could see a chain of ups and downs in their relationship, how they perceived each other, or what I call the gravitational pulls between the two countries. And without this gravitational pull, I do not think that a mature relationship can develop and sustain between two countries. When one goes back and looks at the period after independence, one gets some ideas as how both India and Indonesia shaped up their policies, and one can really establish this gravitational pull and understand how it influenced the relationships between the two countries. Indonesia declared its Independence in 1945, but officially it became independent in December 1949 after Holland transferred formal authority to the republic as well as the other constituent states (sixteen constituent states at that time). It is worthy to analyse why there existed a close relationship between Indonesia and India in the late 1940s as well as early 1950s. I think the gravitational pull played that role. Indonesia was in a relatively weak position as it was facing a lot of pressure from the Western world. Even though Indonesia declared her independence, the Dutch came back and started their military operations against the Republican forces. This made Indonesia quite weak. It really needed the support of another country in the region which could really champion the cause of its independence. India played an important role in mobilizing international support for Indonesia's cause in the international forum. Diplomatically too, India provided a lot of support in the early period. It also provided certain amount of material support during that period. This involvement of India in the freedom fight of Indonesia made their relationship strong, which gradually got matured in the early 1950s. So, a good relationship was established between the two countries. At the same time, India was looking for support from the Asian countries for its policy of non-alignment.

When India got Independence, there was very little economic and military resources to establish itself a leader in the region. But it had the advantage of history, that India had a long civilization and it was a large country at one time. So, the advantage of history prompted India to evolve its foreign policy through which it could mediate a kind of international environment at that time. The best way India found was to adopt a policy of non-alignment. Non-alignment was not an ideal position for India. It was not based on the very realistic assumptions of India's needs and requirements, but it was a political consideration that prompted India to adopt its foreign policy. What India opted to do at that point of time was to adopt the policy of non-alignment and through which it was trying to establish closer links with some of the countries in the region. India pursued a policy, what I call a diplomacy of proclamation, by which it focused on the principles of non-alignment, anti-racialism, anti-colonialism, and tried to build up relationship with the countries on the basis of this diplomatic initiative. In this initiative of India, Indonesia was a strong ally, and that is why in the late 1940s and the early 1950s India and Indonesia collaborated very closely in different areas, especially in the domain of non-alignment. In fact, among all the countries in South-East Asia, the closest relationship was between India and Indonesia.

However, in this relationship, there was hardly any economic content. No relation can sustain only on ideological principles unless it is backed by certain stakes such as economic and trade initiatives. The economic interactions were bare minimum. The lack of economic relationship and inter-dependence resulted in the fast depletion of the relationship. The gravitational pull was no longer there, neither for Indonesia, nor for India. In the early period, Indonesia needed India, and India also needed Indonesia, and that is why there was closer relationship between the two.

But as both began to get involved in the day-to-day nation-building exercise and also get involved in the complexities of the Cold War and similar issues, they diverged at some point of time. I think the first indication of that divergence came in the Bandung Conference. Although this conference was considered a big success in Asian–African solidarity, cracks began to appear in Bandung itself, on many of these issues. Now this is not the time to delve elaborately on those issues, but one point is certain. On many issues of world politics, countries began to differ in Bandung itself. India was trying to bring China into the Asian world order by promoting the cause of China. Indonesia was not willing; none of the Asian countries in the beginning was actually willing to invite China to the Bandung Conference. It was India's initiative that prompted them to accept China. Nehru told everyone to accept China in the committee of Asian nations, but India began to experience problems with China from 1955 onwards. This caused a big gap between what India was talking in terms of international Asian order and its own practice of its relationship with China.

In the case of Indonesia, the domestic politics reached such a stage where Sukarno failed to provide the kind of stability within the country in terms of nation building. He was looking for a foreign policy through which he could make an imprint within the state and that is why he started talking about the new emerging force, the old forces and all that. Now the kind of world-view that India and Indonesia began to develop in 1955 was so different from each other that there was hardly any meeting ground between the two countries. Whereas India's, I mean Nehru's, concept of world was that of accepting the existing world order while trying to reform it by co-operation between the East and the West. Now, Indonesia's view was that this international order itself was defective and there needed a change, and that is why there existed struggle between the older force and the new force. Now, in this kind of a changing world-view between both the countries, i.e. between Nehru and Sukarno, there was hardly a meeting ground between the two. And other issues also strained the relationship. The initial friendship, where Sukarno actually called Nehru his elder brother, didn't last for a long time. In fact, India–Indonesia relations deteriorated quite a bit in the early 1960s and by mid-1960s. The relationship, in fact, was deteriorating day by day. As I said earlier, the gravitational pull was no longer there, and the economic stakes were nil. If the economic relationships were quite strong, even if the political relations were severing, at least the bilateral relations would not have gone so bad as happened in the mid-1960s between the two countries.

Now the entire scenario changed, of course, after the fall of Sukarno. The new dispensation under Suharto made some attempts to develop closer relationship between the two countries. But again, the economic content was still missing in the relationship. There was some improvement in trade relationship; lots of Indonesian teams came visiting to talk about greater economic co-operation but nothing materialized. It is very difficult to say who was to be blamed or not, but that is not the point. The point is that economic relations did not really take off well except that a few Indian businesses were established in Indonesia. I mean, some Indian businessmen and also some Indian local business people had established their economic operations in Indonesia.

But in terms of trade and investment, it was a one-sided development. Indians had invested in Indonesia, but Indonesia had never invested in India. So the stakeholder feeling was absent in both the countries. Then came the Cold War considerations which also created some sort of barrier between the two countries. Kampuchean issue was one, but there was not much fundamental difference between India and Indonesia on this issue. In the 1990s, efforts were made to give a definite shape to the economic relationship between the two countries and some progress was made during that period. Then came the economic crisis of the 1990s. Indonesia itself became a subject of great economic stress during 1997-98. This resulted in non-materializing the gains expected in the economic interactions between the two countries. The post-economic crisis period of course provided a lot of opportunities for economic co-operation between India and Indonesia but somehow again both the countries missed those opportunities.

It was only from 2000 onwards that certain elements of eagerness on the part of the two countries developed in building up strategic partnership. Ambassador Sharma did mention about the strategic partnership signed between India and Indonesia in 2001, but interestingly it took about four to five years to ratify the same. This itself was an indication of the lack of dynamism on the part of Indonesia and India to take their bilateral relationship to a new high.

Now again I would like to go back to the concept of gravitational pull. Although India considered Indonesia as a strategically important nation as the latter controls the two choke points in the Malaccan Strait — the Sunda and the Lombork straits — the link between Indian Ocean and the South China Sea, Indonesia did not really look at India from the same strategic perspective due to Indonesia's defence perspective is based on the concentric circle. In the concentric circle, ASEAN countires come first, then Australia and then the other countries. And India was not part of that concentric circle. The result was that the strategic pull, which could have brought India and Indonesia closer to each other, did not exist at the Indonesian side. The second issue was that while from 2000 onwards, a number of Indian investors, set up businesses and enterprises in Indonesia, there was no similar interest in Indonesia to invest in India. There was an attempt around 2006-07 from an Indonesian business group to set up a facility in West Bengal. But I think problems such as land acquisition and local issues discouraged them from doing so and finally that project did not take off.

Though Indonesia has done some investment in food production/packaging, large-scale economic investments from Indonesia are missing, and I would like to argue that unless and until Indonesia develops that economic stake in India, the relationship we are talking about will just remain stagnant. The strategic partnership, which was established in 2001, got some fillip after Yudhoyono's visit, a number of agreements have also been signed, some institutional set-ups and arrangements are also in motion now. In fact, last year there was a dialogue between India and Indonesia on defence co-operation. But the fact is that all these activities are not sufficient to bring the two countries together.

I would like to reiterate two reasons for the weak strategic partnership between the two countries. One, is the absence of gravitational pull between the two countries and two, the lack of economic stakes from one side. Unless and until the economic stakes are enhanced, the strategic co-operation will not materialize to the desired level.

Some people may argue that both India and Indonesia are keen to talk about greater co-operation essentially because of China's rise. China is a big factor in this region and particularly after 2010, when China started talking about South China Sea as a core issue, things began to change in the region and everybody is now looking for friends; at least the South Asian countries are trying to hedge their interests vis-à-vis China. This may not be an aligned system, but is some kind of an arrangement where there could be engagements with as many countries as possible. So it will be an inclusive system where all the parties would be there, but no party will dominate the institutional structure, and it will function under the leadership of ASEAN.

After China became a little assertive in the post-2000 period, we see a particular trend among the South-East Asian countries that they are getting close to India, who can withstand the challenges from China in the region. But again I would suggest that this could just be a temporary phenomenon because many of these countries are worried due to China's clout and strength. Now if China changes its track and changes its diplomacy towards the region, it can again establish a different kind of relation with this region. Such a development will bring down the compulsion on the part of many South-East Asian countries to look towards India or some other partners outside the region.

Therefore, the only way to sustain relations is through developments in other stake. And that stake could only be the economic stake. Ideological differences and similarities do disappear overnight but economic stakes do not. To make my stand clear, let us look at the relationship between Malaysia and Singapore. If one looks at the perception between these countries, each one has a perception which could even be worse than the perception between India and Pakistan. Singaporeans cannot stand Malaysians and Malaysians cannot stand Singaporeans. But they do not go to war and they try to maintain their relationship intact essentially because of the economic interdependence between the two. Why India–China relations are not breaking down despite having problems here and there such as territorial concerns in Ladakh and Arunachal Pradesh, and issuance of visas? It is the US $ 80 billion trade between India and China that holds the two countries at a more reasonable and decent level relationship.

Coming back to India–Indonesia relationship, we might talk about the various agreements that have been signed between the two. I am sure that somebody will also talk about this strategic relationship in this seminar. I want to refer to an agreement where India will train Indonesian pilots in Mig as Indonesia has also acquired some Migs from Russia and will train Indonesian soldiers in jungle warfare. There are some more collaborations. All these collaborations will not lead into a matured strategic partnership between the two countries unless the economic relations between them progress to a level where each country will say that yes we have a stake in our relationship.

Although Indian investment in Indonesia is quite large, the focus of investment and the trade between the two countries is based only on certain commodities. It has not diversified. Currently, the focus is mostly on palm oil, coal and a few other products. . . . Unless this situation change — enhancing the manufacturing capabilities across the two countries — I don't think the strategic partnership will mature. For the time being, there may be some convergence of interests between India and Indonesia and China — when the real chips are down I think Indonesia will also have a real stake in its relationship with China. The trade with China is much more (US $90 billion), Chinese investment in Indonesia is much larger. Indonesia has a good domestic constituency which propagates better relationships with China, in comparison with India, which does not have much of a domestic constituency. This has been the failure of Indian diplomacy, as India couldn't establish a critical mass in Indonesia through which it could have developed a closer relationship with Indonesia.

Now I shall shift my focus to the area of soft power, which is one of my favourite topics.

Any relationship in Asia will be compared to China, and China has a big advantage over India. China can be generous with its cheque books; its infrastructural development capacities are huge. China has developed infrastructure in the region in such a manner that not only does it become useful for military purposes, but it also creates complete economic interdependence between these countries and China. India has not been able to establish such ties even with Myanmar, so why to talk about other countries? We cannot really compete with China economically in all these areas. The comparative advantage that India possesses lies in its soft power. One of the areas where we can work together is in sharing our multicultural experience. The second area is democracy. Despite all the mess in India in terms of elections, still there are many institutional mechanisms which India can help Indonesia with in terms of capacity building and support. In the last election there were problems of registration of voters in Indonesia. In such an area India and Indonesia can co-operate.

The area in which India has a great advantage over China, however, is in the field of education — especially in terms of English education. When I was in Indonesia, I was talking to the editor of *Jakarta Post* and he was telling me about how China is able to attract a large number of Indonesian students. Especially because of the problems of terrorism, a lot of students from Islamic countries are not getting visas to Western nations. The number of students who are going from Indonesia and other Muslim countries to the West is coming down. He was saying that given the trend, in ten years, the number of students going from Indonesia to the West will be less than the number of students going to China. This will obviously have an effect in the future relationship between Indonesia and China because these youngsters studying there will be the critical mass tomorrow. They will be the leaders of the political parties, they will be working in the government services in Indonesia. This will have a definite impact. And this will happen despite the fact that there is a much stronger English education system in India.

India has provided some scholarships to Indonesian students from ICSSR; however the system is not functioning very efficiently. If someone wants to come to one particular university, we often cannot accommodate that person and the person is put into some other university — so there is a complete mess in that. I think India should make dedicated efforts in those areas. Many Indonesian students have told me that they would love to have branches of IIT in Indonesia. There were even talks of private financing and there was an agreement between India and Indonesia to that effect. But somehow our own politics, our popularism and populist tendencies have not allowed us to follow up on these. Earlier, foreign students used to come to JNU, particularly students from Asia, on the same fees. Now they are charged on foreign currency that is much higher. I think that the Government of India should have made some arrangements by which students of some of these countries could have come and studied at the same level as Indian students are allowed to do. But these are not politically enticing decisions. Thus few takers.

I think the only way India can develop a much closer relationship with Indonesia lies in its capability to use its soft power in the latter. Also, both the countries should make dedicated attempts and create a friendly environment to develop a much closer people-to-people contact.

KEYNOTE ADDRESS

3

India–Indonesia Bilateral Ties: Prospects Ahead

Rizali W. Indrakesuma

Through this presentation, I would like to share some details about the recent development in the relationships between India and Indonesia. Since Navrekha Sharma and Baladas Ghoshal have talked in detail about the bilateral ties and collaborations, I need not have to go for a detailed deliberation on the same. Rather, I would prefer to give a brief overview or an update on the same as seen from the Indonesian government's point of view.

My talk will be mostly centred around the visit of Indian Prime Minister Manmohan Singh to Indonesia in October 2013 and the subsequent developments. It was the third visit of the Indian prime minister to Indonesia, but first as an official visit. It was for the first time that the Indian prime minister visited Indonesia as a state guest. He visited Indonesia for the first time in 2005 to attend the Asia–Africa Conference in Bandung. The second visit was in 2011 to attend the East Asia Summit in Bali. The third visit, the official one, featured not only the ceremonial aspects but also the bilateral talks between the two nations. The meet, led by the leaders of both the countries, discussed many an important issue, but the focus was on simply solidifying what was already agreed before -- starting with the strategic partnership signed by both the leaders in 2005 and then followed by the visionary statement in 2011, again by the two leaders.

During the last visit of Indian prime minister in October 2013 to Jakarta, there was a special joint statement which gave the details of how far we have advanced in our bilateral relations within less than a decade. It did specify the development on economic co-operation since the signing of strategic partnership agreement. The trade volume per annum is approx 20.1 billion (2012-13), very high as compared to the same in the entire history of bilateral trade between the two countries.

Although the partnership on investment is something we are still working on, the eleven Memorandum of Understanding (MoUs) between our private sectors envisage a great prospect for us to really work together in realizing the projects of India and Indonesia, amounting to about $ 13 billion. Though this volume looks significant to start with, we have to really work hard in order to realize the full potential of joint ventures and investments so that we may achieve our trade targets.

All the eleven MoUs I have mentioned above are in the initial stages, and one of them is the building of an airport in Jogyakarta. The paper work has already begun and the agreement between the two parties has already been signed. It is time now to roll out the project in full steam, giving fillip to our bilateral trade and economic relations.

Political Aspect

On the political side, Indonesia and India share the same viewpoints in responding to international affairs and to other developments taking place all around the world. There prevailed no serious problems between us ever since both the countries got independence from the colonial rule, expect few personal issues which turned the relationship a little critical.

If I say, there was no major political issue between both the countries in the past and what really happened in the course of sixty years after independence was probably due to simple negligence. It was a time when both the countries had other priorities to address. India and Indonesia were focusing more on their neighbouring countries. If we look back to 1960-1990s, we are convinced of one thing that only after the turn of the twenty-first century that both sides began to realize the importance of mutual co-operation and the need to take the bilateral relations to a higher level.

The bilateral ties between the two nations started taking proper shape only after 2000, during the presidency of Abdurrahama Wahd, Megawati and now Susilo Bambang Yudhono, and now it is on a high pedestal.

On the political front, I think we are doing pretty well. Joint co-operation in defence is going on, although we need to further our joint operations. Though political co-operation is just one aspect of the mechanism of our bilateral ties, we have covered all the layers of governance. In October 2013, both our leaders agreed on having bilateral meetings annually between our leaders. Now the president of Indonesia and the prime minister of India will be meeting on a regular basis in addition to their meetings at other international forums like ASEAN, G-20, the UN and so on.

In addition to the high-level meetings of the Indian prime minister and the Indonesian president, the ministers of both the countries, on a biannual basis, will have a joint commissioned meeting, which will be held alternatively in India and Indonesia. We had such a meeting here in Delhi in 2012 and hopefully next year we will have the same in Jakarta between the delegations led by our foreign ministers. And even at a lower level, there is a joint foreign consultation meetings conducted and led by officials from the Ministry of External Affairs (MEA) in Indonesia and India, besides the meetings at the joint secretary level from the Indian side and the director level from the Indonesian side.

In addition to these three forums of bilateral relations there are other forums in other fields of co-operation. The trade ministers of both countries have agreed to meet once in every two years since 2011 although the 2013 meeting is yet to be decided. Probably, we wouldn't be able to make it this year, but may take place next year. Anyway, they have agreed to have meetings on a regular basis between our trade and commerce ministers, something very encouraging since we are also focusing on trade and commerce. And as I mentioned earlier, there is a joint commission on defence co-operation as agreed by the defence ministers of India and Indonesia.

Economic, Social and Cultural Aspects

Moving away from the political aspects of our relationship let us have a look at the third aspect of our relationship — economic, social and cultural. Ladies and gentlemen, we have plethora of opportunities in this domain as we have never addressed this issue seriously and thus were taking things for granted. India's historical–cultural ties with Indonesia started two millennia ago, bearing a strong imprint on the Indonesian arts, culture and temple building. Indian religions such as Hinduism and Buddhism made their significant presence felt in Indonesia in the early centuries of the first millennium. Even Islam got migrated to Indonesis through India. But only a few know about all these past links. At present, if you ask any Indian about the Indonesian art, culture or temples, I think you wouldn't get a satisfactory reply and that reflects the gap that got into our close relations that existed long back. I think more and more engagements need to be done on the social and cultural fronts to bring the people of both the countries closer.

At the embassy level, we are encouraging the Indonesian students to pursue their studies in India. I think Indonesia is yet to send a large number of students to India for education, as one of the best educational destinations in the world. Though we are putting in a lot of hard work, it is also the responsibility of other stakeholders in India and Indonesia to encourage Indonesian students to make India their educational destination.

Tourism is an area where I see lots of potential for bilateral relationship. Being so, I am surprised to note that there is no direct air link between India and Indonesia. The lack of direct flights brings sufferings to both the parties, and is an obstacle to scale up our relationship. There are three million Indians every year visiting South-East Asia, though this volume is divided among Malaysia, Singapore and Thailand. Out of the millions of Indians who travel all over the world, the data collected in the year 2012-13 shows that approximately 200,000 visited Indonesia. Ideally speaking, Indonesia would have attracted lots of Indians as tourists given its cultural and religious harmony with Indonesia. However, as I understand, the lack of direct flight service between India and Indonesia plays the spoilsport. It is time that the Indian and Indonesian governments take up this issue seriously and introduce daily direct flight services between the countries.

During my last visit to Indonesia to do preparation for Indian prime minister's visit in October 2013, I got a chance to meet the officials of the Indonesian aviation industry, and the board chairman and board of directors of Batik Air, the recently designated airline by Indonesian government to have flight service to India. I was told that they were waiting for more aircrafts to come and once they have all set, they would start the flight service between India and Indonesia, possibly early next year. Of course, many due diligent needs are to be taken care of before we see the flights take off from Jakarta to Delhi/Mumbai. For us, it is our duty to push forward the process and keep monitoring the same. I recall our bad experience in 2008 when Garuda was set to fly from Medan to Chennai and at the last moment it could not happen. An office with all the paraphernalia was set up in Chennai and suddenly they left. I was called upon by the representative of the airlines; he told me that he was leaving for Indonesia and, upon asking the reason, he updated that the flying plan had been postponed.

Let that be a lesson for all of us and let it not happen again. To fly means to connect India and Indonesia, because that is also one of the ways of making the social and culture association more meaningful and significant.

The low attraction of tourists is an issue associated with promotion. It is important for Indonesia to take a cue from Malaysia in promoting tourism worldwide. The TV channels like CNN in Malaysia do a wonderful job of promoting their tourism. Indonesia is yet to follow suit.

Art

Art is another area that can propel our relationship. Indonesia always shared some sync with India when it comes to arts and culture. Having given such a background, we are trying to make more Indonesian artists to visit India. Similarly, initiatives are to be taken to encourage Indian artists visit Indonesia and meet their counterparts and have expression, talks and discussion. Such associations may pave the way for their better collaboration in the days to come. India and Indonesia had collaboration in *Ramayana* dance in 2011 in Prambanan in Central Java and I hope to have the same programme performed here in India next year.

The small events that we organize like this would really help in shaping up more comprehensive political, cultural and social bilateral relations. Of course, there are many other aspects too. But my opinion is that at the university and academic level, we need to put more efforts in really showcasing to the world that we are bound by the deep historical and cultural backgrounds and we are also bound by the current intensity of relationship in the socio-cultural as well as economic and political fields. We have assembled here with the same determination of our leaders — i.e. our president and prime minister who met in Jakarta in October 2013 to solidify what they have already been agreed to — to keep track on the developments of all agreed projects and to take the mechanism of bilateral relations to a new zenith.

4

India–Indonesia Relations

Need for New Areas of Co-operation

Ganganath Jha

INDONESIA–INDIA co-operation and partnership are considered important as both have similar socio-economic background and quest for development. Their urge for peace, progress and stability is similar, and any socio-politico-economic turmoil/setback to them will have serious implications not only on the two nations but on all the countries in the neighbourhood.

The landmark developments in Indonesia, such as the adoption of guided democracy, financial crisis or tsunami had adverse effects on Indian mind. On the other hand, the developments in India like Chinese aggression, clamping of emergency and increasing poverty rate had adverse impact on Indonesian mind. Although the relations are guided on the basis of objective conditions and national interests, they were not complementary at domestic and international levels. After gaining independence India and Indonesia tried to advocate the case of Afro–Asian solidarity but they had their differences in the post 1955 period as India supported Soviet Union and Indonesia backed America. When the Cold War of the two superpowers came to an end, initiatives were taken to foster closer ties but the constraints were yet to be resolved. The mindset of the Cold War era, the economic downturn and the emergence of the Jemmah Islamiyah proved as major constraints.

India and Indonesia are connected culturally, strategically and geo-politically. Their proximity can be understood by the fact that when the Japanese occupied Andaman during the Second World War, the Indian government handed it over to Indonesia to be ruled. Indonesian island of Sumatra lies adjacent to Andaman within a distance of 100 km, and nationals of India and Indonesia have on many occasions trespassed into each other's territory. The socio-economic conditions of the two also suggest that both are mainly agricultural societies, having patriarchal system in social structure. There have been lopsided economic developments in both the nations and both are in need of better management and technology for sustainable development. Although our anti-colonial agendas were similar, the development agendas very often differed. The development plan and foreign policy adopted under the stewardship of Prime Minister Indira Gandhi and President Suharto were completely different as India supported the Soviet and Indonesia supported the American viewpoints. On many occasions, Indonesia became embroiled in ideological matters and India displayed pragmatism and sometimes the reverse situations existed. The role of the Indonesian Communist Party (PKI) during 1957-65 and Indian Communist Party during 1969-84 influenced the government policies in Indonesia and India, respectively, which diluted the system of the mixed economy. Besides, the populist slogans and socialistic drives did not help either in bringing about a welfare state or equitable social order. The poor became poorer and the rich became richer in India and the dilemma of the relevance of the political system persisted.

It is a fact that if Asia has to emerge a power centre in the new world order, Indonesia and India have to develop rapidly and simultaneously. However, the experiences since 1945 have shown that when India shows economic buoyancy, Indonesia is sluggish and when Indonesia improves, Indian progress is less satisfactory. Bound by nature and geography, the developments in one part cannot be sufficient if other is left underdeveloped. The resources and policies are to be synchronized to evolve a cohesive common policy to emerge both the countries as important partners in progress. As two large nations of Asia, these two have to match the developments in China and Japan. If these two nations develop in proportion to their potentials side by side, they will contribute to evolve Asian resurgence, which is the need of the hour. These nations must act as two important pillars of the regionalism and strengthen the dynamics of cultural co-operation and joint ventures to the extent possible.

The post-Cold War era has thrown serious challenges and opportunities as well. The issues of democracy, human rights, environment, terrorism and WTO have raised substantive issues and most of the Third World countries are at the receiving end. Hence there is a compulsion to work together. India and Indonesia are collaborating through partnership in the ASEAN, ARF, EAS and IOR-ARC platforms. Though they have signed several MoUs, the balance sheet of these co-operations suggests slow progress in terms of trade and investments.

It is known that the two have democratic system and both are committed to promote human rights. Although democratic institutions in India are old compared to Indonesia, their performances are not much different. There are secessionist and terrorist movements in both the countries with transnational support. Both have ethnic diversity and discord. They have lack of consensus on their nationhood. India is concerned about the developments in Kashmir and so Indonesia over West Papua. However, there is no effective modus operandi for conflict resolution because of the lack of trust in the political leadership. But, it is taken for granted that if there is an amicable solution in one part, it will be a trendsetter for resolving many conflicts in the region. However, one solution should not give birth to the rise of new conflicts as witnessed in the case of East Timor.

Indonesian archipelago is huge and it has diverse ethnic groups. The people in Java, comprising 65 per cent of the population, are different in lifestyle and customs from the people in Ambon, West Papua and Kalimantan. Their social orientation, food habits, language and history are different. Their mysticism, folklores and speaking style differ. The emphasis or silence of certain words while speaking, the force of arguments and articulations create confusion and misunderstanding even amongst the natives. Their contributions in freedom struggles were not equally complimentary. The leaders in West Papua and Ambon had contrary visions about their integration in Indonesia. Again the role of Islam in the emerging state system was either strongly supported or opposed by the nationalist leaders. The Soekarno–Hatta combination insisted on resilience and secular path but Darul Islam wanted Islam to be the state religion. In retrospect, we find that although the issue remains alive even today, the consensus to adopt a secular democratic path is rational and pragmatic. But the style of the governance during Soekarno and Soeharto years kept the issue of Islam in the forefront. Islamic groups supported the rise of Islamic radicals and became their spokespersons. These radicals were profusely applauded and supported by some West Asian countries. President Soekarno and his successors did not devote much time attending to the sensitivities of Acehnese. Soekarno talked of Pancasila and national resilience and believed that Islamic factor will deter the Acehnese ultimately from the indulgence in the secessionism. Indonesian leaders believed that Aceh will be simply a case of "diversity for unity" and will not remain alienated with the Islamic adherents in different parts of Indonesia.

The arguments for creation of a Islamic state and violent means (*jihad*) to attain it were projected simply as a law and order problem and tackled accordingly. The radical Muslims felt dejected with the treatment of the government forces. They felt marginalized and demanded separate homeland. These radicals were not deterred by the reality that Islamic adherents were everywhere in Indonesia and that the majority of Muslims were synergetic in nature and secular in outlook. They ignored that fact that if in case Aceh is seceded, the largest Muslim country of the world will disintegrate into several parts. They ignored all elements promoting unity between state and the nation, i.e. common history, common anti-colonial struggle, contiguous territories, cultural heritage, literature and religion. They started crusade against the central authorities and thus mistakes were committed on both the sides.

However, the occurrence of tsunami in Aceh offered an opportunity for peacemaking and the situation has gradually come under control of the government.

India, on the other hand, has had similar experiences. Jawaharlal Nehru, the chief architect of modern India, believed in Pancasila. He was a modernist and was secular in approach. He opposed the idea of having a state religion in the constitution and his vision of independent India was a secular democratic republic. However, nationalist leaders in the fight against British colonialism had always used religion to arouse the feeling of patriotism. If we examine the evolution of our freedom struggle, the first war of independence in 1857 was fought because of the possible use of pork and beef in the gun powder supplied to the Indian soldiers which was abhorred both by Muslims and Hindus. Later Lokmanya Tilak of Indian National Congress promoted Ganesh Puja to mobilize anti-British movement and Mahatma Gandhi believed in daily prayer, Ram-Rajya and Ramdhun. Both Tilak and Gandhi were outstanding nationalist leaders who understood the importance of religion in mobilizing public opinion. However, majority of the nationalist leaders were secular in outlook. Nehru thought that India was multi-religious and multi-ethnic and like Soekarno he also believed that secularism could be the best option. During the period of the emergency 1975-77 Prime Minister Indira Gandhi included secularism in the preamble of the Indian constitution. But the inclusion of the word "secularism" in the constitution did not prevent the use of religion in the politics of the country. It has been found that whenever any groups feel marginalized or justice is denied to them, they try to mobilize opinion on the basis of religion or ethnicity. There are some instances of the religion-based movements in certain parts of India and Indonesia, where minority ethnic groups have posed serious challenges to the state system. The nation builders are concerned about their activities and there are some who believe that disturbances are caused by minorities because of the absence of the state religion. Indonesia's Jemmah Islamiyah is presently fighting for the creation of an Islamic state. In the past Darul Islam preached that Islam should be the state religion of Indonesia. However, Islam alone cannot prove a unifying factor.

We find that although Islam was the state religion of Pakistan, its eastern part seceded in 1971 to form a sovereign independent nation, Bangladesh. The religion may be important to mobilize support, but popular support and developmental issues are crucial for maintaining the state system. India and Indonesia have witnessed the rise of political parties advocating greater role of religion in the politics of the nation and the decision makers are constantly trying to evolve middle ground to steer clear off the obstacles in nation building and modernization, but challenges are insurmountable.

Indonesia is undergoing democratization process, in which multi-party system has been promoted. India, on the other hand too, has multi-party system. Some of them have nationalist agenda but some have only local agenda in mind. If Congress, BJP or Communist Party have nationalist agenda, Akali Dal, RJD, JMM, DMK or National Conference have regional agenda. In Indonesia IDP and NAP have nationalist agenda, whereas parties like GAM and OPM have regional agenda. In India, regional parties have very often worked in the national coalition government led either by Congress or BJP, but GAM or OPM remains isolated so far. If they take part in the democratic process and are inducted in the decision-making process, the scenario will start changing.

India has a parliamentary system where the legislators decide the formation of the government and the leader of the largest group in the Lok Sabha become the prime minister, whereas in Indonesia various parties nominate their candidates for the presidency and general election is held to elect the president. The system of having directly elected president in Indonesia was introduced in 2004 to stop horse trading in the parliament (MPR & DPR) on the eve of presidential election.

There is immense scope of co-operation in the areas of human resource development but the two countries are yet to explore co-operation in the secondary and higher education, pharmaceutical research, information technology, biotechnology and agricultural sciences. The two countries have immense potentials to compliment developments in various areas of trade, investment and culture, and sincere efforts are needed to exploit them. India and Indonesia have similar orientation towards religion and their lifestyles have common features. Both of them find it very homely in the areas of food habits and culture and this point is illustrated more pointedly by personal integration of the two.

India and Indonesia are gripped with problems of terrorism in certain areas. Kashmir, situated at the Pakistan frontier, is a typical case of ethno-religious divide. Most of the Hindu population have been forced to move out of that area and made homeless. There is a crusade for the creation of an Islamic state through violent means. The various issues to resolve the issues are so much politicized that the government institutions and political organizations have lost credibility. There are differing perceptions and no consensus has reached over the methodology to be pursued for resolving the conflict. Kashmiri militants are getting military training in Pakistan and their guerrilla warfare and intermittent efforts to destroy selected sensitive targets in Jammu & Kashmir have given sleepless nights to the security personnel. The building of roads, bridges, railways and highways are disrupted and the development plans remain unfulfilled. On the other hand, terrorists feel injustice and isolated. Various actors, who can contribute to conflict resolution and confidence building, have their own agenda and because the government institutions lack credibility, there is no centrifugal force to bring them together and evolve a consensus. The separatists continue to speak secession and nationalists continue to advocate integration.

There has been numerous reports to suggest that Al-Qaida and Taliban forces are thriving in Kashmir. They are indoctrinated militias with sophisticated weapons and networking. Hence the nature of the conflict has become complicated and it is not helping either the Kashmiris or integration of the region with national mainstream.

Indonesia is facing serious problems of integration with Aceh, West Papua and Maluku, where secessionists are active. The central government tried military means to subdue secessionists but failed in that endeavour. East Timor was fighting for creation of a homeland for the Timorese and seceded in 1999. This precedent inspired secessionists in other areas to accelerate their activities so that they too get an opportunity to secede. If their objectives are fulfilled, Indonesia will disintegrate fully and it may create vacuum in the region, which will neither be in the interests of the region nor in the interests of those who preach secession because the outside forces jump in the fray to dominate.

Jemmah Islamiah, which came into existence to promote Islamic regimes in South-East Asia through violent means, is projecting that there should be the Union of Islamic people in the region to establish a separate state comprising Indonesia, Malaysia, Brunei, Thai territory of Yela, Narathiwat, Satun, Patani and also Philippine area of Sulu and Mindanao. Singapore, inhabitat in the middle, is not Islamic, but because of geopolitical reasons, it should be incorporated in the projected Islamic state by hook or by crook. There is no scope for the display of diversity and sustainability of a small state. As Islamic Sharia laws are codified by the Arab thinkers and supposed to be the law of governance, the dissent against it is considered illegal. This may not be in tune with the democratic processes in the twenty-first century when we are supporting globalization; Islamic groups should understand their limitations. It is necessary on their part to give up the trust in *jihad* (holy war) against their adversaries and stop giving it any religious sanction. Some of the noted militant reactionary outfits have emerged in response to Islamic terrorist activities and normalization is needed for bringing about peace and development.

Various Dakwah organizations like Laskar *Jihad*, Laskar Jundullah, Abu Sayyaf Group (ASG) or Kumputan Militant Malaysia (KMM) or Jemmah Islamiyah are supporting violence and hatred not only towards non-Muslims but also against Muslims who disagree with their theology or methodology. The dilemma of the Acehnese Muslims are that they are fighting their case despite the opposition of Jemmah Islamiyah or Laskar

Jundullah in Indonesia. Although Gerakan Aceh Merdeka (GAM) is advocating for the creation of an Islamic state, their ideals are not complementary to Jemah Islamiyah, which have a grand design to establish a unified strong Islamic state incorporating large chunks of the territories of South-East Asia, which may influence the course of events in the Asia Pacific. Their objective of supporting pan-Islamism may be inspiring one section but it is against the spirit of unity in diversity and it is not a practical solution.

Kashmir, on the other hand, has also become a victim of grand design of Islamic militants. If Pakistan is supporting its secession for the creation of an Islamic state it believes that Islamic civilization of Arabs will directly join through Kashmir with Muslim dominated province of Sinkiang (China). In that scenario, it will not only promote Islam in the region, but at the same time it will strengthen Pakistan's position vis-à-vis India. It is an irony that India is projected as homeland of Hindus for fanatics in Pakistan but the reality is that India is the homeland of the Muslims as well. There are millions of Muslims in India whose contribution in nation building and secular polity are immense. The secession of Pakistan in 1947 and following communal riots on religious grounds disturbed equation and understanding between Hindus and Muslims and to envisage another round of secession and communal riots are neither reasonable nor tenable. The resolution to the conflict is possible through constitutional means and avenues are to be searched through dialogue and negotiated settlement. The special regional autonomy proposal of Indonesia for Aceh and West Papua may be relevant for Kashmir too if the two conflicting sides agree to negotiate.

The problem of international terrorism got complicated especially after 9/11. The bomb blasts in Bali in 2002 proved the extinct of terrorist networks in South-East Asia. Jemmah Islamiyah, regarded insignificant in the region, was suddenly recognized as the major terrorist group and its leaders were arrested and questioned. It was revealed that the Jemmah Islamiyah-supported terrorists were active in different parts of South-East Asia. They had their training centres in Sulu and Mindanao, information centres in Singapore and Malaysia and main experimentation centre in Indonesia. They found Indonesia — a country of more than 17,000 islands — a safe place to hide, escape and strike at the chosen targets. However, the reality at the ground level is that majority of Indonesians are peace loving. They had evolved the policy of resilience and "unity in diversity". It is, therefore, that they are endeavouring at the national and international level to forge an alliance to crush terrorism of any type. There are several moderate elements among the adherents of Sufism in Indonesia, who will ultimately succeed in curbing the militancy of fanatic elements and pave the way for harmonious living.

Finally, it is necessary to examine the economic contents in our relations that contribute substantially in sustaining long-term interests. The value of the two-way trade between India and Indonesia, which stood at US $ 1,575.8 million in 2001-02, increased to US $ 2,212 million in 2002-03. In 2008, the bilateral trade volume increased to US $ 10 billion and in 2010, the figure further increased to $ 13.2. The target for 2015 has been fixed at US $ 25 billion for bilateral trade.

Although the trade ties have been increasing, it is not commensurate with the potential of the two countries. It has to go a long way to prove themselves as important trade partners for both of them. Both the countries can prove important markets for each other because India will always like to import palm oil, paper and paper board, wood pulp, synthetic fibres, organic and inorganic chemicals, oil and gas, etc. and Indonesia can export them. On the other hand, Indonesia needs drugs and pharmaceuticals, hydrocarbons, cotton and cotton yarn, automotive parts, engineering goods, etc. which can be exported from India. There is an immense scope for co-operation in science and technology, agriculture, ecological conservation, information technology, biotechnology, tourism and hotel industries between the two.

The connection between two via Andaman islands is a geographical reality but the construction of a highway through this passage is yet to be worked out. If trade interactions between the two are facilitated and new trade routes are explored, globalization will get a meaningful support. In this connection it is necessary to point out that the investment relations have remained, marginal so far. Indian investment in Indonesia constitutes 0.10 per cent of the total approved foreign direct investment. On the other hand, Indonesian investments in India constitute 0.18 per cent of the total foreign direct investment. Indonesia has made investment through Sinarmas group in paper and pulp products and they have yet to explore other profitable areas for joint ventures. The areas to co-operate are many and requirement is to explore and convince investors about profits and long-term benefits.

To conclude, it can be stated that India–Indonesia relations are improving but the experts have to search new avenues of co-operation in economic, political and strategic areas. India attaches importance to relations with Indonesia under the framework of Look East Policy and it has to evolve some innovative initiatives to promote India–Indonesia partnership in the twenty-first century.

References

Aderson, Benedict, 1972, *Java, in a Time of Revolution, Occupation and Resistance, 1944-46*, Ithaca: Cornell University Press:

Boland, B.J., 1982, *The Struggle of Islam in Modern Indonesia*, The Hague: Martinus Nijhoff.

Budiman, Arif, ed., 1990, *State and Civil Society in Indonesia*, Clayton: Monash University.

Emmerson, D.K., 1976, *Indonesia's Elite: Political Culture and Cultural Politics*, Ithaca: Cornell University Press.

Jha, Ganganath, 2003, *Indonesia: Society and Politics*, New Delhi: Shipra Publications.

Jha, Ganganath, 1996, "A Brief Survey of India-Indonesia Relations, Contemporary Southeast Asia", *Quarterly Journal of International and Strategic Affairs*, Singapore, March, **17**(4): 389-405.

Lee, Khoon Choy, 1999, *A Fragile Nation: The Indonesia Crisis*, Singapore.

5

India–Indonesia Bilateral Trade and Investment Relations

T.S. Vishwanath

OVER the last few years, two large economies in Asia — India and Indonesia — have been aspiring to build a strong trade and investment partnership that is mutually beneficial.

Over the last five years or more bilateral trade has witnessed a spurt though it still remains below the potential. Figures for financial year (April–March) 2011-12 show a bilateral trade of US $ 21.3 billion, which is well within the realm of US $25 billion target set for 2015. With some push, the two countries can bolster trade significantly, especially since they have put in place a free trade agreement since 2010 as part of the India–ASEAN comprehensive trade and investment agreement covering goods, services and investment.

This paper identifies specific areas where the two sides can build complementarities and bring about an exponential increase in trade and investment ties. It highlights the need for the two sides to study and push services trade that today has a huge potential in building regional and global value chains. Industry in both countries will stand to gain by building stronger global and regional value chains.

The two sides will have to look beyond the traditional methods of boosting trade, and identify new and dynamic issues that help boost bilateral trade in a highly-competitive and interlinked world.

Both the countries will have to make use of the fact that they are important players in the most promising region of the world and also account for a very large and growing market in the region.

New Delhi and Jakarta also need to increase their co-operation at the multilateral forums like the World Trade Organization (WTO) where they are part of similar groupings. The upcoming ministerial meeting of the WTO in Bali can be a good platform to intensify their partnership at the multilateral trade forum.

Finally, India and Indonesia should consider adopting a sectoral approach to deepen the partnership for building regional value chains that can boost trade, investment and employment opportunities in both the nations.

Introduction

India and Indonesia share a strategic partnership, which they announced in November 2005 during the state visit of the president of Indonesia, Susilo Bambang Yudhoyono, to India. This notion received a further boost in 2011 when the two sides adopted a joint statement for defining the "Vision for the India–Indonesia New Strategic Partnership over the Coming Decade".

Strategic partnerships, though comprehensive in form and covering a wide range of subjects, always have strong trade and investment elements. The India–Indonesia strategic partnership is no different. The visit by Manmohan Singh, prime minister of India, to Indonesia in October 2013 has provided a further stimulus to the partnership with the two sides agreeing to adopt a five-pronged initiative for strengthening the strategic partnership with the "objective of taking the robust, multifaceted co-operation to even greater heights".

The two sides have agreed to follow a five-pronged approach that will cover "strategic engagement, defence and security co-operation, comprehensive economic partnership, cultural and people to people links and co-operation in responding to common challenges".

The two sides have also set up an Eminent Persons Group headed by former foreign secretary of India, Shyam Saran to build a Vision Document 2025 for India–Indonesia relations.

Economic Partnership

New Delhi and Jakarta are confronted with similar issues regarding economic development. Both have a growing urban middle class, both are faced with the need to boost investment into infrastructure and are looking to identify natural resources within and outside the country for boosting industry and growth. Skill development is a challenge and global economic challenges in the last few years have impacted domestic growth.

The two sides, therefore, are looking to build strong partnerships globally with important trade partners to help focus on the issue of inclusive growth and improving market access for goods and services.

On the bilateral front the two countries have in October 2013 agreed to establish a High-Level Task Force to effectively "monitor implementation of business-to-business Memorandum of Understandings (MoUs); facilitate investment in each other's national infrastructure development plans, including PPP mode; and identify specific projects for joint investment in India, Indonesia or Third World countries".

With the target for bilateral trade fixed at US $ 25 billion for 2015 it will be important for the two countries to look at building investment-led trade so that growth in an inclusive fashion is fostered.

To identify possible ways of boosting trade and investment ties it will be essential to first identify the platforms that have been set up at the bilateral front by the two countries for boosting economic growth.

Platforms to Boost Trade and Investment

The strongest platform to boost bilateral trade is the India–ASEAN comprehensive free trade agreement that covers all aspects of trade and investment issues and will help liberalize trade in goods and services. While the liberalization of goods trade was set in motion in 2010, it is important to note that recently the two sides have been able to finalize the ASEAN–India Trade-in-Services Agreement, and the Trade and Investment Agreement, which would be signed in Bali on the sidelines of the WTO ministerial conference in early December 2013.

Another platform that can provide a stimulus to bilateral trade is the Biennial Trade Ministers' Forum (BTMF). The third is the India–Indonesia CEOs Forum.

Importantly the two sides are also keen to kickstarting the process of establishing an India–Indonesia Comprehensive Economic Co-operation Agreement that will enhance the offers to liberalize trade in goods and services that have been provided by the two sides under the ASEAN–India Comprehensive Agreement. The Eminent Persons Group will provide a further impetus to boosting trade and investment opportunities.

Making the Platforms Relevant

It is, therefore, clear that there is no dearth of opportunities for trading ideas for boosting trade and investment. What is now required is the will at the political and industry level to substantially boost bilateral relations. There is a need to look at new ideas to tap into each other's strength to boost bilateral trade and deepen the partnership.

One such idea to boost trade and investment is to help industry sectors across the two countries build regional value chains or collaborate to join global value chain.

Given the current trend across the globe, companies in India and Indonesia have to look at the possibility of building regional or global value chains through the joint venture route in select sectors to strengthen the partnership.

Global and Regional Value Chains

One significant benefit of the fall of tariff walls across regions due to trade agreements has been the growth of global value chains that help companies cut costs and move goods across borders freely.

Value chains today help bind nations economically while providing tremendous opportunities to companies from across the globe to source best products from the cheapest source to benefit the customer. It is turning out to be a win–win for all parties.

However, it is important to note that global and regional value chains can be a challenge when companies have to meet "just-in-time" schedules. Therefore, there is a need to create a knowledge network across countries where the company's value chain extends. This will aid better understanding of policy and regulatory issues of different countries.

This is an area that the two sides have to identify as an important deliverable under the various policy platforms that have been developed over the years. Governments in both the countries have to aid companies by building knowledge networks as such value chains cut costs for companies and make them more competitive.

Services in Manufacturing Value Chains

India and Indonesia need to recognize the fact that services contribute to nearly 50 per cent of the foreign direct investment that comes into the country. The role of services in manufacturing has not received adequate attention in developing-country markets like India and Indonesia and they now need better recognition and support.

Relevance of Services Sector in Bilateral Trade and Investment Flows

Manufacturing activities across the globe are increasingly getting fragmented, and transnational and even medium-sized corporations are increasing their global footprint to acquire raw materials and goods to acquire competitive strength in global markets which, as discussed above, lead to the creation of global and regional value chains.

Concurrently, contribution of service-inputs in manufacturing has been rising both in terms of volume as well as value. As a consequence of this fundamental shift in manufacturing practices, a new trend is emerging. Today, "services trade" is fast growing into a significant and integral part of "trade in goods" in the manufacturing sector. More than 60 per cent of the global trade involves trade in intermediates.

The importance of services in manufacturing is evident in a document prepared by the WTO,[1] which states:

> It is impossible for any country to prosper today under the burden of an inefficient and expensive services infrastructure. Producers and exporters of textiles, tomatoes or any other product will not be competitive without access to efficient banking, insurance, accountancy, telecoms and transport systems. . . . The benefits of services liberalization extend far beyond the service industries themselves; they are felt through their effects on all other economic activities [. . .].

Liberalization and increased competition have led to "splintering" of in-house services from formerly integrated manufacturing firms and, at the same time, to an increase in

1 WTO GATS Facts Book of 2005.

"outsourcing" of services related to manufacturing sector. These two trends have caused a stronger linkage in services and manufacturing.

Empirical evidence suggests that most multinational corporations procure high-value services (such as R&D, designing, consulting and business services). Consequently, the share of value addition from foreign service-inputs is rapidly growing relative to the corresponding domestic component. Given the increase in the number of firms in India and Indonesia, which are increasing their global footprint, there is a need for greater understanding of this growing concept in markets across the world.

This opens up a completely new area of partnership for the two countries, which needs better understanding and study. Given India's strength in the services sector it can reap rich dividends. However, Indonesia too with adequate focus on skill development can tap this growing segment to boost its economy.

Building on the Noodle Bowl of Global FTAs

Global value chains have been aided and supported by the increasing number of comprehensive Free Trade Agreements (FTAs) covering goods, services and investment. Indonesia has signed six bilateral and regional FTAs. These include agreements as part of ASEAN with China, South Korea and India, and a bilateral with Japan.

India, on the other hand, has already signed or is negotiating comprehensive agreements with seventeen different regional or bilateral partners including bilateral agreements with South Korea and Japan, and regional agreements with ASEAN and the European Union. Further, the two countries will be part of the ongoing negotiations under the Regional Comprehensive Economic Partnership (RCEP), which is billed to be one of the most liberal of trade agreements that countries would sign.

It is not just India and Indonesia but the world at large is negotiating and signing FTAs to increase market access and liberalize investment. There are over 550 regional trade agreements notified at the WTO of which over 350 are in force. The better known regional trade agreements are European Union, North American Free Trade Agreement (NAFTA), Association of South East Asian Nations (ASEAN), the Southern Common Market (MERCOSUR) and the Common Market of Eastern and Southern Africa (COMESA). These along with other bilateral agreements cover over 70 per cent of countries across the globe.

Collaborating at the WTO

Though the world is witnessing a spurt of bilateral and regional trade agreements it is imperative to note that the Geneva-based multilateral trade body provides a perfect setting for the two countries to push the agenda of the large developing countries and benefit from the new opportunities that will emerge over the next few years. The next ministerial meeting of the WTO is slated for December 2013 in Bali, Indonesia.

The agenda for possible agreements in Bali is limited and countries have been fighting hard to ensure that their interests are completely met. One such area that the two sides need to give a close look is the emerging agreement on trade facilitation. This is one area of negotiation, which can be a win–win for industry in all countries. While India and Indonesia need to ensure balance across the negotiating spectrum in Bali and also keep the development flag flying under the Doha Agenda, it will be important to push for a trade facilitation agreement that will balance the needs of the developing and developed countries. While the developed countries will bring this subject to the forefront for discussion in the Bali ministerial, countries like India and Indonesia need to support it. A strong harmonized trade facilitation agreement has the ability to tremendously boost bilateral and regional trade for the two countries. However, the two sides also need to balance the deliverables under the Doha Agenda to ensure that the gains do not get lopsided for some countries.

Sectoral Focus

Prime Minister Manmohan Singh's visit has led to the identification of several sectors for deepening bilateral co-operation. India and Indonesia have agreed to develop a roadmap for concrete collaboration in agreed areas of co-operation, such as biotechnology, marine, agriculture, information and communication technology, health and medicine, energy, disaster management, aeronautics and space technology. Each of these areas provides tremendous scope for increasing trade and investment as they represent areas where the potential is largely untapped.

Third Country Ventures

If New Delhi and Jakarta agree to look at providing policy and other stimulus for building global and regional value chains for sectors of interest to the third countries then there is a need for the two countries to also consider looking at helping private sector benefit from third country joint ventures for tapping global markets. This has to be a completely private sector-led approach and the governments in both countries only need to provide strategic inputs and tweak policy to support the setting up of such joint ventures. Third country joint ventures between companies in India and Indonesia will be a natural corollary to the creation of regional or global value chains by companies on both sides in sectors of interest. Food processing, textiles and engineering are three sectors, which can provide the basis for creation of such value chains.

Removal of Non-Tariff Barriers

Non-Tariff Barriers (NTBs) have always remained a significant reason for holding trade flows. Despite the removal of tariff walls, countries have noticed that trade has failed to take off due to lack of understanding on technical regulations and standards. In this context the recent initiative to intensify co-operation between the Indonesian National Standardization Agency (BSN) and Bureau of Indian Standards (BIS) in the area of Standardization and Conformity Assessment Co-operation is an important step to iron out NTBs. Technical barriers to trade contribute to nearly 70 per cent of the NTBs worldwide and such co-operation can address that problem. Co-operation in this area can lead to mutual recognition of agreements that facilitate trade of goods and services across borders.

Conclusion

The intent of the two countries to raise bilateral trade and investment flows is a good sign as an increase in trade and investment will be beneficial for both the countries.

However, what will be important for New Delhi and Jakarta is to let the economic aspect of the relationship be led by the private sector. The government role in the building this partnership has to be limited to the creation of adequate platforms and, where needed, provide the policy support for such partnerships.

6

Indonesian Democracy and Islam
Challenges Ahead

Gautam Kumar Jha and *Son Kuswadi*

INDONESIA enjoys a unique position in terms of the multiplicity of religions and the relative peaceful coexistence of varied customary religious practices. For centuries, adherents of Animism, Hinduism, Buddhism and Islam have lived together with least acrimony and have borrowed liberally from each other's practices. This imparts to Indonesia a unique identity in the comity of Islamic states in the world. There are many scholarly works dealing with different aspects of the Indonesian society and religion, political Islam and impact of the new waves of pan-Islamic culture. However, critical gaps emerge when it comes to dealing systematically with various nuances of the present Islamic image of Indonesia. The present work strives to portray the socio-economic religious composition of the Indonesian society, complying with the new emerging democratic set-up in the country.

My (the first author's) stay in Indonesia for a year, during 1994-95, followed by a number of short visits provided me an opportunity to understand the society empirically. In 1994, observing the construction of multi-layered flyovers was an indicator of economic development, but it also reflected a haphazard way of development process, visible from the chaotic traffic jams in Jakarta. When I moved to Bandung, my perception got changed. It was a new experience for me seeing rickshaw pullers reading daily newspapers, Muslim women offering prayers with the men in the same mosque and participation of more women outside of home locations in the daily chorus. All gave me reasons to stay in the country and observe Indonesia closely.

The annual economic development during the Suharto period was 7 per cent. That may be the result of a stable government of Golkar party led by President Suharto which always won the general elections for People's Consultative Assembly during 1973, 1978, 1983, 1988, 1993 and 1998 as the civil liberties were completely restricted.[1] As days passed by, my interaction with the general public grew and more facts started surfacing. The country was reeling under the dictatorship of Suharto-led government and it had controlled over all walks of its citizen. The freedom of expressions particularly of the university students, think tanks, theatre artists, musicians, painters and intellectuals were completely arrested and they were constantly monitored.[2] For example, one had to seek permission from the local police just for arranging a small family function of just ten people. As a student from India, I had to report at the local police station in Bandung every two months and sign few documents agreeing I had constantly been staying Bandung and not going anywhere else. Being a part of an art school I could make out from the theatre performances as how Indonesia was craving for change from a complete autocratic system to a democratic one.

As the process of globalization heralded, a new era of economic prosperity and political freedom in the South-East Asian region, coupled with newer threats to internal and global

---

1 http://www.britannica.com/EBchecked/topic/572060/Suharto

2 http://www.apcss.org/Publications/Edited%20Volumes/RegionalFinal%20chapters/Chapter12Bhakti.pdf (Consulted at 18.21 Hrs, 27 February 2014.)

security and ever-increasing quests for identities, Indonesia also underwent a metamorphosis in the last decade. A breathtaking transition from an autocratic rule to a more liberal and democratic system of governance has ensured multi-level changes in its image.

Almost after fifteen years of my regular visits to Indonesia I see a big change in terms of infrastructure development as I had guessed it could be. Among the other changes I see now more towers are concentrated in the mid of the city of Jakarta without leaving ample space for the road which adds complete chaos to the traffic system.

On the social front, I see more Muslim women wearing headscarves and hear more news about the youth jumping into the bandwagon of fundamentalists, particularly in Central Java and other places. However, the design of the headscarves are changing giving somehow a trendy look, different from the pan-Islamic world. And this development is a clear indication that direct infusion of pan-Islamic wave into the Indonesian society is somewhat impossible.

The emergence of Islam as a political force in Indonesian polity was almost inevitable, although, Sukarno as the leader of the nationalist secular wing successfully tried to lay the foundations of the nascent Indonesian state alongwith modern secular principles. While postulating "Pancasila" as the secular basis for the country's constitution he tried to mould the multi-ethnic culture of Indonesia in a single organic unity. Thus during

the initial years, a general consensus on the nature of Indonesian state and to some extent a common post-independence euphoria had prevented the Islamic forces from making any significant progress towards fulfilling their Islamic aspirations. Second, in order to fight the bigger enemy — the Dutch colonial powers — they had assembled under a single umbrella ignoring their internal differences. In such a condition there was hardly any space for a communal and sectarian political agenda as the national movement was fought largely under the nationalist banner, although the presence of right-wing Islamist forces was never in doubt.

However, the post-independence euphoria could not last long and a sizeable population soon got disillusioned. Nationalists' capability to deliver good for the country came under serious criticism in the wake of the government's inability to fulfil public aspirations. This disenchantment was instrumental in provoking the Islamic forces to turn towards the medieval theocratic panacea both as a viable alternative political model and as a common code of conduct for the general masses. Thus far dormant fundamentalist forces found Islam as a lucrative rallying banner for the masses in a primordial society like Indonesia. *Ulamas* (religious preachers) proclaimed Islam a special doctrine that can be fitted into all walks of life. Nothing could be beyond Islam and Islam had a solution for all phenomenal and non-phenomenal problems. The worldwide resurgence of Islamic forces also had a profound bearing on the new upsurge of fundamentalism in the archipelago.

In the 1960s, an exaggerated optimistic view of the government and Muslim relations was advocated by a number of Muslim intellectuals, including Upsep Fathudin and Utomo Danadjaja from the Pelajar Islam, Ahmad Wahib, Dawam Rahardjo and Djohan Effendi from the "Limited Group" discussion circle in Yogya, and Nurcholish Madjid from the

Jakarta headquarters of the Islamic Students Organization (HMI — Himpunan Mahasiswa Islam). As alumni of Islamic students' movements of 1965-66, these men were neither dependent on nor committed to the party organization of the 1960s. Hence in the face of continuing government restrictions on political parties in the late 1960s, they distanced themselves from mass politics in favour of a new strategy of the revitalization of Islam. At its heart lay the conviction that a long-term "cultural" approach to Islamic revitalization had to be formulated, one capable of neutralizing military concerns while slowly deepening the roots of Islam in the nation as a whole.

In the pan-Islamic world, Islam as an assertive political force began to be recognized in the late 1970s and early 1980s when its universal popularity as a source of social, ethical and spiritual power began to upsurge in the political horizon. A section of Muslims felt that the Islamic revolution in Iran was an important development and the same mode in which Ayatollah Khomenie captured power could be applied to their own country. The events in Afghanistan, which resulted in the installation of a Taliban regime, together with the rise of Osama Bin Laden as the champion of the Islamic cause, have impacted Islam worldwide and Indonesia was not an exception. People began to think of Islam in terms of a potential soteriology for spiritual as well as mundane predicaments. In the beginning of the 1970s a general consciousness towards the revivalism of political Islam started to surface.

The *ulama*s were being segregated by the elite privileged section of the society who did not have time to become involved in the religious chorus. Being religious and adopting a pan-Islamic ethos were considered to be rural and conservative as the Dutch-ruled urban population in Indonesia was still shrouded itself in Western values which were quite conspicuous till recently. Thus the role of the *ulama*s in politics was not significant though they had good support in the rural areas.

During and after the late 1970s, the revivalism of Islam was so fast and forceful throughout the Islamic world; the privileged class could not be left entirely untouched by its resounding impacts. Islam became a dominant factor in the day-to-day business of Indonesian people. The increased facilities of communication invited a mass exodus as people from the rural areas flocked to the urban areas in order to get a better livelihood. Facing the challenge of direct social segregation from the urban people the rural workers started attending general religious gathering which provided them with a feeling of unity and also of belongingness to the town.

By the late 1980s the Indonesian political leadership could no longer afford to ignore the growing demands for incorporating Islamic principles in the constitution. After two decades of pushing modernist Muslims into the political wilderness, Suharto suddenly became more responsive to the Islamic demands. Without relaxing the strict curbs on Muslim political activity such as letting the United Development Party (PPP) return to its Islamic roots he began to provide space for communal demands and tried in many ways to exalt his own Muslim credentials. The government toned down the restriction on the use of the *jilbab* (headscarf) at public schools, introduced more Islamic elements into the national school curriculum, and gave more authority to Islamic courts. Suharto went on a pilgrimage to Mecca with his family, and his eldest daughter, Tutu, gave a speech at a public place wearing the *jilbab*, attracting more media attention.

During the late 1990s Suharto recognized the potential threat from the growing Islamic consciousness among the general masses. He started taking interest in religious chorus by establishing a religio-political association called Indonesian Association of Muslim Intellectuals (ICMI) and set aside huge funds for the welfare of Muslims, such as special arrangements for Haj pilgrims, and allowed for the establishment of an

Islamic bank. He generously allowed the reconstruction of mosques and revitalized the hierarchical status of the *ulama* and the caretakers of the mosques, fixing their salary. All these developments provided promising career prospects for the lower middle-class youths and encouraged them to go for the study of theology. At the same time he also maintained his silence on the series of interreligious violence particularly by the Islamic zealots in the late 1990s.

The foundation of ICMI by Habibie was Suharto's final bid to win over the Muslim intellectual class. The tumultuous events of the previous years had made Islam, more than ever, a force to be reckoned with in South-East Asian politics. Yet, far from being a rigid, monolithic force, its manifestations in the region are richly varied and more often characterized by tolerance and notions of social justice than by the quest for an Islamic state. In Indonesia, with the world's largest Muslim population, *reformasi* has led to the flowering of thirty Islam-inspired parties.

The aspirations of Muslims were reflected in the 1999 general election when a large number of newly-established Islamic groups participated. However, they could not muster the support of the majority. The reason was primarily the Golkar's strong base. Suharto's Golkar still was very well established and financially sound even after his messy fall and ignominious ouster by the youth of the country. Golkar also gained second position because it had earlier showed that it was equally interested in the welfare of Muslims by establishing ICMI. The secondary reason was the relatively disorganized state of the Islamic groups and parties.

There always existed a clash between the two forces with "liberal" Islam on the one hand and "literal" Islam on the other. Islamic scholars like Nurcholish Madjid, Azyurmadi Azra and the Dean of the leading Indonesian seminary, IAIN (State Academy of Islamic Sciences), Syarif Hidayatullah, are among the leading moderates. The three men are known for their willingness to address the challenges of modernity, their tolerance of other faiths as well as their sensitivity to gender rights. There are also a number of young generation figures, such as the Nahdlatul Ulama's irrepressible head of human resource development, Ulil Abshar-Abdalla, and the academician Lutfi Assyaukanie. On the other hand, there are ultra-conservative leaders such as Hidayat Nur Wahid of the Justice Party and Ja'afar Umar Thalib of Laskar Jihad who wish to see the imposition of the Sharia.

During the late 2000, the Laskar Jihad leader was quoted in the Indonesian news weekly *Gatra* as saying, "The difference between us and them (the liberals) is the same as between the followers of Islam and non-believers". However, the two largest organizations of Muslims, NU and Muhammadiyah, have more commonality than differences and they cover most of the Javanese Muslims. The NU, with its roots in the privately owned *pesantrens* (religious schools) of East Java, has had a long history of autonomy. Both the organizations with an estimated membership of 30 million apiece have managed to retain their credibility in the eyes of the people. The NU has also directed a great deal of their energies towards education. Unencumbered by political ambition NU *kiyai* (scholars), such as Abdurrahman Wahid (or Gus Dur) focused on the pursuit of knowledge. They spent time in striking a balance between Western enlightenment ideas and traditional Islamic precepts. Having been at the receiving end of the Suharto government the NU developed a passionate and enduring commitment to human rights. As Ulil says of the 30-million-strong association:

> Whilst the NU is committed to tradition it has demonstrated a surprising readiness to embrace new ideas. This is due in part to the benign leadership of Gus Dur.

In this respect Indonesia is extremely unusual.

In most Islamic countries religious organizations have formed a kind of solidarity with the government authorities and the liberal Muslims are isolated. For example, in Egypt, Naguib Mahfouz, a Nobel laureate, was even the subject of a brutal assassination attempt in 1994. Indonesia's liberals are free, they have freedom and so far they are very much abreast of the happenings in the Islamic world and their own countries. These liberals are very strong, Western-educated secularists. Most of them have emerged from *pesantrens*. They are fluent in Arabic and trained in *fiqh* (Islamic jurisprudence). Their background gives them the confidence to debate substantive religious issues. They do not retreat from confrontation and these kinds of discussions, related to Islamic jurisprudence, shown on local televisions have left a strong impact on liberal minds as well those who tend to go with the hardliners.

However, the liberals also agree with the demands of the hardliners, as for example, affirmative action in favour of indigenous Islamic entrepreneurs against the Chinese who dominate the economy. Malaysia's New Economic Program could provide the model by redressing the human rights abuses against Muslims in the past, especially the Tanjung Priok massacre of 1984; and by laying more emphasis on Islamic symbols in public life, including disapproval of gambling, abortion, Western consumerism, etc.

No government can afford to ignore these demands the way Suharto did. Islam is no longer seen as the opiate of the uneducated and economically deprived. Professionals and the middle class increasingly are seeing it as a religion, which can provide for their spiritual needs in the context of contemporary society. There is a new sense of pride in being a Muslim among Indonesian Muslims now. Islamic values are not out of fashion rather they have become a fashion. In the small towns a woman with headscarves is considered to be the civilized one rather than one in jeans or skirts. *Ulamas*, who found Islam as a very powerful tool founded various associations such as *dakwah* or any Islamic intellectual association, started receiving funds from Arab countries and various international Islamic organizations. The underprivileged masses who were not able to afford expensive higher education in the country had no choice but to send their children into Islamic schools where Islamic education is free and is the sole substitute for all core disciplines.

There was a general pessimistic view among the people that there would be a turbulent transition after Suharto was toppled in 1998. There was the first free election after almost four decades and Indonesia might have come under a chaotic period in the absence of any effective leader, which was very clear from the fact that the country did not have a large number of middle class as the entire country was reeling under the strict rules for thirty-two years of Suharto, and after forty-four years of not having free elections.[3]

Therefore, it was a challenging moment for Indonesia to have a peaceful transition. Elections in 1999 and 2004 went very well having almost 117 million people voted, and now there is a full democracy for the last twelve years amid a number of challenges.

Indonesia, which witnessed 8-9 per cent of the economic growth during Suharto regime per year, suddenly got hit by the 1997 East Asian Financial crisis and the economic growth suddenly got a jolt. Now the economy is back on track of at least 6 per cent and the government has also started spending major chunk of its entire budget on education and since 2002 it was mandated to allocate at least 20 per cent of its budget to education a figure that was achieved in 2009.[4]

---

3 http://world.time.com/2013/05/21/15-years-after-the-fall-of-suharto-a-mixed-picture-of-indonesias-minorities/was consulted at 16.40 hrs on 18 March 2014.

4 http://www.eastasiaforum.org/2012/11/16/improving-the- →

Terrorism is a major challenge but the government has been very partial and effective in tackling the problems particularly the post-Bali bombing proceedings of the accused, and almost wiping out the strong presence of Jemmah Islamiyah. The country is itself taking cognizance of the racial violence which is reflected in day-to-day media's coverage as the majority of educated higher middle-class Muslims rather keep moderate profile in order to deal in any social issues purportedly associated to the religious one.

Modern Islamic thinkers like Jamal ud-Din al-Afghani and Muhammad 'Abduh (1849–1905) are still very popular in Indonesia for their moderate school of thought who advocated the distance between religion and politics and discarded the theory of miraculous phenomena in Islam.[5] Sufism and its different streams *aliran* which go side by side with mysticism are the strong pillars of Indonesian society today which make enough reasons why Indonesia has not been swayed by the pan-Islamic views.

References

Achmad, Chatib bin Abdul Lathif, 1965, *Fatwa tentang Tharikat Naqsjabandijah,* Medan: Islamiyah.

Azra, Azyumardi, "The Transmission of Islamic Reformism to Indonesia: Networks of Middle Eastern and Malay-Indonesian 'Ulamâ' in the Seventeenth and Eighteenth Centuries", unpublished Ph.D. thesis, Columbia University, New York, 1992.

Baabdullah, M.O., 1990, *Fatwa dan pendirian ulama sunni terhadap aqidah Syiah,* Bangil Mahad Aly Ilmu Fiqh.

Badan Kerja Sama Pondok Pesantren Jawa Barat, 1986, *Fatwa lengkap tentang Porkas,* Jakarta: Panjimas.

← quality-of-indonesias-education-spending/ was consulted at 16.50 hrs on 18 March 2014.

5 http://www.cis-ca.org/voices/a/abduh-mn.htm was consulted at 16.50 hrs on 18 March 2014.

Boland, B.J., 1982, *The Struggle of Islam in Modern Indonesia*, slightly revised reprint, The Hague: Nijhoff.

Chatib Ali (ed.), 1986, *Al-khatima [al-]bahija*, Padang: De Volharding. [Arabic and Malay in Jawi script.]

Department of Information, 1988, *The Constitution of Republic of Indonesia*, Jakarta.

Geertz, Cliford, 1971, *Religion of Java*, Chicago and London: University of Chicago Press.

Hassan, Muhammad Kamal, 1987 (translated into Indonesian language by Ahmaie Thaha), *Modernisasi Indonesia*, LSI Jakarta.

Hazra, Kanai Lal, 2007, *Indonesia: Political History and Hindu and Buddhist Cultural Influences*, vols. 1-2, New Delhi: Decent Books.

Holt, P.M., Ann K.S. Lambton, and Bernard Lewis, 1970, *The Cambridge History of Islam*, vol. 2, Cambridge: Cambridge University Press.

Hurgronje, Snouck C., 1906, *The Acehnese* (tr. A.W.S. Sullivan), vol. II, Leiden: E.J. Brill.

Kemp, Herman C., 2004, *Oral Tradition of Southeast Asia* (bibliography), Indonesia: Yayasan, Obor.

M. Federspiel, H., 1976, *Soekarno and his Muslim Apologists: Accommodation between Traditional Islam and an Ultra-nationalist Ideology*, Leiden: Brill.

Madjid, Nurchalish, 1985, *An Islamic Appraisal of the Political Future of Indonesia*, Jakarta.

Mcvey, Ruth T., 1965, *The Rise of Indonesian Communism*, Ithaca: Cornell University Press.

Meglio, R.R., 1970, "Arab Trade with Indonesia and the Malay Peninsula from the 8th to the 16th Century", in D.S. Richards (ed.) *Islam and Trade of Asia*, Philadelphia: University of Pennsylvania Press.

Nakamura, Mitsuo, 1976, "The Crescent Arises over the Banyan Tree: A Study of the Muhammadiya Movement in a Central Javanese Town", Ph.D. dissertation, Cornell University.

Noer, Deliar, 1958, *The Rise & Development of the Modern Muslim Movement in Indonesia*, Oxford.

Peacock, J.L. 1978, *Purifying the Faith: The Muhammadiyah Movement in Indonesian Islam*, California.

Wahid, Abdurrahman, 1984, *NU dan Islam di Indonesia, Dewasa ini* (Islam and Nahdatul Ulama Today), Jakarta.

7

India–Indonesia
Co-operation Challenges and Way Ahead

Vikas Saharan

For most Indonesian elites, South-East Asia and ASEAN constitute the main area of interest in Indonesia's foreign relations. While the region has been described as "the first concentric circle" of Indonesia's foreign policy, ASEAN is referred to as its *sokuguru* (cornerstone). Consequently, the stability, security and prosperity of South-East Asia are Indonesia's core strategic interests. Indonesia continues to promote the idea of an independent South-East Asia, capable of maintaining its autonomy in the face of rivalry and competition for influence among extra regional powers. It presents itself as a strong advocate of "regional solutions to regional problems" and affirms that the security of South-East Asia cannot be genuinely attained through military alliance and collective defence arrangements either among regional states or between a regional state with extra-regional power. Indonesia instead believes that such regional vision can only be attained through a co-operative security system among regional countries, such as ASEAN, and between ASEAN and its regional partners, such as in the ASEAN Plus Three (APT) process and the ASEAN Regional Forum (ARF). However, the context within which Indonesia has to pursue its vision of regional order has become more complex. East Asia in the twenty-first century is an area of increasingly diffuse power, with significant implications for regional and global power structures. Power shifts taking place in the region point to the redistribution of influence among key players. The rise of China constitutes the most salient aspect of such changes. Along with its economic development, China's military capability has also improved significantly. As its economic power and military might increase, China has now emerged as the most influential actor in the region. India is also catching up as a major player. Japan, while still in deep domestic political and economic trouble, cannot be written off yet. Other regional powers such as South Korea, Australia and ASEAN are not inactive bystanders. Moreover, power is also diffusing to non-state actors the private sector, civil society organizations, organized crime and terrorist groups.

Indonesia, like many other regional countries, recognizes the potential implications of such changes for the region. That has been manifested in Indonesia's concerns over a number of issues. The important concern primarily relates to the question of China's rise, particularly how China is going to use its new stature and influence to pursue its national interests and objectives in the region. Indonesia, therefore, remains anxious about how China is going to use its newly-acquired wealth and military power. The pre-eminent role of the US in East Asia remains beyond doubt. However, its role and influence in the region are increasingly being limited by the rise of China, both in terms of Anti-Access/Area Denial military capabilities and the incentives China's sheer economic size creates for regional states. The US is, therefore, confronted by the necessity to maintain and ensure its political primacy, economic interests and military preponderance, and has declared a renewed commitment and interest to play a more active role in the Asia-Pacific, especially in East Asia. This new intention has been reflected in the Obama administration's "pivot" strategy towards the Asia-Pacific.

Indonesia has responded to these emerging dynamics by relying on three approaches. First, ever since the revolution, Indonesia's foreign policy has been committed to abide by the principle of *bebas-aktif* (free and active). This normative principle, first declared in 1948, requires Indonesia not to take sides in any rivalry between great powers. Indonesia's second approach elevates the principle of *bebas-aktif* to the regional level and seeks, together with other ASEAN states, to create a "dynamic equilibrium" among major powers in South-East Asia. Indonesia realizes that no regional country can address emerging security challenges by working alone. In this regard, regional co-operation becomes relevant and important to address security challenges stemming from strategic uncertainties brought about by geopolitical changes. Indonesia has played an active role in shaping up the emerging regional architecture in the region by ensuring ASEAN's centrality while encouraging greater participation by other major and regional powers in the regional processes. It supported the inclusion of India, Australia and New Zealand in the East Asia Summit (EAS) and, in 2010, invited the US and Russia to become members of the grouping. Indonesia has also taken steps to encourage the consolidation of ASEAN. Through the EAS process, together with other processes such as APT, ARF and the ASEAN Defence Ministerial Meeting Plus (ADMM-Plus), Indonesia supported ASEAN's initiative to provide an institutional framework that would hopefully facilitate a co-operative relationship among the major powers, especially between the US and China.

The ties between Indonesia and India date back to the times of *Ramayana*. (Yavadvipa (Java) is mentioned in India's earliest epic, *Ramayana*.) Sugriva, the chief of Rama's army, dispatched his men to Yavadvipa, the island of Java, in search of Sita (Kapur, 2010). Indians had visited Indonesia since ancient times, and ancient Indonesians had embarked in maritime trade in South-East Asian seas and the Indian Ocean. The ancient Indians spread Hinduism and many other aspects of Indian culture including Sanskrit and the Brahmi script. India had played a big role in Indonesian culture, which is a fusion of Indian, Chinese, South-East Asian and indigenous Indonesian culture. The trace of Indian influences is most evident in great numbers of Sanskrit loanwords in Indonesian languages. The name Indonesia derives from the Latin *Indus,* meaning "India", and the Greek *nesos,* meaning "island" (due to the similarity of the culture in both regions) (Tomascik et al. 1996). The name dates to the eighteenth century, far predating the formation of independent Indonesia. During the Srivijaya era, many Indonesians studied at Nalanda University in India (jnicc.com). Throughout their shared history, most of relations between ancient India and Indonesia were harmonious and peaceful; however there was one exception when ancient India and Indonesia were involved in warfare against each other. In 1025 Rajendra Chola, the Chola king from Coromandel in south India, launched naval raids on the ports of Srivijaya and wrested Kadaram from Srivijaya and occupied it for some time (Lockard 2006). The Indian epics — *Ramayana* and *Mahabharata* — play an important role in Indonesian culture and history, and are popular amongst Indonesians to this day. In the open theatres of the Prambanan in Java, Javanese Muslims perform the *Ramayana* dance during full-moon nights. Examples of deep Hindu–Buddhist influence in Indonesian history are the ninth-century temples of Borobudur and Prambanan. Even after the adoption of Islam, the link between two countries remained strong. Indonesian Islamic architecture, especially in Sumatra, has been deeply influenced by the Mughal architecture, evident in the Baiturrahman Grand Mosque in Aceh and Medan's Great Mosque. Cultural admiration is not one-sided, however. Indians also relate closely to Indonesian culture. In the 1945-49 period, during Indonesian National Revolution and the formation of the republic, India and Egypt were among the earliest nations that supported and recognized Indonesian independence and fostered diplomatic relations with the Republic of Indonesia. In addition, prior to Indonesia's independence, Muhammad Ali Jinnah, the founder of Pakistan, who at that time was the president of the All India Muslim League, encouraged Indian Muslim soldiers serving in British Indian army to join hands with Indonesians against their fight against the Dutch Empire colonization of Indonesia. As a result, 600 Muslim soldiers of the British Indian Army deserted the colonial forces putting their lot at stake, and allied with Indonesia (*The Jakarta Post* 2008). India and Indonesia officially opened the diplomatic relations since 3 March 1951 (*"India Perluas Kerjasama Ekonomi, Energi dan Hukum"*, *Antara News*). In 1955, Indian Prime Minister Jawaharlal Nehru and Indonesian president Sukarno were among the five founders of the Non-Aligned Movement (NAM). During the 1965 Indo–Pak War, Indonesia offered to provide Pakistan with military help and "to seize Andaman and Nicobar islands" of India so as to distract it from the Kashmir front, eventually mobilizing submarines to help Pakistan. A maritime boundary agreement between the two countries was issued in New Delhi on 14 January 1977 (Foreign Affairs Record 1977).

The relationship between India and Indonesia was warm and cordial since the beginning. Borobudur, a Buddhist Temple built during the Sailendra dynasty of Indonesia, temple's design in Gupta architecture reflects India's influence on the region (Paul Michel Munoz, 2007). The Prambanan Temple of Central Java, reflects the Dravidian architectural influences. It is the largest Hindu temple of ancient Java (Sastri, 1955). The Balinese script in a Hindu temple. Indian people spread Hinduism, Buddhism and helped to spread Islam in Indonesia, as well as introducing the first form of writing to Indonesia, which evolved into the writing scripts still used in Bali and

Java (http://www.omniglot.com/writing/balinese.htm). *Idli*, an Indian savoury cake especially prevalent in south India, may have been an imported idea from Indonesia (*Outlook*, 4 Febuary 2014).

Indian–Indonesian relations refer to the bilateral relations of India and Indonesia. India and Indonesia are neighbours. India's Andaman and Nicobar islands share a maritime border with Indonesia along the Andaman Sea. The Indian–Indonesian relationship stretch back for almost two millennia. In 1950, the first president of Indonesia — Sukarno, called upon the peoples of Indonesia and India to "intensify the cordial relations" that had existed between the two countries "for more than 1,000 years" before they had been "disrupted" by colonial powers (*Foreign Policy of India: Text of Documents 1947-59*, p. 54). In the spring of 1966, the foreign ministers of both the countries began speaking again of an era of friendly relations, which was disturbed during the Indo–Pak War in early 1960s. India regards Indonesia as a key member of ASEAN. Both nations had agreed to establish a strategic partnership. Indonesia and India are member states of the G-20, the E7 (countries), NAM and the UN. According to a 2013 BBC World Service Poll, 79 per cent of Indonesians view India's influence positively, with 21 per cent expressing a negative view, one of the most favourable perceptions of India in the world.

India and Indonesia, the two major regional powers, have in the recent past initiated intimate bilateral relations. With globalization as a key driver, the two countries have reconfigured their relationship particularly in the economic and defence spheres. The signing of the strategic partnership in 2005 has been critical to strengthening of the bilateral ties. Security relations are complimentary. While India needs to safeguard its interests in South-East Asia, Indonesia needs a benign power like India for its security concerns. Some issues of strategic importance for India vis-à-vis Indonesia are maritime security, energy security and co-operation in counter-terrorism. India is one country with which Indonesia has rapidly deepened its bilateral co-operation within diverse areas, particularly defence. Indonesia, the sixteenth-ranking economy in the world with a nominal Gross Domestic Product (GDP) worth almost a trillion dollars, is an emerging economy considered so important that the world is talking about expanding BRICS into BRIICS, with the second "I" denoting Indonesia. Indonesia is the nearest neighbouring country from Andaman and Nicobar islands, nearer than even mainland India. Indonesia is the largest and the most influential country of the ten-member ASEAN, which is so vital for India's Look East Policy.

Often in diplomacy what is not said or written is more important than what is being said or written. This should be the yardstick in examining bilateral relations between any two powers in the world. Ahead of his Brunei and Indonesia visit, India prime Minister Manmohan Singh had said that India's sees its "ties with Indonesia as an essential part of India's integration with the broader region". "I intend to utilize this visit also to re-emphasize our commitment to building a stronger partnership with ASEAN. We will also have the opportunity to exchange views on regional and global issues of common interest," he said, while committing to create an institutional framework to further enhance the content of our co-operation in the years ahead. "Our engagement with ASEAN and its member countries is the cornerstone of our 'Look East' Policy and has evolved into a strong, comprehensive and multifaceted partnership in recent years," the prime minister said in his departure statement as quoted by (*TOI*, 9 October 2013). New Delhi wants to develop its relations with South-East Asia with its Look East Policy, in which Indonesia is considered a very important country. So there are a lot of things in common we can look at, both in terms of strategic location and our economic growth. The policy, adopted by India in 1991, seeks to establish closer ties with East Asian economies. The current India–Indonesia engagement is also strengthened by the first bilateral visit of Prime Minister Manmohan Singh to Indonesia. A 2640-word joint statement on India–Indonesia Strategic Partnership (in place since November 2005) was released after Singh's talks with Indonesian president Susilo Bambang Yudhoyono. The first point that needs to be mentioned upfront is that India and Indonesia have agreed to hold annual summits, including on the margins of multilateral events. This is a giant leap forward in bilateral relations between New Delhi and Jakarta. There are only two nations thus far with which India has an institutionalized mechanism of holding annual summits — Russia and Japan — in the chronological order. However, the India–Indonesia bilateral relations still have some way to go to reach the depth, maturity and substance that is visible in India's bilateral engagement with Russia and Japan. That is because Singh and Yudhoyono agreed to hold annual summits, but not in each other's capital as is the practice with Russia and Japan. The joint statement makes it clear that the annual summits can even be held side-by-side at multilateral events in other countries. This means that Indonesia is still not there as prominently on the Indian strategic calculus as Russia and Japan are, though India–Indonesia bilateral trade is over US $20 billion, almost as much as India–Japan trade and nearly double than the current India–Russia trade. But then it is just the beginning of a deeper and more substantive engagement between New Delhi and Jakarta.

Sample the decisions by the two heads of governments as reflected in the joint statement. They stressed the importance of continuing regular bilateral consultations through the robust architecture of dialogue in place, including the ministerial and working group mechanisms. They agreed to hold the Joint

Commission Meeting on an annual basis. They directed the two foreign ministries to continue to hold regular consultations on bilateral, regional, multilateral and international issues, and to co-ordinate co-operation activities. Overall, India and Indonesia agreed to intensify co-operation in such vital areas as defence, space, nuclear energy, agriculture and transportation.

In the entire joint statement, released after Singh–Yudhoyono talks in Jakarta on 11 October, the two sides refrained from using the "C" word. They also did not mention the South China Sea issue, though it is on the forefront of the two nations' international agenda, more so with Indonesia. The reason is obvious. Indonesia is not Vietnam or Philippines, the two nations who are most vocal about their trepidations with regard to China's South China Sea diplomacy which Beijing embarked upon in 2009. Though Indonesia is as much concerned about the China factor in its diplomatic engagements with the rest of the world, it has been treading a cautious line and not exhibiting bellicose diplomacy with regard to China. China has a sizeable presence in South-East Asia with more than 50 million of ethnic Chinese accounting for 10 per cent of the region's population. As much as two thirds of retail trade in South-East Asia is controlled by ethnic Chinese; and Indonesia is no exception to this trend. If China is missing from the two leaders' open statements, it is because it is intended to be so a covert diplomacy till the two sides explores each other. It does not mean that the two sides are afraid of China. A more reasonable way of looking at it would be that the two sides are still trying to discover each other, know each other's positions and intentions and leave a more pronounced joint position for an appropriate time in the future.

India and Indonesia have found common ground in sea, air, land and space to take their strategic relation to the next level. Manmohan Singh and Susilo Bambang Yudhoyono bonded well in Jakarta to give a push to the existing arrangements. The discussions resulted in the signing of six agreements and co-operation in different sectors including defence, space, maritime security, food security, trade, health and culture. This is one bilateral relation in India's proximity which is working, growing and is recognizing its potential. The joint statement issued after the talks elaborated:

> The leaders agreed to adopt a five-pronged initiative for strengthening the strategic partnership with the objective of taking the robust, multifaceted co-operation to even greater heights.

These five areas are: strategic engagement; defence and security co-operation; comprehensive economic partnership; cultural and people-to-people links; and co-operation in responding to common challenges. Both countries have decided to have robust co-operation in maritime security. The joint statement said that both countries have stressed the importance of closer collaboration on capacity building and exchange of best practices in the field of maritime security and holding joint exercises. Navies of both countries already hold joint navy exercises to safeguard their ships from pirates in Malacca Straits. From India's Andaman and Nicobar islands, Indonesia is just 90 nautical miles away. Both countries continue to emphasize the need for maritime co-operation. The two countries also agreed to enhance air connectivity. One of the agreements under the trade negotiations has been about, "recognizing the significance of connectivity for enhancement of trade and tourism. The leaders welcomed the agreement to establish direct flights by Batik Air and code-sharing services between Jet Airways and Garuda Indonesia", said the joint statement.

Greater co-operation can be expected between the countries in the area of space too. The joint statement said:

> Leaders acknowledged the increasing intensity of collaboration between the Indian Space Research Organization (ISRO) and the National Institute of Aeronautics and Space of Indonesia.

ISRO might help Indonesia with its launch vehicles to put Indonesian satellites into space. The statement said Indonesia welcomed India's offer of further upgradation of the Biak Telemetry, Tracking and Command Station to receive data from its Ocean Sat and Resource Sat satellites that have applications in hydrography, weather forecasting, disaster management, crop forecasting and resource mapping. Indonesia is playing a significant strategic role in helping India enhance its association with ASEAN. Many ASEAN countries, including Indonesia, look forward to India's active role in the region, as China grows its presence rapidly in and around East Asia. India and Indonesia share not just history but contemporary issues too. Both are plural, both have adopted liberalization and have fast-spaced economies. Both countries have a growing urban middle-class, issues related to growth, lack of funding for infrastructure, both are looking for investment in better technology to exploit natural resources, issue of food security, *jihadi* terrorism, the issue of maritime security in surrounding sea bother them. All these common challenges have been discussed today between both countries. Prime Minister Singh said:

> Indonesia is one of India's most valued partners in our Look East Policy. Our bilateral relations are rich in potential and growing rapidly.

Besides the issue of trade imbalance due to India's import of oil, coal and palm oil, there has been few trade-related issues regarding Indian private investment in Indonesia. Some of it has been recently on shaky ground because Indian businessmen like the Ambanis, Adani and other business groups are finding the going tough. They want "transparent, stable and predictable regime in Jakarta". Decision has also been taken to expedite trade-related issues on both sides. The joint statement said that to solve the pending business-related issues both sides have agreed to form "a high-level task force to effectively monitor implementation of Business-to-Business MoUs; facilitate investment in each other's national infrastructure-development plans, including PPP (Public–Private Partnership) mode; and identify specific projects for joint investment in India, Indonesia or third countries". Both the countries are also exploring the possibility of joint defence equipment production. India, the world's second most populous country, and Indonesia, the world's fourth most populated country, with the largest Muslim population, enjoy cordial relation which was visible in the joint addresses of both leaders. Both leaders have welcomed the constitution of the India–Indonesia Eminent Persons Group and tasked the group to prepare, within a year, a vision document 2025 for India–Indonesia relations. India and Indonesia have put their best footsteps forward in mutual interest with commitment to take the US $ 20 billion trade to US $ 25 billion by 2015.

This visit has further deepened India's strategic partnership with Indonesia. India and Indonesia inked a strategic partnership agreement in 2005, about a year after both Singh and Yudhoyono assumed leadership in their respective countries. Singh's scheduled meeting with Yudhoyono may be the last one during the latter's tenure as the president of Indonesia. Presidential elections are expected to be held in Indonesia in April 2014 after Yudhoyono completes his second term. The India–Indonesia bilateral trade has grown by nearly five times since this partnership; to about US $ 20 billion currently, while it is targeted to reach US $ 25 billion by 2015, as we have seen earlier. India's relationships with ASEAN and other Asian countries are now moving towards more strategic partnerships as areas of co-operation have expanded from only economic issues to security, defence, intelligence sharing, etc. Even on trade, the relations would grow multifold after the FTA on services and investments is signed with ASEAN later this year and gets implemented by July 2014. The issue of maritime security was also discussed by both leaders, while other areas where co-operation is expected to increase include counter-terrorism measures, non-traditional security threats, and disaster mitigation and management. On South China Sea dispute, India made its position clear that the freedom of navigation should be there as per international norms and an early resolution should be worked by first making early progress towards adoption of Code of Conduct norms. Asked about a different approach taken by China on this issue, officials said, India was very clear on its position irrespective of any other country's view. They said that there were certainly some differences among countries on the issue of sovereignty, but India was firm on its stance that these issues should be resolved through consultations as per international norms.

Yudhoyono and Singh bilateral meeting had broadened relations between Asia's two largest democracies. Singh's visit has not only consolidated and expanded strategic relations between the two countries, but also in bilateral trade. Foreign Direct Investment (FDI) from Indian firms totalled US $ 78.1 million across fifty-eight projects last year, while it amounted to US $ 57.1 million in fifty-nine projects from January to June 2013. Both countries have set the target of US $ 25 billion in bilateral trade by 2015. This target of US $ 25 billion is now appears to be achieved by end of 2013 itself. Infrastructure, power, textiles, steel, automotives, resource-mining, banking and manufacturing are the attractive investments for Indian companies. Another important issue for the two countries is free trade. India is very "keen" to have a FTA on services and investment between ASEAN and India. An FTA on goods between India and ASEAN was signed two to three years ago and that has resulted in positive expansion.

Conclusion

India is looking for stronger ties with Indonesia in economic and other areas of co-operation. Besides being a key ASEAN member, Indonesia is an important bilateral partner of India. The areas of co-operation between the two countries range from economy, culture, energy, security, space and development. The relation between Indonesia and India has strengthened and deepened. There have been various co-operation schemes under the current strategic partnership. There has been strategic partnership inked by the two countries in 2005, aiming to make Jakarta–Delhi one of the most thriving bilateral relationships in the region.

References

Craig, A. Lockard, 2006, "Societies, Networks, and Transitions: A Global History", *Cengage Learning*, 27 December, p. 367.

Foreign Policy of India: Text of Documents 1947-59, p. 54.

http://www.embassyofindiajakarta.org

http://www.indonesianembassy.org.in

http://jnicc.com/doc/Ramayana%20to%20films.pdf

http://www.omniglot.com/writing/balinese.htm

"India–Indonesia Maritime Boundary Agreement", *Foreign Affairs Record*, **XXIII**(1), 2, January 1977.

Kapur, Kamlesh, 2010, *Portraits of a Nation: History of Ancient India*, New Delhi: Sterling Publishers.

"Pakistan Aims for Better Relations with Indonesia Beyond Politics", *The Jakarta Post*, 24 June 2008.

Paul Michel Munoz, 2007, Early Kingdoms of the Indonesian Archipelago and the Malay Peninsula. Singapore: Didiermillet, p. 143.

"RI-India Perluas Kerjasama Ekonomi, Energi dan Hukum", *Antara News*.

Sastri, K.A. Nilakanta, 1955, *A History of South India*, Oxford: Oxford University Press, pp. 424–26.

The Invention of Tradition in Indian Food, *Outlook*, Febuary 4, 2014. (http: / / www.outlook-india.com / article / the-Invention-of-Tradition-In-Indian-food / 223131)

Times of India, 9 october 2013 (http: / / times of india.indiatimes.com / india / Prime-Minister-Manmohansingh-leaves-on-four-day-visit-to-Brunie-Indonesia / articleshow / 23779015)

Tomascik, T., J.A. Mah, A. Nontji, M.K. Moosa, 1996, *The Ecology of the Indonesian Seas — Part One*, Hong Kong: Periplus Editions.

8

India–Indonesia Relations in a Changing World

Yuvaraj Gogoi
Junuguru Srinivas

Abstract

India and Indonesia relationship has a long history. While the former is the largest country in South Asia, the latter is the largest country in South-East Asia. The two countries have several commonalities like cultural affinity, colonial past and geographical proximity. India and Indonesia are already part of G-20 and share the same spirit in WTO negotiations. Both the countries had acrimonious relationship with China once. But, in spite of these commonalities, the bilateral relationship between the two countries has several ups and downs and has a chequered history. The India–Indonesia relationship reached its pinnacle during the establishment of Non-Aligned Movement (NAM) under the leadership of Jawaharlal Nehru and Sukarno along with Gamal Abdel Nasser of Egypt and Tito of Yugoslavia in 1961. But in the subsequent period, especially during the Indo–Pak war of 1971, the relationship between the two nations suffered a setback. However, in the recent years both the nations are again coming closer. Indeed, they have reached such a juncture that they cannot afford to ignore one another. Both the countries have liberalized their economies and the trade between the two countries are ever expanding in the post-1990s. in October

2013, during Prime Minister Manmohan Singh's visit to Indonesia, six Memorandum of Understandings (MoUs) have been signed between the two nations. In 2011, eleven MoUs/treaties were signed by the leaders of the two countries. In the same year, India and Indonesia completed six decades of their diplomatic relationship. This bears an ample testimony to the fact that the relationship between the two nations has come of age.

Both the countries have shown prudence in foreign policy making and diplomacy. India is a key member of BRICS, while Indonesia is the driving force of ASEAN. Indonesia has even the potential to be a part of BRICS in future. Both the nations can take the lead to transform the "Look East" Policy into a success story of prosperity and solidarity.

This paper thus tries to explain why India and Indonesia can and should have robust political ties with each other. It also seeks to analyse how these two nations can take their bilateral ties to a new level in this changing world. The paper argues that strategic, economic and cultural interests can bring the two nations closer in the coming years. It emphasizes that India and Indonesia should come forward hand-in-hand to tackle problems like terrorism, corruption, narcotics and illegal drugs. The two nations can be a profound voice of the global south in the world forums like World Bank, IMF and the UN Security Council.

Introduction

INDIA and Indonesia relationship has a long history. India and Indonesia are said to have maintained cultural and trade relations with each other for thousands of years. While the former is the largest country in South Asia, the latter is the largest country in South-East Asia. The two countries have several commonalities like cultural affinity, colonial past and geographical proximity. Since the period of independence from the yoke of colonial rule, the relationship between the two countries has witnessed several ups and downs. This paper tries to explain why India and Indonesia can and should have robust political ties with each other. The first part of the paper tries to highlight the commonality between the nations. The next part deals with the changing dynamics of India–Indonesia relations. The article ends by suggesting that the two nations can take their bilateral ties to a new level in the years to come.

Commonalities between the Nations

India and Indonesia have got certain commonalities.[1] These include cultural affinity, geographical affinity and post-colonial history. These common features can act as catalysts in proliferating ties in the political and strategic areas. These features are briefly highlighted hereunder:

> As an Asian neighbour of India, Indonesia shares certain cultural similarities with the former. As already stated, the cultural relation between the two nations goes to the remote past. Indonesia's traditional puppetry and drama tradition called *Wayang* has been influenced by the narratives of the *Ramayana* and the *Mahabharata.* — Trivedi 2010: 56 n. 4

In fact, the epics *Ramayana* and *Mahabharata* have greatly influenced the folk narratives of Indonesia. The Hindu temples in Bali also amply reflect the influence of Indian culture in Indonesia. In addition to this:

> (B)oth Java and Sumatra were subject to considerable cultural influence from the Indian subcontinent during the first and second millennia of this era. — Ibid.: 54

The national motto of Indonesia is "Bhinneka Tunggal Ika" which means "unity in diversity, although different still one" (Portal Nasional Republik Indonesia. Web. 10 November 2013). And this spirit is also found in the Indian constitution. The national symbol of Indonesia is the Garuda bird which finds mention in *Ramayana.* Its national symbol also contains a

---

[1] However, there are several differences between the two countries as well. For detailed analysis of similarities and differences between India and Indonesia, see Lankester 2004: 291-304.

banyan tree and a bull head. While banyan tree is the national tree of India, the bull is also there in the national symbol of India — the Ashoka Pillar of Sarnath. This reflects that the culture and mythology of one country have influenced the other in certain ways.

Indonesia is the largest Muslim country in the world though officially it is not a Muslim state. Though 90 per cent of the population is Muslims, there are Hindus and Buddhists as well among other minority religious groups. A writer has observed that "Hinduism and Buddhism had cast a penetrating influence on Indonesia's cultural life" (Trivedi 2010: 54). As far as India is concerned, it has the highest Hindu population but it is not a Hindu state. Both the nations are ethnically diverse. While India is the world's largest democracy, Indonesia holds the third rank.

India and Indonesia have also certain common elements of history. Both the countries were under colonizing powers for centuries. The British ruled India for more than 200 years. Similarly, Indonesia was also under the Dutch rule; it proclaimed independence just two years before India in 17 August 1945 and became fully independent in 1949. It became a republic in 1950. Seen in this way, both the countries had a colonial history and attained independence in the same decade and became republican states in the same year. In the post-independence period also, both the countries faced the same kind of problems and issues like nation building, corruption, sectarian violence and economic development to cite a few. India got divided from Pakistan, likewise Indonesia suffered with its division from Malay, an archipelagic island in South-East Asia. India acquired Pondicherry from French rulers in 1954, Goa from Portuguese in 1961. Similarly, Indonesia took over Dutch New Guinea in 1963, and Portuguese East Timor[2] in 1975. Indonesia–India countries fought against ethnic and religious

[2] East Timor became an independent country in 2002.

separatism within their respective borders to build cohesive and secularism (Brewster 2011: 223). Indonesia has international borders with India along the Andaman and Nicobar islands. It is noteworthy that this geographical contiguity helped in the establishment of trade relations with each other.

After independence, both India and Indonesia tried to maintain cordial relations with China. But after the 1962 Indo–China war, there appeared an indelible strain in the bilateral ties between India and China. From 1960s Indonesia's relation with China also started deteriorating over certain conflicting issues. Though both India and Indonesia have resumed their diplomatic relations with China, now they have started adopting a more cautious approach towards China. The rise of China is a matter of concern for both the countries. Indian–Indonesian strategic ties are influenced by this China factor to a certain extent.

The Changing Dynamics of India–Indonesia Relations

L.P. Singh has divided the contemporary history of India–Indonesia relations into four periods:

> the years of extreme cordiality, 1947-58; emerging differences, 1959-61; strained relations, 1962–winter 1966; and the current phase of reestablished friendship.
>
> — Singh 1967: 655

Singh points out that during the period 1947-58:

> (T)he most important factor contributing to the cordiality was India's mobilization of international support for the cause of Indonesian independence. — Ibid.

This factor brought the nations closer to each other. However, during the period 1959-61, rifts emerged between the two nations particularly with regard to the image of China. During the Indo–Pak war of 1971, the relationship between the two nations suffered a setback. But in the recent years two nations have reinvigorated their bilateral ties. They have reached such a juncture that they cannot afford to ignore one another.

The disintegration of Soviet Union greatly paved the way for emergence of new international order. It is well known how this event led to the formal end of the Cold War. During this phase, India was striving hard to stand as a nation with enormous economic, political and societal challenges. Since then India has started engaging actively and giving importance to the "extended neighbourhood" regions like East Asia, Central Asia, Persian Gulf and Middle East (Raja Mohan 2008: 45). The then prime minister of India P.V. Narasimha Rao liberalized the Indian economy and also brought certain changes in foreign policy objectives, for example, India established formal diplomatic relations with countries like Israel for the first time. Rao also launched the Look East Policy with a view to establish strong trade relations with East Asian countries. Indonesia is the largest country in the region and naturally India's focus on Indonesia is quite evident and understandable. Since the 1990s onwards, the trade relations between the nations have been increasing as never before. The trade also grew immensely with the India's active engagement with the ASEAN region. The increasing trade relation between India and Indonesia is evident from Table 8.1. It clears that the total trade between India and Indonesia was US $ 92 million in the year 1987. It got increased to US $ 286 million after the introduction of the Look East Policy. The total trade between the two nations touched the US $ 10 and US $ 15 billion mark in the years 2010 and 2012, respectively.

In the last few decades, India's aspiration to become a global power has been increasing rapidly. This is discernible from India's growing voice on a multitude of global issues. India's nuclear deal with the US, its stand on CTBT, Palestine issue in the United Nations (UN), and its role in the southern multinational forums like BRICS, SCO, BRICS BANK, and also

Table 8.1: India-Indonesia Two-Way Trade (US $ million)

Year	*India's Exports*	*India's Imports*	*Balance of Trade*	*Total Trade*
1987	29	63	- 34	92
1988	35	67	- 32	102
1989	79	51	+ 28	130
1990	149	59	+ 90	209
1991	226	56	+ 170	282
1992	216	70	+ 146	286
2010*				10 **
2012*				15 **

* Ministry of External Affairs, Web. 10 November 2013. ** Billion US $.

Source: Indonesian Trade Figures, Embassy of the Republic of Indonesia, New Delhi (cited in Jha 1996: 396).

extension of support for south–south co-operation are the real indicators of its influence in global affairs at par with other aspiring nations like China, Brazil and Russia. Emergence of China, India, Brazil and many other countries from south and its increasing voice on a plethora of global issues have been clearly indicating the emergence of a multipolar world order.

At this critical juncture, David Brewster (2013) says, India wants a direct political and security role in South-East Asia as part of its evolution as a regional power since the recent past as never before. In this context, the help of Indonesia is indispensable. The two nations can transform their relations to a win–win situation.

Vibhanshu Sekhar points out:

> There has been a growing realization on the part of these two countries that they have common stakes in a peaceful, stable, and co-operative Asia, a vision once shared together by the founding fathers of these two countries — Nehru and Sukarno — and enshrined under the Bandung Spirit.
>
> — 2010: 77

The strategic relationship between the two nations has been informed by this vision. Sekhar has also viewed the India–Indonesia strategic relations as a cumulative outcome of the following factors:

> Changing geopolitical realities of Asia during the post-Cold War era and the first decade of the twenty-first century.
>
> Multi-pronged strategies of engagement pursued by India under Look East Policy since 1992.
>
> The dynamism of greater economic integration and multilateral co-operation.
>
> A shared understanding of prevailing security discourses in the region. — Ibid.: 78

The year 2005 was a milestone as far as the Indo–Indonesian strategic partnership is concerned. The Indo–Indonesian strategic partnership was signed in that year during the visit of the Indonesian president Susilo Bambang Yudhoyono to India. The same year in April, the Indian Prime Minister Manmohan Singh visited Jakarta to attend the 50th anniversary of the Afro–Asian Bandung Summit. During the visit these two countries signed a new strategic partnership and the two leaders noted:

> Asian continent is emerging as a leading space for global economic and politics, it gives opportunity to these two countries for their mutual co-operation . . . and as free and open societies sharing a common commitment to democracy and pluralism, in this context India and Indonesia should promote peace and stability in Asia and in world at large as never before.
>
> — Ministry of External Affairs, Web, 10 November 2013

Thus, the strategic relationship between the two countries is increasing in the recent years.

In 2011, eleven MoUs/treaties were signed by the leaders of the two countries. In the same year, India and Indonesia completed six decades of their diplomatic relationship. This bears an ample testimony to the fact that the relationship between the two nations has come of age. Such south–south co-operation can usher in a new era in the South Asian region. Both the countries have shown prudence in foreign policy making and diplomacy. In 2013, six MoUs have been signed between the two countries, during Prime Minister Manmohan Singh's visit to Indonesia in October. The two nations have also agreed to strengthen their "co-operation on space, research and training and education" (*Jakarta Post*, Web, 13 November 2013). Such south–south co-operation can usher in a new era in South Asian region.

The role of India and Indonesia is also evident in multilateral forums. India is a key member of BRICS, while Indonesia is the driving force of ASEAN. Indonesia has even the potential to be a part of BRICS in future. Both the nations can take the lead to transform the Look East Policy into a success story of prosperity and solidarity. It is an unpalatable truth that though two decades have passed, the Look East Policy of India has not achieved any spectacular success. But, being a key actor of the Asian region, Indonesia's help and participation would be indispensable for the successful implementation of the Look East Policy.

In the changing world scenario, the two nations can help each other in tackling the problems of corruption, economic underdevelopment, narcotics and illegal drugs and assist each other in upholding the democratic spirit. The two nations can be a profound voice from global south in the multilateral forums like the World Bank, IMF and the UN Security Council. Indonesia has huge amount of oil and natural gas reserves. It can help India in meeting its energy needs. All these explain why the two nations can and should have robust political ties with each other.

Conclusion

The dynamics of world politics was rapidly changing in the last two decades. In this new emerging multipolar world order, countries like China, India, Brazil and Indonesia, among others, are expected to play a key role. In a nutshell, world is moving towards a multipolar world order. These emerging countries are striving hard to bring about reforms in the global institutions like World Bank, IMF, WTO and UN Security Council. In this changing world scenario, the commonalities that India and Indonesia share can help in bringing them closer. The two nations can take their political, economic, strategic and cultural relations to a new level in the years to come.

References

Brewster, D., 2011, "The Relationship between India and Indonesia", *Asian Survey* (March/April), **51**(2): 221-44.

"Indonesia, India take Further Steps to Strengthen Relationship", *Jakarta Post*, Web, 13 November 2013.

Jha, G.N., 1996, "A Brief Survey of India–Indonesia Relations", *Contemporary Southeast Asia* (March), **17**(4): 389-405.

"Joint Declaration between the Republic of India and the Republic of Indonesia", Ministry of External Affairs, Web, 10 November 2013.

Lankester, T., 2004, "'Asian Drama': The Pursuit of Modernization in India and Indonesia", *Asian Affairs*, **35**(3): 291-304.

Portal Nasional Republik Indonesia, Web, 10 November 2013.

Raja Mohan, C., 2008, "India's Geopolitics and Southeast Asian Security", *Southeast Asian Affairs*, 43-60.

Sekhar, V., 2010, "India and Indonesia: Reliable Partners in an Uncertain Asia", *Asia-Pacific Review*, **17**(2): 76-98.

Singh, L.P., 1967, "Dynamics of Indian–Indonesian Relations", *Asian Survey* (Sept.), **7**(9): 655-66.

Trivedi, S., 2010, "Early Indian Influence in Southeast Asia: Revitalising Partnership between India and Indonesia", *Indian Quarterly*, **66**(1): 51-67.

9

India–Indonesia Strategic Partnership

Defining Contours of Engagement

Pankaj K. Jha

INDIA and Indonesia, the two large democracies of the southern Asia, have witnessed similar historical legacy in terms of civilizational interactions, pluralistic multicultural and multi-religious societies, and incrementally decentralized federal structure. Strategically, the two nations sit astride important Sea Lines of Communication (SLOCs); have large coastlines and vast Exclusive Economic Zone (EEZ). In terms of foreign policy perspective also, the views are nearly identical.[1] Given the pre-eminent position, both geographically and strategically, these two nations are bound to play an important role in maintaining regional order and peace. The strategic partnership signed between the two in 2005, exemplifies this objective and underlines a need for defence and strategic co-operation which would enable the armed forces of the two nations to work together for protecting national sovereignty and interests. However, in terms of tangible results, the two nations can be called as hesitant players in the regional strategic

[1] India espouses the concept of the world as a family (drawn from the Sanskrit term *vasudhaiv kutumbkam*) while Indonesian foreign policy professes "thousand friends and no enemy". Both the nations also believe in concentric circles approach in their foreign policy priorities.

configuration. Moreover, the strategic partnership has not gained the necessary impetus from both the countries owing to their respective reservations and apprehensions about each other on a number of issues related to security of Malacca straits, defence co-operation and bilateral defence exercises. As a result, the only visible co-operation between the two has been co-ordinated patrol and occasional exchange of military officers apart from the defence dialogue which has been less frequent. The chapter would highlight the historical backdrop of the strategic understanding between the two nations; the inherent structural bottlenecks and the reasons for a lack of futuristic perspective from both sides. It would propose a future roadmap for the strategic partnership between the two nations and how the mutual trust could be enhanced through capability building and joint co-operative mechanisms.

Indonesia, having the highest Muslim population[2] in the world, is slowly emerging as a fledgling democracy and a fast developing nation. Importantly, India has been enhancing ties with Indonesia in defence, economic and trade areas. The signing of the strategic partnership in 2005[3] between the two countries highlighted that perspective. The contours of this partnership are kept vague so as to keep it in an open-ended evolutionary phase. The high-level visit of Indian Prime Minister Manmohan Singh to Indonesia in October 2013[4] highlighted the need and the urge of India to engage it as one of the closest maritime neighbours. The visit led to the signing of six MoUs ranging from energy

[2] Saleh 2001: 1. Also see Suryadinata et al. 2003: 106.

[3] Joint Statement on five initiatives for strengthening the India-Indonesia Strategic Partnership, 11 October 2013, Jakarta, Indonesia at http://pmindia.nic.in/press-details.php?nodeid=1713 (accessed on 13 October 2013).

[4] Joint Statement on five initiatives for strengthening the India–Indonesia Strategic Partnership at http://pib.nic.in/newsite/erelease.aspx?relid=100004 (accessed on 13 October 2013).

security, space, education, academic interactions, to anti-narcotics co-operation, etc. Two leaders agreed to expand their strategic partnership by holding annual summits and proposed an eminent persons group to expand the relationship. New areas of co-operation have been identified such as space, nuclear energy, food security, counter-terrorism, transnational threats from religious *jihadi* forces. Co-operation would be expanded in areas like defence and maritime, and a comprehensive action plan would be developed for security co-operation.[5]

India–Indonesia ties have been one of the most touted relations in the recent history. The engagements have been robust but undermined by the lack-lustre bureaucratic approach from both sides. The initiatives and declarations have been promising but the tangible results were somewhat absent from the ground. The strategic partnership document, signed between the two sides in 2005, outlined the core areas of engagement such as shipbuilding, trade, investment, defence co-operation and multilateralism. However, the initiative and the contours of engagement were largely undefined. Subsequently, it was the business and private sector interests which proliferated in terms of investment and trade, and compelled India to engage the largest archipelagic nation of South-East Asia. Moreover, Indonesia acts as a cradle to the South-East Asian geopolitical construct. In the recent times, the importance of maritime trade routes and sea lines of communication were highlighted in the two maritime strategy documents of India[6] which stressed on the need to engage maritime neighbours like Indonesia.

---

[5] Jha, 2013. http://www.dnaindia.com/india/report-prime-minister-manmohan-singh-leaves-for-home-after-4-day-visit-to-brunei-indonesia-from-barun-jha-1902470 (accessed on 13 October 2013).

[6] Two maritime strategy documents of India were released in 2004 and 2007, respectively. These two documents amplify India's naval thinking in terms of future and its likely role in maritime domain.

For India, the major reason for engaging Indonesia has been a fourfold strategy. First, in order to expand its horizons to the eastwards of Indonesia, the country needs to be engaged. Second, the "Indo-Pacific" construct, to which both the countries have started their subscription is another viable reason, closely connected to the United States rebalancing strategy towards Asia. Thirdly, the energy requirements of India especially in terms of power generation through thermal power plants have made Indonesia as a lucrative destination for coal imports. Fourthly, the increasing imprints of Indonesia both in terms of multilateral institutions like G-20 and East Asia Summit (EAS) as well as its increasing stature in Muslim organizations like Organization of Islamic Countries (OIC) and Developing–Eight (D-8) has made it a indispensable partner for India. Moreover, the defence and strategic co-operation germinating because of India's urge to develop blue water navy has created a natural reason for India to reach out to Indonesia.

The chapter while outlining all the facets of the relationship would also scrutinize the future of the relations, given the fact that India wants to subscribe to the ASEAN centrality in multilateral structures while China is not so willing subscriber to that role. This argument germinates from the fact that China has been trying to negotiate with the claimant countries on a bilateral level while the ASEAN nations are advocating a multilateral solution to the problem through the formal mechanism like Code of Conduct (COC) on South China Sea.

From Non-Aligned Movement (NAM) to East Asia Summit (EAS)

During the Indonesian struggle for independence, the vulnerabilities fragmented social and physical geography of the Indonesian state were exposed, an experience similar to newly-independent Afro-Asian nations. Indonesia's untapped bountiful natural and energy resources made it a lucrative destination for external powers. Furthermore, its strategic location between the Indian and Pacific Ocean reinforced its importance in Asian geo-strategic configuration. Pride in its revolutionary achievement, multi-cultural distinctiveness, a awareness of vast territorial area, large population, myriad natural resources reinforced the belief that Indonesia was entitled to play a leading role in the management of regional order within South-East Asia.[7] Even the conciliation process with Dutch, in the aftermath of the Second World War was fraught with tensions and divisions within Indonesian society. British, apprehensive about the future scenario, contemplated sending British Indian troops to control escalating internecine tensions in Indonesia. This was the first interaction, in terms of defence between Indonesia and India. In terms of cultural and religious ties, the links were historical. Syncretic form of Islam that is prevalent in Indonesia is being influenced by India's tolerant ethos and was exported to the country through Indian traders and religious thinkers.

With regard to political interactions, on the issue of anti-imperialism, anti-apartheid and non-aligned movement, there was convergence of opinion between the two nations. In order to buttress Afro–Asian solidarity, India took initiative to convene pan-Asian conferences such as the 1947 Asian Relations Conference and the 1949 Conference on Indonesia to combat colonialism. The latter was meant to condemn Second Dutch "police action" in Indonesia and urged effective UN intervention to drive the Dutch out of Indonesia. In India's opinion not only was India's freedom, was of material significance to these new states but equally their freedom was important to India, if it wanted to develop independently. Sukarno's Indonesia therefore appealed to the Indian elites primarily because it was perceived as

---

7 Liefer, 1983: xiv.

ferociously nationalistic and non-aligned.[8] Even during the outbreak of the Korean War, the Indonesian government refused to adopt a position of either approval or disapproval towards the belligerents and correspondingly resisted pressures from the United States to become a party to its global policy of containment.[9] This non-aligned position had been encouraged by India's prime minister, Jawaharlal Nehru, who had strongly advocated Indonesia's national cause.[10] Mohammed Hatta, Indonesian prime minister, was extremely sensitive to the domestic political atmosphere which gave rise to such a position. Within the United Nations, Indonesia's delegation identified itself with measures for a peaceful settlement in Korea and with support for anti-colonial movements.[11] Right since the Bandung Conference in 1955; the ideas mooted by the leaders of the two countries had found a stable ground in developing countries.[12]

India–Indonesia relations took off to an impressive start with India's unflinching support for the new Indonesian republic. In the early 1950s both countries showed a remarkable level of co-operation in foreign affairs as they spoke with one voice of non-alignment, Panchsheel (Five Principles of Peaceful Co-existence), colonialism, etc. and more specifically on Indo–China, SEATO and the Suez crises.[13] But by the late 1950s, due to their differing images of China[14] and due to a personality clash between Nehru and Sukarno there developed an unbridgeable chasm between the two countries. The 1961

8 Sridharan 1996: 24.

9 Ibid.

10 Ibid.

11 See Finkelstein 1951.

12 Sridharan 1996: 24.

13 Jha 2013; also see Sridharan 1996: 24-27.

14 Sukma 1999: 1-2.

Belgrade Conference proved a forerunner to the tensions that marked their relations. During the conference Sukarno and Nehru differed over the primary objective of the non-aligned gathering. The former insisted on the anti-colonial line while the latter felt that world peace was the more pressing issue facing the countries. Even during the Fourth Asian Games due to non-participation of Israel and Taiwan, an Indian vice-president of the Asian Games Federation, sought to have the status of the games nullified. This initiative was construed as a personal insult to Sukarno and a national insult to Indonesia. As a consequence, Indian embassy was attacked by an infuriated mob and its participants as well as national flag were booed.[15]

These differences got magnified, concurrently with the Sino–Indian conflict, and the progressive intensification of the Sino–Soviet dispute, Indonesia and India themselves parties to competing structures of alignment. The same intensity highlighted the 1964 Cairo Conference where India and Indonesia clashed over the principle of peaceful co-existence. President Sukarno championed the Chinese view of that principle[16] which annoyed India and led the latter to conduct a spirited campaign in defence of its own version of peaceful co-existence. At the more intermediate level, India–Indonesia relations took a beating owing to India's instance on Malaysia while Indonesia was nurturing a *konfrontasi*. Later, during the 1965 Afro–Asian conference, India lobbied to get the support from sufficient number of members for Malaysia's admission at the conference. This incensed President Sukarno to such an extent that the Jakarta mob violently attacked the Indian embassy in retaliation. Relations worsened when Indonesia diplomatically supported Pakistan during the Indo–Pak War

---

15 Sridharan, 1996: 27.

16 Sukma, 2009: 591-94. Also see Jha 2013.

(1965) and branded India as the provoker.[17] During this period Indian strategic discourse referred to Beijing–Jakarta–Rawalpindi axis in operation against India.

The estrangement in relationship ended after Suharto came to power in 1966. China became suspect in the eyes of the Indonesian elite owing to its alleged complicity in the 30 September coup,[18] as it has earlier become in the eyes of India. This provided the foundation for rebuilding the relationship. This led to the visit of Indonesian foreign minister Adam Malik in 1966 with a view to restore friendly ties. India reciprocated with offer of rupees 100 million worth of credit facilities to Jakarta. Indian foreign minister also visited Indonesia in January 1967 which further strengthened the bond between the two countries.[19]

In the 1969 after the Sino–Soviet clash on the Ussuri River, Soviet Union proposed the Asian Collective Security framework. Mrs Gandhi when visited Indonesia and Japan in 1969 found very little support for the Brezhnev plan for Asian Collective Security system and was asked to clarify India's stance. Mrs Gandhi clarified that if the plan projected a military alliance or pact then India would disagree but if it is for economic co-operation then India would consider it differently. Indonesia was also annoyed by the absence of India from the Thai-sponsored Vietnam peace conference in 1966 and also stayed away from the 1970 Jakarta Conference on Cambodia.

---

17 Sridharan 1996: 27; Jha 2013.

18 The unsuccessful coup by a group of army dissidents led ostensibly by Lieut. Col. Untung in September 1965 in which Communist Party of Indonesia (PKI) was implicated. Along with the destruction of the PKI in the domestic arena, the army also moved to eliminate the party's external ally China, by charging it with supporting the abortive coup. For further details, see Sukma 1999: 33; Sridharan 1996: 26.

19 Sridharan 1996: 28.

In a way these were attempts to restore order in the region but India saw them in a different light.[20] Indonesia was annoyed with India's decision and Indonesian Foreign minister Adam Malik implied that India followed the Soviet lead in this matter. Such a stance was further strengthened with the signing of the Indo–Soviet Treaty and also Soviet support to India during the Bangladesh War.[21]

In the 1980s the situation mellowed down between the two countries but there were issues of contention like India's recognition of the Vietnamese-installed Heng Semrin Regime though President Suharto agreed that Vietnam would be one of the instruments of controlling China. Although there were some difference of views over Kampuchea, India probably felt more at ease with Indonesia's restrained stance over Kampuchea.[22] A *Far Eastern Economic Review* report in May 1986 which mentioned India's plan to build a major naval base on great Nicobar Island perturbed the Indonesians. However, the apprehensions were more about the possibility of Soviet using the facilities in the Nicobar base.[23]

Earlier during the late 1980s, the discussion about India's hegemonic designs was projected, when it was stated that India intents to reinforce its presence in the Andaman and Nicobar islands through the proposal of an Andaman and Nicobar Command. It compelled India to undertake diplomatic initiatives to assuage the apprehensions raised by the littoral nations including Indonesia and Australia. In the post-Cold War phase after the withdrawal of the US forces from the

---

20 Sridharan, 1996: 61.

21 Ibid.: 61-67.

22 Ibid.: 66-71. Also see *Hindustan Times*, 3 December 1980 and *Times of India*, 2 December 1980.

23 Sridharan, 1996: 130-39. For details see *The Straits Times*, 13 October 1986.

South-East Asia, the South-East Asian states were wary of a different kind of strategic rivalry between the three major Asian powers namely Japan, China and India. Indonesia, in particular, was apprehensive about Indian intentions following the latter's efforts to bolster its naval strength in and around subcontinental waters. Indonesia's proximity to the Andaman and Nicobar group of islands was a prime factor for such an uneasiness on the part of Indonesia. An additional cause for concern was India's pursuit of a naval modernization programme. The Indian Navy's blue water status was projected through the acquisition of a second aircraft carrier in August 1987 and a leased nuclear powered submarine from the Soviet Union in February 1988.[24] ASEAN states in general and Indonesia in particular felt at unease with the flurry of Indian naval activities. With its naval base at Vishakhapatnam and at Port Blair, Andaman, India was seen by Jakarta as extending its subcontinental policeman role further east. Now, the same development of Integrated Command in Andaman and Nicobar islands is seen as a force multiplier and a prerequisite for regional security. Moreover, the most compelling reason has been the challenges related to piracy and maritime security. Also, these issues have become the reason to develop trilateral understanding between Australia, Indonesia and India especially when the three countries can boast of strategic partnerships among themselves — at the bilateral level.[25] To dispel the notion of threatening blue water Navy was also one of the motives of India to initiate LEP. India's elevation to Dialogue Partner status in ASEAN and the institution of informal mechanisms like EAS defined a new phase of partnership between the two nations. The relationship between India and Indonesia graduated to a strategic partnership, and

---

24 Young 1988: 4-18.

25 Jha 2013.

the fact that Indonesia was open to the few countries with which India signed the strategic partnership, revealed the significance of their partnership.

Strategic Partnership: Defining Contours of Engagement

In order to develop relations with the extended neighbourhood, India projected a safe terminology to project its non-aggressive intentions and cultivate its benign image among the security-conscious nations of South-East Asia. The adverse effect Indo–Soviet Friendship Treaty in 1971 created doubts about India's commitment to NAM and its aversion to power-bloc politics. Drawing lessons from the past; India initiated the policy of strategic partnership.[26] In the post-Cold War era, the leaders of China, India and Russia have dogmatically engaged in a quest for an enhanced role in the regional politics. With their own goals for status and power tempered by pragmatism, the secondary powers have also sought mutual ties that bind them in functionally co-operative endeavours. The attempts of Chinese, Indian and Russian leaders at developing more defined and formal bilateral strategic partnerships and trilateral ties, while seeking neither to antagonize nor fully embrace each other or the United States, demonstrate the challenges to peace and security, and opportunities for co-operation embodied in their strategies.[27]

Strategic partnerships call for greater engagement between parties than mere ad hoc bilateral relationships that ensue as a result of normal diplomatic intercourse between states. They are, however, less inflexible than defensive military alliances, since they are neither explicitly targeted at a specific country

---

[26] Strategic partnership is increasingly seen in India's foreign policy discourse as the flexible approach to meet the long-term foreign policy objectives.

[27] Nadkarni 2010: 25.

nor contain binding defence commitments. These partnerships have emerged as a safe policy option for secondary powers in a complex and globalizing world.[28] Incidentally, barring few exceptions India has signed strategic partnerships with those countries with which it has not signed the (FTAs) or on a slow track of negotiations. The case in point is that of Vietnam and Indonesia.

On the issue of regional security and stability, Indonesia has developed harmonious relations between different communities and more recently taken initiatives to maintain peace in the region. The case in point is the extensive shuttle diplomacy[29] done by Marty Natalegawa to diffuse the tensions in South China Sea in 2012. Indonesia role in counter terrorism efforts both domestically and at regional level has been widely appreciated. Indonesia has for long been the fulcrum of any regional initiatives be it the formation of ASEAN or even ARF. Indonesia has contiguous maritime boundary with India and due to Andaman Nicobar Joint Command emerging as a major strategic move of India in the region, Indonesia comes as a strategically important country for India. Also India's move in the region in the past has been observed keenly by Indonesia during the Cold War years be it the formation of Bangladesh or even the plan to form the Andaman command in 1980s. It can be stated that these issues were raised by United States, so as to thwart any attempt by USSR to find a footing in the strategically important Indian Ocean region. In the current context it has been in both India and Indonesia's interest to have greater strategic partnership so as to secure Indian Ocean and even Malacca Straits of any external power domination. Indonesia has been taking steps in this regard with help from Malaysia and to a certain extent by Singapore while in order

---

28 Nadkarni 2010: 48.

29 Nehru 2012.

to secure Indian Ocean, Indian Navy is also enhancing its strategic reach. These steps are not mutually exclusive as India has time and again reiterated its stance with regard to the security of sea lanes and has also wanted the security of South China Sea without annoying any of the claimants of the Spratlys islands.[30]

Indonesia also gains importance with regard to the alternative routes it provides in case of any accident in Malacca Straits. Indonesia has also seen influx of radical Islamic organizations like Hizb ut Tehrir (HUT) which has endorsed establishment of Islamic caliphate across the Muslim majority countries in Asia and the conference though did draw a large crowd but the influx of radical Islam has been refuted by Indonesian population. This has been projected by the loss of radical Muslim candidates in the local and provincial elections in Indonesia, barring the case of Aceh which has resorted to autonomy under Indonesia. The question arises that time and again radical elements in Indonesian society has projected democracy to be main culprit in terms of the suffering of people, though the reason was refuted by the general public.[31]

Indonesia has shown keenness to co-operate with India for the security and stability in the region and also a number of scholars have pointed out to India as an example of the more tolerant and developed society as the basic framework of prosperity. India and Indonesia being the two big nations geographically in southern Asia have a mutual interest in maintaining security in the region and also within the nations. The interaction between the two nations recently point to the fact that Indonesia's enhanced capability both in terms of defence and economic acts to the benefit of India. As companies like TVS and Bajaj have already opened their manufacturing

---

30 Jha 2013.

31 Ibid.

units in Indonesia, companies like Tata acquired stakes in Indonesian coalfields to secure supplies for their western coast power projects. Indonesia does act as a major energy supplier to India. Indonesia itself is keen to develop nuclear energy but has been facing problems with regard to placement of nuclear power plants and also does not possess necessary skilled workforce and scientists for this venture. Also Radical Islamists and even moderate Muslims in Indonesia have been raising apprehensions about the nuclear power projects in Indonesia which is to an extent justified but more palm oil and even vital resources like oil and gas would be freed in case Indonesia develops alternative fuels. As regards to geothermal energy, Indonesia has the world's second largest potential but has not got necessary human resource for exploiting the same. The amount of geothermal capability is around 37,500 kWh/year.[32] In terms of internal politics also the present president has marginalized both the military and the radicals in terms of political mileage. It would be imperative for India to strengthen Indonesian society, economy and defence so as to have a formidable and stable country in its strategic perimeter which nurtures good relations in the past and also present. Moreover, there are new constructs such as Indo-Pacific which have highlighted the need to engage bilaterally.

Indo-Pacific Construct

The latest construct "Indo-Pacific" has created a larger debate on the outcome and viability of security complexes which has geo-political and geo-strategic implications. In the contemporary times, the multilateral institutions are also becoming more inclusive and strive for building common consensus on regional security and developmental issues. As a result, a debate has started that whether multilateralism would define security constructs or vice versa.

---

[32] Jha 2013.

Tracking evolution of multilateralism and geopolitical constructs in the historical annals, the concept even though not articulated as "Indo-Pacific" construct, first resonated in the writings of the legendary strategic thinker K.M. Panikkar. Panikkar has made references about the Yemen (Socotra Island) and Malacca Straits as the two anchorages for India's strategic thought. Subsequently, Indian Prime Minister Jawaharlal Nehru defined a new construct of Afro–Asian unity as a tirade against anti-colonialism, anti-imperialism and anti-apartheid, and organized a conference defining this construct. Subsequently, NAM defined new construct to galvanize south-south co-operation thereby creating a third bloc. In early 1990s Asia-Pacific was a new terminology which defined the formation of Asia-Pacific Economic Co-operation (APEC).

In the more contemporary times, few strategic thinkers and countries such as Australia, Indonesia have shown subscription to the new concept of Indo-Pacific. Prime Minister Manmohan Singh has also outlined the preferred strategic choices for India and has highlighted the "Indo-Pacific" as a new paradigm for enhancing co-operation in the region. Giving preference to the "quest for stability and peace in the vast region in Asia that is washed by the Pacific and Indian Oceans" the Indian leader has enlisted Japan as the preferred partner. Earlier also, during the India–ASEAN Commemorative Summit in 2012, the Indian prime minister has alluded to the term Indo-Pacific.

According to Rory Medcalf, the "Indo-Pacific" terminology was referred in the 1950s to discuss decolonization and was again alluded to in the 1960s and 1970s. The term re-emerged as a consequence of Michael Richardson's paper in 2005 which argued that the inclusion of Australia, India and New Zealand as members of EAS reinvigorated the concept of "Indo-Pacific" region. The term "Indo-Pacific" later found increasing reference in the Australian foreign policy discourse, especially in the speeches by the Australian leaders and strategic analysts. However, the concept is still in its infancy and its applicability and utility in wider security concepts are still debated and discussed. The United States also adapted to this new lexicon, albeit with apprehension and proclaimed that ensuring security in the Indo-Pacific region will be a challenging task for it and liberal nations. The United States has repeatedly endorsed the concept as the fulcrum for developing regional economic and security structures and failure to do so would result in greater uncertainty, insecurity and instability. Given the rapid progress that has been witnessed in the region, it is expected that with its progressive economic growth, military clout and political resilience, the Indo-Pacific is incrementally emerging as the powerhouse of the world.[33] However, there are strands of struggle between the different forms of governance and development which can be witnessed in the form of liberalism, authoritarianism and even totalitarianism. Moreover, with the large number of Global Commons in this geographic construct, increasing co-operation as well as competition would make it a geo-political and strategic area of importance.

Michael Auslin in his report "Security in the Indo-Pacific Commons" states that the Indo-Pacific's unique physical outline makes the balance of regional security most vulnerable in its "commons": the open seas, air lanes and cyber networks that link the region together and to the world. Given the importance of the Indo-Pacific commons to the continued prosperity and stability of the region, the policy objectives of the United States and its Indo-Pacific allies and partners have been to:

- Ensure accessibility for all nations to the Indo-Pacific commons.
- Dissuade or manage conflict in the commons.

33 Medcalf 2013.

- Preserve credible military capabilities that can act as deterrent and even overcome the most likely regional threats.
- Support the liberal-democratic norms that will assist in propagating freedom and promote co-operative behaviour.[34]

The overarching goal of this approach is to replace a security environment that augments stability and development without the use of United States or allied military power. The interests of the United States and its allies and partners are primarily aimed to pre-empt any disorder that would trigger political strain or conflict, negatively affecting global economic activity or hamper the access of any nation to the rest of the region and globe for political or military reasons. However, as a result of China's military modernization in particular, the United States and its allies are apprehensive of maintaining their regional superiority of forces numerically or, eventually, qualitatively. Both India and Indonesia have been cautiously supporting the United States configuration without playing to its strategic plans.

New Avenues for Co-operation

Indonesia becomes a more important partner for India, not only in trade and investment, but also in science, technology, education and health as the two countries have similarities in terms of high population, market and culture.[35] India and Indonesia, the second and third largest economies in Asia after China, have signed thirty-three agreements to promote trade. They are also partners through the FTA signed by the ASEAN. Indonesia is keen on attracting Indian investments in manufacturing and value-added processing than just in

---

34 Auslin, 2013.

35 Aprilianto, 2012.

exploitation of its natural resources, according to Andi M. Ghalib, the Indonesian Ambassador to India.[36] The Indian government has shown keenness to increase investment in Indonesia, particularly in the food, automotive, manufacturing and infrastructure sectors. Indian investment in Indonesia currently stood at almost $10 billion and was mostly concentrated in the mining, textile and automotive sectors.[37] For India, Indonesian coal has been firing its thermal power plants and comprises an important element of making India fully a electrified nation. A number of companies like Adani, Tata and Reliance Power have bought equity in many Indonesian coalfields. However, there have been problems in the recent past when Indonesia hiked the levy on coal mined by foreign companies there to benchmark Indonesian coal price to international market prices and to promote investments in value-addition and manufacturing sectors. According to Leonard F. Hutabarat, Counsellor, Embassy of Indonesia, when companies invest in value addition the levy is lower. For instance, taxes for a company sourcing crude palm oil will be halved if it sets up a refinery in Indonesia. The same applies to other resources like coal. This follows demands by local governments in Indonesia that saw no economic benefit in foreign companies exploiting their natural resources.[38]

Conclusion

The evolving strategic scenario in the Asian context has made it pertinent for both the nations to enhance engagement at all

---

36 Indonesia looks to Indian investments beyond natural resources, *The Hindu*, 22 April 2013 at http://www.thehindu-businessline.com/industry-and-economy/government-and-policy/article-3342616.ece?-homepage=true&ref=wl_home(Accessed on 18 October 2013).

37 Hardum and Kessek 2013.

38 Cf. n. 36.

levels. However, strategic partnership has been rather restraint. The reason has been the inherent bureaucratic inertia from both sides and the lack of visionary approach from the policy perspective. The incremental change is taking place but there is a need for comprehensive policy to enhance engagement. Both India and Indonesia can undertake joint patrols, defence exercises and also create structures to address non-traditional security threats like terrorism, transnational crime syndicates and cerate database for international terrorists at both bilateral and multilateral levels, the two regional powers need to define their role in regional security and undertake responsibilities rather than acting as "free riders". The constrained approach will need more intense scrutiny in the future and the need for greater strategic engagement is foreseen but the domains and level need to be articulated from both sides at appropriate levels.

Note: The views expressed in this paper are the personal views of the author and do not represent the views of the institute or Government of India.

References

Aprilianto, Cundoko, 2012, "Indonesia Becomes More Important Partner for India", 9 March 2012 at http://english.cri.cn/6966/2012/03/09/3123s685975.htm (accessed on 18 October 2013).

Auslin, Michael, 2013, "Security in the Indo-Pacific Commons", *American Enterprise Institute* at http://www.aei.org/papers/foreign-and-defense-policy/regional/asia/security-in-the-indo-pacific-commons/(accessed on 10 October 2013).

Finkelstein, Lawrence S., 1951, "Indonesia's Record in United Nations", *International Reconciliation*, November.

Hardum, Siprianus and Khara Kessek, 2013, "India Keen to Boost Investment in Indonesia, Ambassador Says", 21 March 2013 at http://www.thejakartaglobe.com/business/india-keen-to-boost-investment-in-indonesia-ambassador-says/581115/(accessed on 18 October 2013).

Jha, Barun, "Prime Minister Manmohan Singh Leaves for Home after 4-day Visit to Brunei, Indonesia", *DNA*, 12 October 2013.

Jha, Pankaj, 2013, "India–Indonesia Partnership: Perspectives on Security and Stability", at http://www.scribd.com/doc/19229647/IndiaIndonesia-Strategic-Partnership (accessed on 12 December 2013).

Liefer, Michael, 1983, *Indonesia's Foreign Policy*, The Royal Institute of International Affairs, London: George Allen and Unwin.

Medcalf, Rory, 2013, "The Indo-Pacific: What's in a Name?", 25 October 2013 at http://www.brookings.edu/research/articles/2013/10/indo-pacific-economic-political-asia-medcalf/(accessed on 31 October 2013)

Nadkarni, Vidya, 2010, *Strategic Partnerships in Asia: Balancing without Alliances*, Oxon: Routledge.

Nehru, Vikram, 2012, "Shuttle Diplomacy in the South China Sea", Washington, DC, *Opinion*, 30 August 2012 at http://www.thejakartapost.com/news/2012/08/30/shuttle-diplomacy-south-china-sea.html (accessed on 23 December 2013).

Saleh, Fauzan, 2001, *Modern Trends in Islamic Theological Discourse in 20th Century Indonesia: A Critical Survey*, NV Leiden: Koninklijke Brill.

Sridharan, Kripa, 1996, *The ASEAN Region in India's Foreign Policy*, Aldershot: Dartmouth Publishing Company.

Sukma, Rizal, 1999, *Indonesia and China: The Politics of a Troubled Relationship*, London: Routledge.

———, 2009, "Indonesia-China Relations: The Politics of Re-engagement", *Asian Survey*, **49**(4) (July/August): 591-94.

Suryadinata, Leo, Evi Nurvidya Arifin, Aris Ananta, 2003, *Indonesia's Population: Ethnicity and Religion in a Changing Political Landscape*, Singapore: ISEAS.

Young, P. Lewis, 1988, "India's Nuclear Submarine Acquisition: A Major Step Towards Regional Dominance," *Asian Defence Journal*, Kuala Lumpur, November, pp. 4-18.

10

Being the First among Equals

Indonesia's Emerging Leadership Role in ASEAN

Anushree Chakraborty

INDONESIA's leadership in ASEAN was prominent during the Suharto era. Following the domestic instability with the fall of Suharto and shaken by the 1997 Asian financial crisis, Indonesian leadership weakened in the region. However, under President Susilo Bambang Yudhoyono, Indonesia has once again revived its image of being the first among equals in the region. The ASEAN growth trajectory since the last decade and its recent attempt to emerge from crisis situations, have witnessed Indonesia's active contribution. The Ministry of Foreign Affairs in Jakarta is presently engaged in using their good office to tighten and carry forward the twenty-six-year old regional organization at the stage of its most challenging times.

In early 2010, in an interview Indonesian Foreign Minister Marty Natalegawa was quoted as saying that Indonesia would play a role in a global arena by creating the so-called "dynamic equilibrium" among countries in the world in which "there is not one preponderant country".[1] This statement is significant

[1] Alexandra, 2011.

because it reflects the direction in which Indonesia's foreign policy is shaping for the future. ASEAN in this perspective provides an ideal platform to nurture and play the equilibrium it seeks to play. It must be noted that the term "equilibrium" is not synonymous to "balancer".

Among the ongoing regional initiatives throughout the world, ASEAN has acclaimed the record of carrying out the most successful regionalization process in Asia. After UN, it has emerged as the hub that binds the major power centres while engaging them through various spokes of institutions such as East Asia Summit (EAS) ASEAN Regional Forum (ARF) and ASEAN Defence Ministers Mealing Plus (ADMM-Plus) ASEAN is unique because it is driven by an assembly of small and medium powered countries who bring together the major powers to turn them into stakeholders and contributors to their regional security and stability. Among the small and medium power members in ASEAN, Indonesia stands as *primus inter pares*. This paper examines Indonesia's recent leadership initiatives in ASEAN. It selects some case studies that will highlight the above point. It attempts to explain the source of legitimacy behind Indonesia's leadership role. Some comments on Indonesia's failure are inevitable to have a fair assessment of its success. This paper also addresses the question of whether there is a contradiction between Indonesia's global and regional aspirations. In the end, it will look at leadership position of both India and Indonesia and the lessons that can be drawn from their role of being the big brothers in the region.

History of Indonesia's Foreign Policy and Its Participation in ASEAN

Soon after independence, Vice-President Mohammad Hatta characterized its foreign policy as "free and active" (*bebas aktif*), a guideline that continues to this day.[2] The fundamental

[2] Smith, 1999.

characteristic of Indonesia's foreign policy is non-alignment. Although, there was a marked difference in Sukarno's idealism and his successor Suharto's pragmatic foreign policy pursuits, none the less, both the leaders shared the same vision for Indonesia's regional and global aspirations.[3] However, it was Suharto, who gave priority to the South-East Asian region in its foreign policy. The normalization of relation with Malaysia and subsequently abandoning the "confrontation policy" was in tune with his focus on good neighbourhood relation in the region.

While engaging with the West for trade and assistance and continuing links with the developing countries, Indonesian foreign policy, since the 1960s, began to look for regional engagement with the anti-communist countries. The regional chaos as a result of the Indo–China upheaval during this period and the deep historical mistrust between the South-East Asian countries spellbound the need for regional initiatives. Dewi Fortuna Anwar, one of the experts on Indonesia and ASEAN, noted in her book in 1994 that Indonesia's original motivation to establish a regional organization with its immediate neighbours can be summarized into three broad categories: (1) desire for normalcy in its relations with the non-communist nations of South-East Asia; (2) the need for domestic stability; and (3) less reliance on external powers for regional security.[4]

In the twenty-first century, Indonesia is aware of the need for a pragmatic foreign policy which combines both realism and idealism. A look at Foreign Affairs Ministry's diplomatic co-operation suggests the presence of a series of concentric circles. The first concentric circle is with ASEAN which becomes Indonesia's prime pillar in carrying out its foreign policies. In the second concentric circle lies ASEAN + 3 (Japan, China,

---

3 Smith, 1999.

4 Anwar, 1994.

South Korea). Outside of those circles, Indonesia also builds an intensive co-operation with the US and European Union (EU) which serve as Indonesia's main economic partners. In the third concentric circle lie like-minded developing countries.[5]

Normatively speaking, Indonesia's first major contribution to ASEAN was the emphasis on non-alignment (keeping in line with its foreign policy objectives). The significance of this principle could be understood from the perspective of removing superpower rivalry in the region at the peak of Cold War period. Subsequently, in the years to come, Indonesia played a positive role by accepting Malaysia's proposal of the Zone of Peace, Freedom and Neutrality (ZOPFAN) signed in 1971 as the Declaration of ASEAN Concord. Thereafter, supplementing to the Malaysian proposal, Indonesia forwarded the proposal of Southeast Asian Nuclear Weapons Free Zone (SEANWFZ) in 1983 for the enhancement of regional security.

Indonesia's most important contribution to ASEAN has been its emphasis on ASEAN solidarity despite the differences among the members and the inherent weaknesses within the regionalization process. Working within the ASEAN through consultation and consensus has been the approach of Indonesian foreign policy. One good example is Jakarta's compromised stand in order to portray a common policy among ASEAN members during the Vietnamese invasion of Cambodia in 1979. Despite Indonesia's wariness towards China, publicly Indonesia went by the ASEAN stand of supporting Thailand's foreign policy. At the end of the Cold War, Indonesia played a crucial role in organizing United

---

5 For details, see Ministry of Foreign Affairs, Republic of Indonesia, Accessed on 13 November 2013, URL:// http://www.kemlu.go.id/Pages/IFP.aspx?P=Regional&l=en

Nations supervised elections and normalizing relations with both Cambodia and Vietnam.[6]

In addition, Indonesia played a crucial role in expanding ASEAN, particularly during the inclusion of Vietnam in 1995. At present, Jakarta is working towards admitting East Timor in the ASEAN club despite having differences with other members. Indonesia played an important role in mediating the regional conflicts both within and outside the ARF process. Examples are managing the South China Sea dispute, Vietnam–Cambodia–Laos conflict, and conflict between the Philippines and Moro National Liberation Front (MNLF).

Strength of Indonesia's Leadership Role in ASEAN

Indonesia draws legitimacy from the values it represents, such as its pluralistic society, its moderate Islam and its democracy. Through these values, it wants to pursue its leadership, de facto, in South-East Asia which eroded during the Asian financial crisis in the late 1990s.[7] Its embrace of Islam, commitment to Pancasila and pluralism, and at the same time its ability to fight religious fundamentalism, have set an example for the region. Indonesia is presently the only ASEAN member ranked as a free country by the Freedom House Index (FHI).[8]

Indonesia's economy has been an important propellant of ASEAN stability and prosperity. At present, Indonesia is maintaining a high economic growth rate, looking towards sustainable development and successfully implementing the reforms and infrastructural set-ups. In 2012, Indonesia maintained a stable growth rate of 6.2 per cent.[9] It is working

---

6 Smith 1999: 242.

7 Pakpahan, 2011.

8 Areethamsirikul, 2011.

9 *World Bank Country Report*, Indonesia, accessed on 14 November 2013, URL: http://www.worldbank.org/en/news/feature/2013/10/04/indonesia-economic-quarterly-october-2013.

towards diversifying its export baskets and boosting competitiveness in order to sustain a more rapid pace of growth and development. Indonesia, being the largest economy in the ASEAN region, is attracting its neighbours with the opportunity of huge market, rich natural resources and sufficient cheap labour force. Interestingly, a McKinsey Global Institute report predicts the South-East Asia's most populous nation is on track to become the world's 7th largest economy by 2030, putting it ahead of the developed nations of Germany and the UK.[10] There are speculations about Indonesia being a strong contender of joining the BRIC.[11]

Indonesia has earned reputation from active participation in multilateral forums. It is a member to World Trade Organization (WTO), the G20, Colombo Plan, Developing Eight (D-8), G-15, G-77, IOR-ARC, Non-Alignment Movement (NAM) in addition to ASEAN and EAS. It could be a multiple hub within various institutional levels. It is a regional representative at the G-20. Indonesia has the glorious history of becoming the founding member of NAM. The Asian African Conference held in Bandung in 1955 gave the archipelagic country an international standing. The largest Muslim country in the world also plays a significant role at the Organisation of Islamic Conference (OIC).[12] The Directorate of Multilateral Affairs within the Indonesian Ministry of Foreign Affairs has

10 "The Archipelago Economy: Unleashing Indonesia's Potential", McKinsey Global Institute, September 2012, accessed on 13 November 2013, URL:// *www.mckinsey.com/.../McKinsey/.../The%20archipelago%20economy/*

11 Davies, 2013.

12 Indonesia has been elected as the Chair of the OIC Peace Committee for the Southern Philippines (OIC-PCSP). OIC-PCSP has managed to host tripartite meetings, the latest the 3rd tripartite meeting in Manila on March 2009 which reached an agreement to further peace process in the southern Philippines to achieve peaceful conflict resolution in the region.

set the programme of year 2010-14 under the frame of "Improvement of Indonesia's Role and Diplomacy in Multilateral Affairs". One of their aims includes, becoming host to multilateral conferences.[13] Indonesia was the Chair of Asia-Pacific Economic Cooperation (APEC) in 2013.

Within ASEAN, Indonesia is the most important player, considering that Jakarta is the founding member, the centre of ASEAN diplomacy, where the ASEAN Secretariat is located and the ASEAN permanent representatives and ambassadors to ASEAN reside. This gives Indonesia the leverage to raise attention, discuss issues, call for meetings and create regional direction. Most importantly, Indonesian foreign policy links its national interest with the ideals of building peace and stability in the region. Therefore, idealism in its foreign policy encourages it to go beyond its naked self-interest.

Moreover, Indonesia has built reputation from engaging with the civil society organizations. It makes a conscious effort to involve the ASEAN-based non-state actors to participate and hear their voices in the broader community-building process. Therefore, Indonesia repeatedly emphasizes on building People's Community while talking about ASEAN Community. No other ASEAN member holds such profile.

Indonesian Diplomacy: Recent Incidents Highlighting Its Leadership Role

FIRST CASE STUDY

Despite not being a party to the dispute, since early 1990s, Indonesia played host to series of workshops on the Spratly Islands dispute. During 31 October–2 November 2013, in Yogyakarta, Indonesia held the 23rd Workshop on Managing Potential Conflict in the South China Sea.

---

[13] For details, see "Ministry of Foreign Affairs, Republic of Indonesia", accessed on 12 November 2013, URL:// http://www.kemlu.go.id/Pages/IFP.aspx?P=Multilateral&l=en

SECOND CASE STUDY

The failure to produce a closing statement at the 45th ASEAN Ministerial Meeting in July 2012, a first in its 45-year history, brought the Indonesian diplomacy at the forefront. Indonesian Foreign Minister Marty Natalegawa embarked on a 36-hour diplomacy tour a week later to the five countries including the Philippines, Vietnam, Cambodia, Malaysia and Singapore that resulted in ASEAN member states agreeing on a joint statement on the ongoing disputes in the South China Sea. Marty rejected claims that ASEAN was not united. He noted that "following the AMM and shuttle diplomacy, what we are focusing on now is how to keep the momentum alive in drafting the Code of Conduct (CoC) in the South China Sea". Despite the absence of a joint communique, Marty said that ASEAN is still on track to finalize the items they agreed on during the meeting, such as completing the draft for an ASEAN Human Rights Declaration and the establishment of the ASEAN Institute for Peace and Reconciliation before the next regional summit of leaders.[14]

THIRD CASE STUDY

Democratic transition in Burma and ASEAN's engagement with the country despite international pressure to abandon it. Indonesia has been quietly promoting political reforms in Myanmar, hosting visits by the country's presidential advisory team and sending military reformers, such as Agus Wijoyo, to pass on Indonesia's experience of democratic transition. While other ASEAN members have argued in favour of cutting Myanmar from the group, President Yudhoyono stood firm, insisting that casting the reclusive country out of the organization would only push it toward China, endangering the balance of power in the region. More recently Yudhoyono called on Myanmar President Thein Sein to solve the deadly

---

14 Lutfia, 2012.

communal conflicts between the Rakhine and Rohingya ethnic groups that have led to asylum-seekers flowing into neighbouring ASEAN countries.[15]

FORTH CASE STUDY

Mediation in the border dispute between Thailand and Cambodia. The UN mandated Indonesia to act as a mediator in the dispute. The dispute took the centre stage during the period of 18th ASEAN Summit on 7-8 May in Jakarta. Indonesia while holding the ASEAN Chair at the Summit, confined the Thai–Cambodian dispute to a bilateral meeting between the two parties, thereby not derailing the ASEAN Summit. On the other hand, it worked on back-door diplomacy to encourage continuing with the dialogue between the two disputant neighbours.

Reception of Its Clout in the ASEAN Circle

The expansion of Indonesian leadership together with the increase in its military budget (increasing its military spending from around 1 per cent of GDP to 1.5 per cent by 2014) may shake the balance of power in ASEAN and ignite fears of a self-proclaimed regional leader. Areethamsirikul explains ASEAN has never endorsed the creation of a responsible de facto regional leader like Germany in the EU or the US in NATO.[16] Areethamsirikul further notes, "when a country has obvious newfound power, people certainly expect something out of that privilege".[17]

None the less, Indonesia's diplomatic initiatives have received well among the ASEAN members. Indonesia's neighbours do not see their big neighbour having interest in

15 Lutfia, 2012.

16 Areethamsirikul, 2011.

17 Ibid.

dominating the region. Indonesia's ASEAN diplomacy is well acknowledged since the regional peers understand Jakarta has an interest in making the organization a stronger political voice on the global stage. For example, in July 2012 after Indonesian foreign minister's two-day tour to bring out a common regional statement, the Singaporean government, on its foreign affairs ministry's website stated: "Singapore welcomes the release of the six principles. This is the result of the unceasing efforts of Indonesia. It helps to restore ASEAN centrality in the regional architecture."[18]

Indonesia and India: Gulliver among the Lilliputs

It must be noted that there is no comparison between the two countries and their respective regional set-ups, given that they have different contexts and textures. India is a democracy with its usual domestic compulsions while Indonesia during the formative years of ASEAN was under the authoritative leader. In fact, most of the ASEAN members were governed under authoritative governments, which makes decision-making at multilateral set-up simpler. Moreover, in the initial phase, ASEAN members were faced with common external threat while in SAARC there is no commonality between the members on the concept of external threat.

Nevertheless, given their past shared history, religious and cultural affinity, India and Indonesia share a special relation. Prime Minister Manmohan Singh said that Indonesia is one of India's most important partners in the neighbourhood and a "key constituent of India's Look East Policy".[19] During the period of struggle for independence in both the countries,

18 For details, see Singaporean government, Foreign Affairs Ministry's website, http://www.mfa.gov.sg

19 Full text: Prime Minister's interview to *Kompas* newspaper, Indonesia, accessed on 5 November 2013, URL:// http://ibnlive.in.com/news/full-text-prime-ministers-interview-to-kompas-newspaper-indonesia/427723-2.html?utm source=ref_article.

India's national movement was a source of inspiration for Indonesians. In the recent times, India can draw inspiration from Jakarta's political leadership in its region. Within SAARC, India failed to replicate Indonesia's triumph. India is much detested by its neighbours, similar to the US in North and South America. As C. Raja Mohan observes, India looms large, both physically and psychologically, over its neighbours.[20]

To begin with, Michael Vatikiotis wrote in the *Straits Times* that Indonesia's good intentions and largely selfless diplomatic efforts can be held up as a rare example of a powerful nation putting the interests of others before its own.[21] Although India has been following the Panchasila philosophy, nevertheless, more needs to be done. Second, Indonesia has successfully kept its bilateral issues separate while working through the regionalization process. However, India is caught up with bilateral issues that put a brake in its regional participation. Third, Indonesia under Suharto, strongly believed in regional resilience adding to national resilience. India can work towards the given philosophy. Finally, India lacked Indonesia's spirit for regional co-operation since its policy makers were sceptical that regional co-operation might provide an opportunity for the small neighbours to regionalize all bilateral issues and join with Pakistan to "gang up" against India.[22] This apprehension needs to be addressed and New Delhi must make further efforts to encourage the SAARC members to co-operate while building the environment of shared development and prosperity.

Some Failures

ASEAN's growth trajectory has been following Indonesia's growth trajectory. Indonesian perception determined

---

[20] Raja Mohan, 2003: 12.

[21] Vatikiotis, 2012.

[22] Raja Mohan 2003: 238.

ASEAN's evolution. Anthony Smith observes that in the initial two decades of ASEAN formation, the greatest achievement has been diplomatic co-ordination while resisting functional integration. Indonesia's strategy of economic nationalism, whereby economic reforms were taken out of absolute necessity, but much of Indonesian commerce was sheltered to protect infant industries was an important factor. The lack of ASEAN economic integration was therefore the result of reluctance of Indonesian political elites who feared it as a ploy to exploit Indonesia's huge market without gaining any substantial returns.[23] Therefore, Indonesia acted as a brake to economic integration in ASEAN in the early phase.

Indonesia lost internal stability and as a result international credibility during and after the financial crisis in the late 1990s. One example was its failure to tackle future forest fires and implement the Regional Haze Action Plan agreed on December 1997. Second, during the period, an important issue for the Philippines has been Indonesia's assistance with the Moro insurrection in Mindanao. Given Indonesia's domestic instability, its mediatory role suffered. Similarly, the most serious issue at that period was the dispute between China and the Philippines over Mischief Reef. In 1998, China began to build permanent structures on the reef. None the less, ASEAN members failed to raise this issue with China during the Sixth ASEAN Summit in Hanoi in December 1998. Indonesia, ravaged by the economic crisis, could not afford to mediate between China and the ASEAN countries. China gained goodwill in the region for not devaluing its currency. Clearly, Indonesia failed to establish itself as the neutral mediator that it used to, given its interest in keeping China in good humour.[24]

---

23 Smith 1999.

24 Ibid.: 249.

At present, Indonesian foreign minister's shuttle diplomacy in July 2012 which is otherwise receiving cheers internationally and regionally is not without criticism. A report by Keith Loveard, a senior analyst with the Jakarta-based Concord Security was critical of Indonesia's diplomatic spell in ASEAN. Loveard notes: "Indonesia is acting in its own interests, not those of ASEAN, determined to carve itself a major role in regional diplomacy with or without the organization." He comments that "being friends with all parties is one of the official principles of Indonesia's foreign policy". The report suggested, Indonesia would remain neutral in the battle for influence between the US and China and its policy of being friends to all would continue and put Jakarta in a good position to achieve maximum benefit.[25]

Indonesian and ASEAN: What Does Indonesia Seek to Achieve for ASEAN?

Indonesia's key interests in South-East Asia are to promote stability and ensure that the region retains its autonomy from great power influence. Indonesia has historically used ASEAN as a tool to pursue these goals, and Jakarta's purported ability to lead ASEAN is an important source of its international influence.[26]

The priority area for Indonesia in ASEAN is to maintain its centrality in Asia's regional architecture like EAS. This is primarily because ASEAN is crucial in order to maintain a balance of power between the US, China, India and Russia within EAS. This is the reason behind Indonesia's opposition to the idea of an East-Asian community — comprising ASEAN, China, Japan and South Korea. Instead, it backed the more inclusive EAS, which brings together leaders from ASEAN and its eight key partners — China, the US, Japan, India, Russia,

25 Hunt, 2012.

26 Murphy, 2013.

Australia, South Korea and New Zealand. Indonesia hopes to create a looser and more pluralistic grouping that would not be dominated by one or more powers, thereby allowing ASEAN to continue to play the central role of convener.[27] Pakpahan highlights some of the challenges facing Indonesia. She notes Indonesia can act as an important interlocutor between ASEAN and EAS in trying to find the best solutions for common regional challenges, including the South China Sea issue, competition between the Regional Comprehensive Economic Partnership (RCEP) and the Trans-Pacific Partnership (TPP), and attempts to close the development gap between nations in South-East and East Asia.[28] In addition to this, there are issues of climate change, regional infrastructure building (under "ASEAN Connectivity"), human and drug trafficking, migration, and the protection of low-skilled workers, women, children and the disabled in the region.

One of the most critical areas of concern for ASEAN has been the maritime disputes in the South China Sea. Although the issue is not new, in the last few years, its impact on ASEAN credibility and unity has been enormous. Therefore, managing the dispute and its eventual settlement is a priority concern for Indonesia. Conducting the ASEAN's six-point principles on the South China Sea and commencing the discussion on the CoC between ASEAN and China and work on the continuation of discussions on the COC towards the early conclusion of a Regional Code of Conduct in the East Sea is the path in which Indonesia seeks to achieve within ASEAN.[29] Indonesia has

---

[27] Indonesia's Cautious Confidence, accessed on 14 November 2013 URL://http://www.project-syndicate.org/commentary/asean-and-indonesia-s-foreign-policy-priorities-by-dewi-f—anwar#xHFTfof8AwDHf4zh.99

[28] Pakpahan, 2013.

[29] See ASEAN website, accessed on 4 November 2013 URL:// http://www.asean.org/

come up with the idea of establishing an ASEAN peace-keeping force.

Indonesia is also looking to strengthen the ASEAN Inter-governmental Commission on Human Rights (AICHR), its own human rights commission. But AICHR has only the mandate of promotion, not protection of human rights. The Terms of Reference (TOR) does not give AICHR the power to hear or investigate cases, to make country visits or even produce fact-finding reports. In fact, during its chairmanship in 2011, Indonesia gave priority to the establishment of AICHR. The agreement to establish an ASEAN Institute of Peace and Reconciliation, a structure to manage and resolve regional dispute, as outlined in the Political-Security Community Blueprint is an important milestone yet to be achieved. So far the disputes that have beset between ASEAN members had to be taken to International Court of Justice in order to resolve them. However, the mechanisms in TAC through CoC and established framework have never been utilized. Therefore, the upcoming Institute will be an arena which will determine Indonesia's as well as ASEAN's determination to be efficient and relevant.

Conclusion

Anthony Smith wrote in 1999: "Whatever the outcome of Indonesia's political and economic turmoil, it will take years for Indonesia to resume the role as leader of ASEAN — a position that Suharto held."[30] After a decade, Indonesia seems back to assume the leadership role in ASEAN.

However, in the coming days, its leadership role is not without challenges. With the presidential election due in 2014, the post-SBY leadership is yet to be tested. In addition, with the new government coming to power in Jakarta, there might be the possibility of heightened nationalism and the larger

[30] Smith 1999: 257.

role of Islam, thereby undermining the Indonesia's ASEAN priorities. Most importantly, the present-day Indonesia is different from Suharto's period. An authoritative government can afford to carry out its foreign policy goals without giving heed to domestic audience. But not in a democratic set-up. Barry Desker observes that since the transition to democratization, the Indonesian government has to pay close attention to domestic opinion as expressed through the media, rowdy street demonstrations and fiery speeches by members of parliament.[31] Therefore, policy making is difficult on sensitive issues with neighbours, for example, the elected parliamentarians have blocked ratification of agreements reached by the executive branch such as the Defence Cooperation Agreement with Singapore. In addition, criticism came in the way of the compromises entailed in reaching agreement on the ASEAN Charter. Relations with Malaysia have recently been strained by the strong public reaction to conflicting territorial claims, maritime boundary disputes, treatment of Indonesian workers in Malaysia and the belief that Malaysians regard Indonesians as poor cousins.[32]

Moreover, there is an ongoing national debate on whether with the rising profile Indonesia should look beyond ASEAN in its foreign policy priorities. Although there is no consensus on this subject, nevertheless, there are some prominent voices within the country calling for Indonesia to see itself as a major emerging power like Brazil, South Africa, India and China with global interests and concerns.[33]

Notwithstanding this, Indonesia's foreign policy under the present government has focused on ASEAN in its foreign

---

31 Desker, 2010.

32 Ibid.

33 The most prominent proponents of Indonesia's post-ASEAN foreign policy are Rizal Sukma and Jusuf Wanandi.

policy priorities. The post-ASEAN foreign policy is implausible at present, given Indonesia's security and prosperity closely linked with the region. Indonesian government also realizes that its influence within ASEAN gives informal influence internationally. Most importantly, Indonesia is a developing country with limited resources and capabilities. There are domestic socio-economic challenges that need attention in addition to numerous centrifugal forces acting against the unity of the country. Therefore, looking for a global role will place unnecessary pressure on the archipelagic country.

In conclusion, Michael Leifer could be recalled when he said that Indonesia's foreign policy of prioritizing its leadership role in ASEAN is rooted in domestic strength.[34] The bottom line is: if Indonesia's domestic imperatives are strong, its leadership will equally be assertive in driving ASEAN into a higher plane. One good example is, when economic crisis hit Indonesia in the late 1990s, its diminishing influence was apparent with the rejection of its ambitious initiative to build an ASEAN Peacekeeping Force by other member states due to its potential effect on the sovereignty and non-interference principles of ASEAN. Ironically, given its rising profile and corresponding influence, Indonesia has again taken up the subject with encouraging response from its neighbours. Therefore, in the post-Suharto Indonesia, with a brief hiatus, Jakarta has revived its leadership image. There are challenges ahead; none the less, regional acceptance of Indonesia's initiatives on the ASEAN Security Community in 2003 and currently, its efforts towards constructing the ASEAN Charter, its chairmanship in 2011 and the diplomatic engagement during the crisis in 2012 are indicative of the acceptance of its *primus inter pares* status.[35]

---

[34] Leifer, 1974: 419.

[35] Alexandra 2011.

References

Alexandra, Lina A., 2011, "Indonesia's Chairmanship: What Are the Priorities?", *ASEAN Monthly Commentary*, vol. 1, January.

Anwar, Dewi Fortuna, 1994, *Indonesia in ASEAN: Foreign Policy and Regionalism*, Singapore: St Martin's Press and Institute of Southeast Asian Studies.

Areethamsirikul, Sarinna, 2011, "Can Indonesia Become the Central Leader of ASEAN?", Bangkok, 22, March 2011, accessed on 4 November 2013, URL:// http://www.nationmultimedia.com/2011/03/22/opinion/Can-Indonesia-become-the-central-leader-of-Asean-30151407.html

Davies, Martyn, 2013, "Indonesia and Turkey Top BRICS Contenders", 3 March 2013, accessed on 14 November 2013, URL:// http://www.bdlive.co.za/businesstimes/2013/03/03/indonesia-and-turkey-top-brics-contenders

Desker, Barry, 2010, "Is Indonesia Outgrowing ASEAN?", *RSIS Commentaries*, No. 125/2010 dated 29 September 2010, accessed on 14 November 2013, URL:// http://dr.ntu.edu.sg/bitstream/handle/10220/6676/RSIS1252010.pdf?sequence=1

Hunt, Luke, 2012, "Indonesia Capitalizes on ASEAN Divisions", accessed on 4 November 2013, URL:// http://thediplomat.com/asean-beat/2012/07/25/indonesia-capitalizes-on-asean-divisions/

Leifer, Michael, 1974, "Indonesia's Regional Vision", *The World Today*, **30**(10) (October 1974): 419.

Lutfia, Ismira, 2012, "Indonesia Leads from the Front on Asean", 8 August 2012, accessed on 5 November 2013, URL:// http://www.thejakartaglobe.com/archive/indonesia-leads-from-the-front-on-asean/

Murphy, Ann Marie, 2013, "Indonesia in Asia's Changing Balance of Power", 11 March 2013, accessed on 5 November 2013, URL:// http://www.worldpoliticsreview.com/articles/12779/indonesia-in-asia-s-changing-balance-of-power

Pakpahan, Beginda, 2013, "Indonesia's Role in ASEAN and the EAS", *East Asia Forum*, accessed on 4 November 2013, URL:// http://www.eastasiaforum.org

Pakpahan, Beginda, 2011, "The Role of Indonesia in ASEAN, in East Asia Summit and in G20", *The Jakarta Post*, 4 October 2011, accessed on 4

November 2013 URL:// http://www.thejakartapost.com/news/2011/10/04/the-role-indonesia-asean-east-asia-summit-and-g20.html

Raja Mohan, C., 2003, *Crossing the Rubicon: The Shaping of India's New Foreign Policy*, New Delhi: Penguin.

Smith, Anthony, 1999, "Indonesia's Role in ASEAN: The End of Leadership?", *Contemporary Southeast Asia*, **21**(2) (August 1999): 239.

Vatikiotis, Michael, 2012, "Indonesia's Quiet Diplomacy Triumphs in the Region", *Straits Times*, 6 August 2012, accessed on 14 November 2013, URL:// http://www.thejakartaglobe.com/archive/indonesias-quiet-diplomacy-triumphs-in-the-region/

11

India–Indonesia Trade Relations

Afreen Bano

This paper will analyse the level, trend and composition of India–Indonesia bilateral trade in recent times. India and Indonesia are increasingly seen as emerging Asian economies, and have undergone massive economic reforms in the past two decades. Strong economic fundamentals with a robust financial sector and manufacturing industry have positioned them among the top five investment destinations in Asia. In order to maximize the gains from their bilateral relations, however, the two countries have to tread a middle path, that is a mix of seeking complementarities in the economic field, while competing with each other in terms of attracting foreign investments. During the colonial period, India's connections with Indonesia were in the capacity of two colonies occupied by the British and the Dutch colonial masters, respectively. When India achieved independence, it opted for an inward-looking "mixed economy" model. However, as a result of the continued growth of India's economic transactions with the ASEAN from 1970s onwards, the amount of trade grew in volume. By 1982 the ASEAN countries' share of India's exports, which had been 2.6 per cent in 1970, had risen to 4.2 per cent. During the same period, India's total imports from the region had risen even more, from 0.6 to 5.9 per cent. In the early 1990s, while India was struggling with its "balance of payment crisis", Indonesia and other ASEAN member countries were emerging as powerful economies.

India's opening up of its economy together with the rise of the Asian Tigers motivated India to look for opportunities in the East. India took a big step in that direction with its Look East Policy in 1991. Over the past two decades India has engaged comprehensively with Indonesia and the region by way of signing and implementing several bilateral and multilateral trade agreements. India has also invested in Indonesia.

The economies of both India and Indonesia have undergone massive reforms in the past two decades. Indonesia has emerged to become the second largest trading partner of India in the ASEAN region. India–Indonesia bilateral trade has increased from US $ 6.9 billion in 2007-08 to US $ 20.10 billion in 2012-13. India is the largest buyer of crude palm oil from Indonesia. Other imports are coal, minerals, rubber, pulp and paper and hydrocarbons. India exports to Indonesia refined petroleum products, maize, commercial vehicles, telecommunication equipment, oil seeds, animal feed, cotton, steel products and plastics. However in the present context it argues that the two countries have not been able to realize this potential because of the lack of imaginative planning as well as ignorance on the part of the business communities of the two countries. The financial crisis of 1997 and 1998 had also disillusioned India vis-à-vis Indonesia, which, in the aftermath of the financial crisis, plummeted to an economic low when its currency was devalued against the international basket of currencies. This paper also contains suggestions to overcome these limitations.

Introduction

INDIA–INDONESIA relationship dates back to hundreds of years and continued after the independence of both countries. This was particularly evident when our founding leaders, Sukarno and Nehru who shared the same values of independence, freedom and non-alignment, later translated those ideals into the first Afro–Asian Conference at Bandung in 1955. Since the adoption of India's Look East Policy in 1991, there has been a rapid development of bilateral relations between two countries in political, security, defence, commercial and cultural fields. The multi-faceted relationship got an added boost with the signing of the Joint Declaration on Establishing a Strategic Partnership in 2005 during the state visit of Indonesian president Susilo Bambang Yudhoyono to India.[1]

So far as the India–Indonesia relation is concerned, there have been as many as eight visits by the heads of government to intensify the bilateral ties. From Indian side, prime minister visited Jakarta in 2003 to attend the India–ASEAN Summit in Bali and in April 2005 to attend the celebration of the 50th anniversary of the Afro–Asian Conference in Bandung. The other important visits from the Indonesian to India include those of President Abdurrahman Wahid (February 2000), President Megawati Soekarnoputri (April 2002) and President Susilo Bambang Yudhoyono (November 2005, January 2011 and December 2012). During the celebration, the Indonesian president conferred the singular honour to the Indian prime minister to speak on behalf of Asia. The President of India paid a state visit to Indonesia in November 2008. During the visit, two MoUs were signed on Agricultural Co-operation, and Co-operation in Youth Affairs and Sports.[2]

There have been regular high-level bilateral visits providing momentum to the relationship between the two countries. The Indonesian President Susilo Bambang Yudhoyono's visit to India in January 2011 marked a major milestone in the long history of India and Indonesian relations. India selected the Indonesian president as the special guest at the 62nd Republic Day celebrations. It meant that India was

---

1 http://www.mea.gov.in/Portal/ForeignRelation/Indonesia-Brief_for_MEA_website_decem_2012

2 Ibid.

clearly signalling that it wanted to develop closer relations with Indonesia. In response, President Yudhoyono came to India with a large number of delegations including many Indonesian CEOs.

During the visit, sixteen inter-governmental agreements were signed between the two countries such as an air services agreement, extradition treaty, mutual legal assistance treaty, and MoUs on — exchange of financial intelligence related to money laundering and financing terrorism; establishing a biennial trade ministers' forum; co-operation in oil and gas; co-operation in urea manufacturing; co-operation in the field of micro, small and medium enterprises; co-operation between the BATAM free trade zone and Santacruz Electronic Export Processing Zone (SEEPZ); co-operation in marine and fisheries; weather and climate services; science and technology co-operation; programme of co-operation in science and technology; co-operation between the press councils of the two countries; co-operation in the field of education and a cultural exchange programme.[3] This recent event reflects the growing strategic importance from one to another. The convergence of strategic interests that resulted from geopolitical changes in Asia and the world is bringing the two countries closer together once again. The renewed concerted co-operation and alliance between India and Indonesia will also impact on Asian politics and the world politics at large.[4] President Yudhoyono attended the India–ASEAN Commemorative Summit in New Delhi on 20-21 December 2012 accompanied by several Indonesian cabinet ministers. There has also been a regular exchange of ministerial

---

[3] http://www.mea.gov.in/Portal/ForeignRelation/Indonesia-Brief_for_MEA_website_decem_2012

[4] http://www.asia-studies.org/board/board_download.php?board_uid=1&idx=258

visits and a joint commission process, co-chaired by the foreign ministers of the two countries.[5]

A Historical Overview

During the colonial period, India's relations with Indonesia were in the competence of two colonies occupied by the British and the Dutch colonial masters, respectively. When India achieved independence on 15 August 1947, it opted for an inward-looking "mixed economy" model. However, as a result of the continued growth of India's economic transactions with the ASEAN from 1970s onwards, the amount of trade grew in volume. In 1982 the ASEAN countries' share of India's exports, which had been 2.6 per cent in 1970, had risen to 4.2 per cent. During the same period, India's total imports from the region had risen even more, from 0.6 to 5.9 per cent. In the early 1990s, while India was struggling with its "balance of payment crisis", Indonesia and other ASEAN member countries were emerging as powerful economies. India's opening up of its economy together with the rise of the Asian Tigers (Hong Kong, Singapore, South Korea and Taiwan) forced India to look for opportunities in the East. India took a big step in that direction with its Look East Policy.[6] Over the past two decades India has engaged broadly with Indonesia and the region by way of signing and implementing several bilateral and multilateral trade agreements. India has also invested in Indonesia. Though Indonesian investment in the Indian economy is minuscule compared to India's in Indonesia, things are looking up in terms of bilateral trade and economic co-operation.[7]

---

5 http://www.indianembassyjakarta.com/index.php/2013-05-20-10-02-04

6 http://www.idsa.in/system/files/IB_Indonesia TradeInvestmentComplementarities

7 Ibid.

The centuries-old economic relationship between India and Indonesia has been formalized and firmly established through a number of agreements, declarations and MoUs. The first trading agreement was signed in January 1953, further extended in June 1978, when the two countries agreed to develop mechanisms in order to strengthen and diversify trade and commercial links. Both the countries signed a bilateral agreement on avoidance of double taxation in January 1986. The two countries also signed an agreement for the promotion and protection of investments, during the G-15 meeting in Jamaica in February 1999 and which came into force in January 2004. An India–Indonesia Joint Commission Meeting (JCM) was held in Yogyakarta in September 2003, which mandated the promotion of bilateral economic and commercial relations and the setting up of an India–Indonesia Expert Working Group. During the 2005 visit of the Indonesian president, the two countries also signed an MoU on setting up of a joint study group to examine the feasibility of entering into a comprehensive economic co-operation agreement.[8]

Both India and Indonesia are dynamic market economies and have undertaken a comprehensive economic reforms policy, Indonesia since 1966 and again after the oil boom in 1982, which enabled growth at an average annual rate of 6.7 per cent during the Suharto era (1966-96) before it was hit by the Asian financial crisis of 1997-98 when the Indonesian economy contracted by an unprecedented 13.1 per cent. The economy recovered, at first slowly, in 1999 but it grew faster in the following years; 4.6 per cent in 2009, 6.1 per cent in 2010 and 6.5 per cent in 2011. However, because of the continuing global uncertainty, including the projected slower growth of Indonesia's major trading partners, China being one, the

---

[8] http://mercury.ethz.ch/serviceengine/Files/ISN/95449/ipublicationdocument_singledocument/9069db38-4d1b-442b-ab8f-5f85cd55ddfb/en/IPCS-Special-Report-38

Indonesian economy is predicted to grow slightly slower at 6.2 per cent in 2012. India, on the other hand, introduced sweeping economic reforms in 1991 after it experienced a serious balance of payments crisis. Since then, India has been one of the fastest growing economies in the world along with China, and for the past decade has been growing at 8-9 per cent annually, second only to China, which grew very rapidly since Deng Xiaoping, China's pre-eminent leader since 1978, introduced extensive economic reforms in the late 1970s.[9]

The total assessment of bilateral trade has gone up from US $ 1.12 billion in 1995-96 to US $ 2.5 billion in 2003-04 and reached US $ 4 billion in 2005. The bilateral trade objective has been set at US $ 10 billion by 2010. India imports palm and vegetable oil — crude and processed — coal, petroleum and paper products and spices whereas major Indonesian imports are textile yarn, chemicals, electric power machinery and parts, refined petroleum products, iron and steel goods, wheat, rice and sugar. India is the largest importer of crude palm oil and Indonesia has become India's second largest trading partner in ASEAN after Singapore. Energy is another important area in which the two countries are exploring the possibility of co-operation. During the visit to India in 2002, the then Indonesian president, Sukarnoputri, addressing a joint meeting sponsored by the Federation of Indian Chambers of Commerce and Industry (FICCI) and the Confederation of Indian Industry (CII) in 2002. In meeting she had expressed her country's willingness to supply oil and gas to India. India is now studying the possibility of procuring natural gas from Indonesia through an undersea pipeline from Aceh to the Nicobar islands. The bilateral trade has gone further up with Indonesia's economic recovery and a growing realization between the two countries

---

[9] http://www.riebs.org/documents/fullpaper/2011vol2no2/Paper%20III%20-%20Indonesian%20-Indian%20Economic%20Relations

about the strategic necessity of strong economic bilateral relations.[10]

India and Indonesia: Emerging Trade Partners

Both India and Indonesia have undergone massive economic reforms in the past two decades as a result both economies have emerged as dynamic markets with strong economic fundamentals and a robust financial sector and manufacturing industry after liberalizing their economies. The two countries, due to labour-cost advantage, have positioned themselves among the top five investment destinations in Asia.[11] The commotion and uncertainty fascinating the global financial markets and the world economy during the current global financial crisis affected India also. Growth rates declined to 6.7 per cent in 2008, in contrast to 9.2 per cent in 2007 and 9.7 per cent in 2006. Prompt monetary and fiscal measures were undertaken to enhance demand, boost credit flows and lower interest rates to counter the slowdown. Growth is stronger than expected, across categories, such as transport equipment, metal products, textiles and mining. At the same time, consumer spending continues to gain strength both in durables and non-durables. Though inflation and unemployment have been issues of concern, economists feel that these would be addressed by the growth momentum.[12]

Trade in Goods

Prime minister of India and president of Indonesia inked a bilateral strategic partnership agreement in November 2005.

---

10 http://mercury.ethz.ch/serviceengine/Files/ISN/95449/ipublicationdocument_singledocument/9069db38-4d1b-442b-ab8f-5f85cd55ddfb/en/IPCS-Special-Report-38

11 http://www.idsa.in/system/files/IB_Indonesia TradeInvestmentComplementarities

12 Ibid.

Table 11.1: India–Indonesia Trade (Year to Year Trends) (in millian US Dollors)

Year	*2005-06*	*2006-07*	*2007-08*	*2008-09*	*2009-10*
Export	**1,380.20**	**2,032.96**	**2,164.17**	**2,559.82**	**3,063.36**
Growth (%)	—	47.29	6.45	18.28	19.67
Share (%)	1.34	1.61	1.33	1.38	1.71
Import	**3,008.11**	**4,181.96**	**4,821.25**	**6,666.34**	**8,656.66**
Growth (%)	—	39.02	15.29	38.27	29.86
Share (%)	2.02	2.25	1.92	2.20	3.00
Total Trade	**4,388.31**	**6,214.92**	**6,985.42**	**9,226.17**	**11,720.03**
Growth (%)	—	41.62	12.4	32.08	27.03
Share (%)	1.74	1.99	1.68	1.89	2.51

Source:
Rahul Mishra, 2011, "India and Indonesia: Trade and Investment Complementariness", available at: http://www.idsa.in/system/files IB_IndonesiaTradeInvestmentComplementarities

As part of the agreement, both the sides agreed to increase bilateral trade up to US $ 10 billion by 2010. In 2010 total trade surpassed this target, touching US $ 12 billion; up from US $ 4 billion in 2005. In order to fully realize the trade potential, India and Indonesia have pledged to increase the volume of trade to US $ 20 billion mark by 2015. This is working as the dynamic force behind the accelerated negotiations on Comprehensive Economic Co-operation Agreement (CECA) and is likely to create mutually assuring tariff reduction timelines and increased co-operation in the services sector.[13]

Table 11.1 reveals that India's exports have almost tripled in the last five years, while the share of imports is equally remarkable. Among the important items that India exports to Indonesia are gems and jewelleries, mechanical equipment and raw minerals, while in the case of Indonesia it has been

[13] http://www.idsa.in/system/files/IB_Indonesia TradeInvestmentComplementarities

chemicals, hides and engineering products, minerals and precious stones. These two nations initiated many steps to supplement the infrastructure facilities for increasing the trade and facilitating investment which would prove complementary in the economic development of both the countries.[14]

Indonesia has become the second largest trading partner of India in the ASEAN region (after Singapore) and one of our leading export destinations among developing countries. Bilateral trade was US $ 2.4 billion during 2003, an increase by 24.14 per cent over the same period of 2002. The trade baskets are complementary to each other.[15]

India is the largest buyer of crude palm oil from Indonesia and it imports coal, minerals, rubber, pulp, paper and hydrocarbons reserves. India exports refined petroleum products, maize, commercial vehicles, telecommunication equipment, oil seeds, animal feed, cotton, steel products and plastics to Indonesia. In addition, there is also considerable scope and potential for expanding trade between the two countries in the areas of automotive components, automobiles, engineering products, IT, pharmaceuticals, biotechnology and health care sectors. India exports pharmaceuticals in bulk and formulations to Indonesia.[16]

There are approximately 100,000 Indonesians of Indian origin in Indonesia. Mostly of them are concentrated in Greater Jakarta, Medan, Surabaya and Bandung. They are mainly engaged in trade, dealing in textiles and sports goods. There are around 10,000 Indian nationals living in Indonesia including

---

[14] http://www.idsa.in/system/files/IB_Indonesia TradeInvestmentComplementarities.

[15] http://www.ecaii.org/index.php?option=com_content&view=article&id=22:india-indonesia-trade-and-economic-relations&catid=6:outlook-indonesia&Itemid=8

[16] http://www.indianembassyjakarta.com/index.php/2013-05-20-10-02-04

engineers, consultants, chartered accountants, bankers and other professionals. The Indian community is very well regarded in Indonesia. They are generally prosperous and include individuals holding senior positions in local and multinational companies. An Indian Diaspora Meet was organized by Overseas Indian Facilitation Centre in July 2013 in association with the Embassy and the Ministry of Overseas Indian Affairs in Jakarta and Medan to strengthen Indian diaspora's engagement with India's growth story.[17]

Investments and Joint Venture Projects

The overall investment circumstance for India in Indonesia is very hopeful. It is an attractive destination for Indian investment in the region. The first Indian project approved in Indonesia was in 1972, five years after the Suharto government had opened the door to Foreign Direct Investment (FDI) by the ratification of its Foreign Investment Law in 1967. By the end of 1978, a total of eighteen Indian investment projects had been approved by Indonesia's Investment Co-ordinating Board, the Badan Kerjasama Penanaman Modal (BKPM).[18]

The massiveness of these investments was made in the 1970s and 1980s, and in fact in 1985. Indian companies have made significant investments in all the sectors including infrastructure, power, textiles, steel, automotive, mining machinery, banking and consumer goods sectors. The top Indian companies such as Tata Power, Reliance, Adani, L&T, GMR, GVK, Trimex, Videocon, Punj Lloyd, CG Power, Madhucon, Spice, Aditya Birla, Bombay Dyeing, Jindal Stainless Steel, ESSAR, TVS, Bajaj, BEML, Godrej, Balmer &

17 http://www.mea.gov.in/Portal/ForeignRelation/India-Indonesia_Relation

18 http://www.riebs.org/documents/fullpaper/2011vol2no2/Paper%20III%20-%20Indonesian%20-Indian%20Economic%20Relations

Lawrie, SBI and Bank of India which have established fully-owned joint ventures in Indonesia. In 2013, Tata Motors set up its assembly line for production of Tata Ace and Tata Nano. Apart from heavy industries these two countries have decided to invest and undertake joint ventures in several medium and small businesses. Many IT companies such as Tata Consultancy Service (TCS), Tech Mahindra, Satyam, Wipro, HCL and Polaris have business interests in Indonesia. In general, Indian investors hold around US $ 1.5 billion in assets in Indonesia and the annual output of these companies is between US $ 1-1.5 billion.[19]

Many Indian companies have been involved in supplying apparatus to Indonesia. They are also undertaking projects in Indonesia. These include WAPCOS, Ircon, RITES, STUP Consultancy India, TCIL, Punj Lloyd, KEC International, Telk, BHEL and Bharat Heavy Plates. The companies like NIIT, Aptech and LCC Infotech have also established IT education centres in Indonesia. Reliance, Kirloskars and Thermax maintain representative offices in Indonesia. Bajaj Auto is in an advanced stage of setting up a joint venture for the assembly production of three wheelers and two wheelers in Indonesia. Ircon International is an engineering and construction company, specialized in transport infrastructure which is currently bidding for road construction projects in Indonesia and exploring railway rehabilitation and construction projects as well as prospects for leasing locomotives. The Society for Technical Communication (STC) and Metals and Minerals Trading Corporation of India (MMTC) have been active participants in trade with Indonesia.[20] The Adani Group has

---

19 http://www.mea.gov.in/Portal/ForeignRelation/India-Indonesia_Relations

20 http://www.ecaii.org/index.php?option=com_content&view=article&id=22:india-indonesia-trade-and-economic-relations&catid=6:outlook-indonesia&Itemid=8

signed a Head of Agreement with Bukit Assam, which is a state coal mining company for constructing and operating a 200-km railway line and a port in South Sumatra. The project is worth US $ 1.6 billion. The Anil Ambani Group has acquired three coal mines and will construct a 233-km railway line and port in the Jambi and South Sumatra provinces in South Sumatra. The project is estimated at US $ 2 billion. In May 2012, India's Madhucon Sirwijaya Power, an energy consortium, signed an MoU with State Electricity Company (PLN) to build a US $ 455 million 300 MW power plant in South Sumatra.[21]

For deeper economic engagement between the two countries, the Indian Embassy in Jakarta launched the India Business Forum (IBF) on 18 July 2012. The Forum brought together Indian CEOs, entrepreneurs and professionals in Indonesia for a rigorous effort towards an enhanced economic engagement with Indonesia. IBF organized its first interactive session with Chatib Basri, Chairman, and Indonesia Investment Co-ordinating Board (BKPM) on 4 September 2012.[22] Numerous high-profile commercial events have been held in Indonesia to give a boost to bilateral trade and investment relations between the two countries. In March 2011, the Embassy of India and the Economic Association of India and Indonesia jointly organized a Seminar on "Partnering for IT Sector Excellence". On 21 January 2013 a Buyer and Seller Meet was organized in partnership with CHEMEXCIL India (The Basic Chemicals, Pharmaceuticals & Cosmetics Export Promotion Council) on dyes, agrochemicals, speciality chemicals & cosmetics and the Embassy of India, Indonesia, organized a

---

[21] http://www.ecaii.org/index.php?option=com_content&view=article&id=22:india-indonesia-trade-and- economic-relations&catid=6:outlook-indonesia&Itemid=8

[22] http://www.indianembassyjakarta.com/index.php/2013-05-20-10-02-04

Table 11.2: Signed Mega Business Contracts during the Yudhoyono Visit in 2011

Items	*Related Parties (Indonesia/India)*	*Value* (bln.)
Steel Mill Plant	MoU between Kalimantan Govt. and International Coal Ventures Ltd.	3.50
Power Plant	MoU between PT Mega Urip and Adani Global Ltd.	3.00
Railway Project	MoU between PT Bukit Asam and Adani Global Ltd.	1.65
Fertilizer Project	MoU between PT Pupik Sriwidjaja and National Fertilizers Ltd.	1.65
Seaport Project	MoU between South Sumatra Govt. and Reliance Coal Resources Ltd.	1.50
Rail/Port Project	MoU between Jambi Government and Reliance Coal Resources Ltd.	1.50
Airport	MoU between PT Pembangunan Bali and GVK Ltd.	1.00
Military Equipment	MoU between PT PAL and Pipavava Shipvard Ltd.	1.00
Heavy Minerals	MoU between Ministry of Industry and TRIMEX Stands Ltd.	1.00

Source: Seung-Yoon Yang, 2012, "Rejuvenating Indonesia–India Relations in the 21st Century: Security and Economic Cooperation." Availble at: http://www.asia-studies.org/board/board_down-load.php?-board_uid=1&idx=258. * US $ billion.

Seminar Series on promoting co-operation between India and Indonesia in the health care and pharmaceutical sectors. CII and the Ministry of Commerce and Industry organized an "India Show" in Jakarta during 6-8 March 2012. An India–ASEAN Business Seminar was held on 24 October 2012 in Jakarta in partnership with International Cricket Council (ICC), Kolkata, and Jakarta Chamber of Commerce. Business seminars were held in Bali and Manado in October–November 2012 in association with ICC, Kolkata, and FICCI, respectively. Gem & Jewellery EPC held a roadshow in Jakarta on 10 January 2013 with participation by twenty companies. Indian pharmaceutical

SMEs participated at the Convention of Pharmaceutical Ingredients–South East Asia (CPI–SEA) held in Jakarta during 20-22 March 2013. These companies represented various segments of the pharmaceutical industry ranging from APIs and generics to machinery and packaging. India–Indonesia Roundtable was organized by the Embassy jointly with Indonesian Chamber of Commerce (KADIN) and INVEST India on 21 March 2013.[23]

In January 2013 the visit of Indonesian president Yudhoyono was accompanied by a large number of Indonesian CEOs. President Yudhoyono and the Indonesian business delegations succeeded in signing eighteen major business deals with Indian counterparts.

Table 11.2 shows the important deals between the two countries in the areas of power plant, mining, fertilizer, seaport and military weapon. These projects reflect the shortage of infrastructure in Indonesia and Indian companies but now energetically participate in that sector. In addition, many smaller projects signed between the two parties are mainly concentrated to the development of natural resources in Indonesia. There is a reason for optimism following the visit of President Yudhoyono to India. Trade volume between the two countries is balanced to grow from US $ 12 billion in 2010 to US $ 25 billion in 2015. The visit also saw Indian companies committing to invest US $15 billion in Indonesia. These deals mean that in the twenty-first century, economic relations between Indonesia and India are being advanced through mutual co-operation in the construction of infrastructure and in natural resources development.[24]

---

23 http://www.mea.gov.in/Portal/ForeignRelation/India-Indonesia_Relations

24 Ibid.

The India–Indonesia Joint Working Group (JWG) interpreted that the two countries are destinations of FDI inflows; they have also emerged as sources of external investment in different sectors. JSG adds that the planned CECA would facilitate more investment within a co-operative framework to promote increased investment flows between the two countries alongside stronger investment facilitation. Some of the sectors in which Indonesia can invest in India include chemicals, infrastructure, hotel, hospitality and tourism, hybrid seeds, processed food, electrical and non-electrical machinery, etc. There some specific areas of mutual interest which both the countries can exploit in close collaboration include energy (oil and gas exploration), agriculture and fisheries, forestry, transportation, Special Economic Zones (SEZs), etc. The two nations need to outline the priority areas for co-operation both in terms of investment and growth.[25]

On the other hand, Indonesian investment in India is rather low and ranks 36th in the FDI inflow to India. Though there has been increasing participation by Indonesian groups especially in West Bengal, the strict regulatory climate in India is perceived as a primary deterrent for Indonesian companies looking to invest in a large way. Limited direct flights between the two countries and restrictive visa requirements by India have further proved to be a hindrance to greater Indonesian participation in India.[26]

Co-operation in the Energy Sector

In recent times, energy collaboration among developing countries has emerged as one of the most important areas

---

25 http://www.asia-studies.org/board/board_download.php?board_uid=1&idx=258

26 http://www.idsa.in/system/files/IB_IndonesiaTradeInvestmentComplementarities

since the problems such as limited access to energy resources, the widespread use of traditional biomass and dependence of imported energy constitute a significant obstacle to social and economic development. The Indonesian government has introduced policies aimed at increasing investment in the country's upstream sector by providing various incentive programmes for firms to develop marginal oil resources throughout the country that would not otherwise be attractive to international companies. PT Pertamina is an Indonesian state oil company which plans to spend US $ 10-11 billion on boosting Indonesia's downstream sector over the next five years. As part of this effort, there have been various proposals to promote existing refineries or build new facilities, as well as to expand the country's transmission, distribution and marketing networks.[27]

Coal accounts for over half of India's total energy generation. More than 50 per cent of India's domestic coal production is utilized for power generation as three-quarters of India's electricity is generated from more than eighty coal-fed thermal plants. According to India's minister of state for coal, Shriprakash Jaiswal, coal imports are likely to rise by 21 per cent over 2011. He added that though local production has augmented by about 8 per cent, energy requirements have risen by 15 per cent. This clearly indicates that India is in dire need of reliable and long-term coal imports, without which domestic demand cannot be met. India's major source of imported coking coal is Australia, while Indonesia is the main source for non-coking coal. The close proximity of Indonesia to India compared to other source countries gives it a freight advantage. In August 2007, Tata Power acquired a 30 per cent stake in the Indonesian energy giant PT Bumi Resources, by paying close to US $ 1.3 billion (Rs. 6,000 crore). Anil Dhirubhai

---

[27] http://www.ipcs.org/article_details.php?articleNo=2650

Ambani Group's Reliance Power also acquired three coal mines in Indonesia and plans to invest over Rs. 3,000 crore in that country. In June 2010, it announced that it plans to buy two Indonesian coal companies through its unit, Reliance Coal Resources. Coal from Indonesia will be used for the Krishnapatnam Ultra Mega Power Project and others. GMR Energy has acquired full ownership interest of the Barasentosa Lestari coal mine in Indonesia, by investing Rs. 400 crore. With the acquisition of the Aries mines, the Essar Group has become the fourth Indian business house to buy coal mines in Indonesia. In the past two years, almost all power giants NTPC, Essar Power, Adani Power, JSW Energy, Indiabulls Power and Lanco Infratech — have been exploring options to own coal mines in Indonesia, to fuel some of their proposed projects.[28]

Emerging Challenges and Opportunities

Whereas the "China threat" theory has helped India gain Indonesia's co-operation in regional strategic negotiations and entry into forums such as ASEAN, ARF and the EAS, the Pakistan factor has restricted their bilateral co-operation. Although India and Indonesia have worked together in international forums such as WTO, they have adopted competitive approaches on certain issues such as the issue of Asian contention in an expanded UN Security Council. The existing visa regime has also been a matter of unease between the two countries. In the economic sector, issues of wide-ranging trade agreement or preferential trade agreement have been delayed due to differences over the listing of protected goods. While Indonesia wants palm oil in the free trade list, India has kept it in the list of protected items to provide security to palm oil producers in south India. The limited nature of international transportation between the two countries has

28 http://commerce.nic.in/trade/india_indonesia_jsg_report_2009

been another matter of concern in the area of bilateral economic and trade links. While Air India flies only once a week to Indonesia, Air Garuda, Indonesia's national carrier does not have any flight to India.[29]

Recently, the two countries have been at loggerheads over differences pertaining to the India–ASEAN FTA. Indonesia has been approaching for greater access of its palm oil exports to India while India wants an alternative of the negative list put forward by Indonesia. Further, at a bilateral level, there are also issues pertaining to the Indian demand for the removal of non-tariff barriers on its exports of meat and processed foods. Though India is one of the largest exporters of *halal* bovine meat in the world, Indonesia continues to ban India's bovine meat and milk products on the grounds that India is not free from Foot and Mouth Disease (FMD).[30] Yet, over the years the two countries have moved closer to each other and busy in co-operative initiatives on bilateral and multilateral issues. In spite of challenges, both countries also have reassured each other of continued co-operation in different sectors without letting divergences hinder their bilateral engagement. For example, during his visit to India in 2000, the then Indonesian president, Abdurrahman Wahid, decided not to go to Pakistan as a major political nod to Indian establishment. Thus, India's raising profile in the ASEAN region has come about not only because of its great power projection but also because of the acceptance of that stature by the major ASEAN countries such as Indonesia.[31]

Even though the above-mentioned issues exist between the two countries, there is also optimism about the potential

---

29 http://www.ipcs.org/pdf_file/issue/477138183IPCS-Special-Report-38.pdf

30 http://www.idsa.in/system/files/IB_Indonesia TradeInvestmentComplementarities

31 http://commerce.nic.in/trade/india_indonesia_jsg_report_2009

that exists for greater economic ties. With both countries facing intimidating infrastructural and energy challenges, there is tremendous opportunity for investments on both sides. With opportunities and forum for co-operation in place, it is important that economic actors in both countries step up and work towards enhancing economic partnerships. Companies in both countries need to actualize potential synergies for their mutual benefit and ensure that attempts at co-operation are not limited to inter-governmental meetings and commissions.[32]

Optimal Solution

The joint study group came up with a better idea of having bilateral trade through special market access, whereby both nations can make a substantive and high-quality commitment. Further, for maximizing the gains, both India and Indonesia would focus on:

- Setting up of a bilateral Trade Negotiations Committee (TNC).
- Commencement of negotiations on trade in goods, trade in services, investment and other areas of co-operation as a "single undertaking" by TNC with a view to establishing a CECA.
- Have considerable sectoral exposure measured in terms of number of sectors, volume of trade and modes of supply.
- Provide for the best possible market access and national treatment both horizontally and sectorally.
- Develop rules and disciplines on trade in services based on General Agreement on Trade in Services (GATS) provisions and improving on them further wherever possible including disciplines on domestic regulation.

---

32 http://www.ipcs.org/article_details.php?articleNo=2650

- Give priority to areas with greater potential and complementarities between both the parties.
- Facilitate better dialogue between the regulatory bodies of the two countries for possible Mutual Recognition Arrangements (MRAs).

Conclusion

In the overall analysis, it can be said that economic and trade complementarities between India and Indonesia are enormous. Therefore, there is a need for the two countries to sort out the irksome issues and clarify doubts. The two nations should also work to sort out issues related to MRAs in a spirit of co-operation. Because India and Indonesia have large, rapidly growing economies, they can reap the benefits of their demographic dividend, a consequence of their young population. Indonesia and India have also been growing rapidly from opening up and liberalizing their economies, India since 1991 and Indonesia since 1967. These economic reforms of both countries have made both economies more competitive and outward-looking, opening up great potential gains from closer economic relations. Indonesia is a geographical neighbour of India and both share a maritime boundary. Like India, Indonesia is also a diverse, multi-ethnic, multi-religious and democratic country. In the context of our Look East Policy, it is the largest and most influential member of the ASEAN. As India prepares and works towards political and economic convergence with the region, Indonesia's role is critical and its support is vital. These closer economic relations will also be underpinned by the long historical and cultural links between India and Indonesia and by the mutual admiration that both countries are democratic, India since its 1947 and Indonesia since mid-1998.

12

India and Indonesia in the Indo-Pacific Imagination

Krishnendra Meena

Introduction

CONCURRENT to the recent phase of globalization, there has been a clear geopolitical shift in favour of the developing world which has facilitated a recent spate of regionalization. A prominent feature of this geopolitical shift in the world system, resulting from the globalization of the world space in the last two decades, is the emergence of a few developing states as economic powerhouses (China, India and Brazil). This complicates the conceptual clarity about the world political system, which was a feature of the Western discourse, as these economies challenge the traditional dominance of the industrialized states and new geographies take shape. The emergence of China as the second largest economy of the world in recent years has defied the traditional notions of civilization, culture and development. This has led to a reimagination of the world system which partly is a post-Cold War situation wherein the bi-polarity is missed and there exists an indication of a general momentum towards a multi-polar situation with regional groupings of states playing an ever-increasing role in world politics. New regional formations are imagined which defy the logic of geography and are increasingly legitimized through constant repetition by statesmen, media and academic institutions. BRICS is an example which by its expanse negates the traditional conceptions of "region". This chapter, therefore, in general is marked by three distinct but related themes which run as undercurrents in it. First, the recent phase of globalization, which has impacted the human perception of time and space significantly as the global linkages, economic, social, political and cultural improved at a heightened pace, which has been termed by David Harvey as "Time–Space Compression" (Harvey 1992) which shapes the way in which we understand spaces immediate to us and the spaces beyond. Second, and the related theme, is that of the emergence, arrival or rise of some of the developing economies due to the accrual of benefits of globalization, which informs the regionalization processes concerning us in the chapter. Third, the "rise" of China and its impact on the shifting geopolitical alliances, which also impinges upon the theme of regionalization and related processes. Within this context the chapter attempts to locate the new imagination of the "Indo-Pacific" space. The term has been frequently used during the last decade to describe an area extending from the eastern coast of Africa to the eastern coast of Asia littoral to the Pacific. The study argues that the term is a geopolitical imagination without a sound basis in geography. Indo-Pacific has found immense usage in the statements emanating from Japan and Australia and has later on been evoked by the United States of America which also during the Cold War years and after have defined the space as Asia-Pacific and indicate that United States (US) foreign policy will direct considerable resources toward the region.

In an interesting article in the journal *Foreign Policy* in October 2011, reflective of the geographical shift of the strategic orientations of the US from Trans-Atlantic to the Asia-Pacific, Secretary of State Hillary Clinton begins with an immediate futuristic objective:

> One of the most important tasks of American statecraft over the next decade will therefore be to lock in a substantially increased investment — diplomatic, economic, strategic, and otherwise — in the Asia-Pacific region. — Clinton 2011

The geopolitical shift is underlined by the economic emergence of China during the last three decades and the effort to actively surround China geo-strategically by engaging traditional allies in the region, as Agnew summarizes:

> that Asia-Pacific is really a code for China and that this focus on China involves reinforcing existing alliances to contain China. — Agnew 2012

Though it is notable that Agnew disagrees with this perception of reformulation of US policy, as he argues that in the first instance the notion that the US policy has totally been Atlantic centric to contain the USSR and now it has shifted to the Asia-Pacific is a fallacy as the strong US alliance with Japan and South Korea during the Cold War suggests (Agnew 2012). None the less, there is a significant reimagining of the world space through such labels and geopolitical codes since the end of the Cold War and the advent of the recent phase of globalization. Sidaway is explicit in saying that:

> a series of high profile intergovernmental and corporate reports have reinforced impressions of a shifting global economic geography that reconfigures maps of development/underdevelopment. — Sidaway 2012

These geopolitical visions which emanate from particular biases and advantaged conceptions of the world are then embedded in the popular psyche and the geographical terms like the "Asia-Pacific" take root. For example, the nomenclature of Asia-Pacific is contested by the Chinese academia. Zhu Feng attests the argument with the assertion that:

> the conceptualization of "region" is still debated and the term "Asia-Pacific" is a Westernized usage to define a broad

> area, geographically situated within the bounds of the Pacific Ocean. In historic and cultural explanations, such a region never actually existed. In economic and political terms, the notion of Asia Pacific is a foreign one for most of the inhabitants on the western edges of Asia-Pacific.
>
> — Feng 2008:

The scepticism and apprehensions about the US policy toward the Pacific Ocean space aside, it is true that in terms of the economic growth in the recent decades, which coincide with the recent phase of globalization, some "developing" economies (China, India and Brazil) have registered very high growth rates. If Asia-Pacific has dominated the literature emanating from the US, Japan and Australia have been instrumental in reviving this controversial term.

The Indo-Pacific Geopolitical Imagination

The history of the term Indo-Pacific extends back into the nineteenth century during the 1850s, when it was used to identify the people inhabiting the people in the islands of Indonesia as Indo-Pacific islanders (Medcalf 2012). However, the first instance of its use since the ascendance of geopolitics as a discipline in the late nineteenth and twentieth century is by the discredited Nazi geopolitical thinker Karl Haushofer, who has the notorious distinction of advising the Fuhrer, Adolf Hitler, during the inter-war period in Germany. Therefore, the term has a long geopolitical history, even prior to the application by Haushofer, as a part of his book *German Culture Politics in the Indo-Pacific Space* in 1939. For him the context was clear as the Germans sought to emulate the British Empire, charted out a course for global military domination. For Haushofer, the inspiration came from the fact that on the basis of a strong naval base the British had built a global empire and the Dutch during the same period were present in South-East Asia. To address the German dream to be present globally, Haushofer intended to examine the viability of such a presence in the region. Since the end of the Second World War, the term "geopolitics" came in place of the German term Geopolitik, as the ideas of Karl Haushofer were discredited because of their Nazi association. The discipline of geopolitics suffered as the term invoked references to the Second World War and the Nazi ideology. The term was also used by noted American geopolitical thinker Spykman in his work *America's Strategy in World Politics* (1942) while explaining his formulation of "rimland". Spykman argued that the Indo-Pacific was "a great maritime circumferential highway". Geopolitics began its revival in the 1970s and the term Indo-Pacific is now being reinvigorated in the academic circles as new strategic and geopolitical constellations in the wake of emergence of China. Most recent instance of its use is by the Japanese Prime Minister Shinzo Abe in 2007. Let us examine the geographical validity of this term in this section.

The term "Indo-Pacific" itself can be put to scrutiny for its geographical validity. Authors like Robert D. Kaplan, in his work *Monsoon: The Indian Ocean and the Future of American Power* (2010) argues that the Indo-Pacific entity will cater to the rising trade in the region due to the rise of China and India as a basis to establish its unity. His basic argument is that Indo-Pacific is a bio-geographical region alluding to the similar flora and fauna from the East African (Madgascar) coast to the Asian lands littoral to the Pacific (Japan). Second, for Kaplan, these regions have similar climate, the unifying climatic type is that of the monsoons. Both the claims can be put to scrutiny, the first one is specially intangible, since the bio-geographical basis is still not vigorously scrutinized to become a geographical category, the only evidence could be found in a paper published as recently as 2007 (Spalding et al. 2007). Kaplan's explanation in climatology also lacks intense research as the two most accepted climatic classifications in the field do not support his thesis. The most accepted climatic classification that is of Wladimir Koeppen which he developed from 1900 to 1936 and which by the scholars of climate is considered to be the most relevant to explain and classify the world into climatic zones. His basic categories are:

- A Tropical forest climates; hot all seasons
- B Dry climates
- C Warm temperate climates
- D Cold forest climates
- E Polar climates
- F Undifferentiated highland climates (Koeppen cited in Critchfield 2001).

The classification is completed with various sub-categories in each of the above-mentioned categories. But the Indo-Pacific extending from the east coast of Africa to the islands of Japan shows tremendous diversity with categories A to D all present in the Indo-Pacific. Thus, the climatic classification does support the unity of Indo-Pacific as a single climatic zone. A close look at the regions littoral to the Indo-Pacific reveals that the climatic zones present on the eastern coast of Africa are the A and B category, i.e. (tropical forest climate and dry climate). The region from the Horn of Africa to the Persian Gulf to Pakistan surrounding the Arabian Sea has the dry climate (category B). The Indian subcontinent supports the first four (A, B, C and D) categories due its extremely diverse physiography. The South-East Asian region falls under the A category (tropical forest climate). Then northwards on the Asian landmass the majority of the countries have either of the two categories, i.e. C and D (warm temperate climates and the cold forest climates). The western coast of Australia again displays the two categories of A and B types of climate. The sub-categorization of these regions elucidates much more diverse climatic zones which exist in the Indo-Pacific. Another very prominent climatic classification used by geographers is that of C. Warren Thornthwaite. The Indo-Pacific zonation can be discussed through this classification and it also falls short of scrutiny there.

The idea can be contested on other grounds as well:

> Some will argue that this super-region is too big to be a coherent strategic system. To be sure, some of Asia's most serious security flashpoints — from the Korean Peninsula to the India–Pakistan relationship — seem principally sub-regional. — Medcalf 2012

There is a commonality to these conflicts though, as the principal powers (India, China and the United States) of the region has a stake in these security flashpoints and these powers could safely be considered to have an influence in the wider Indo-Pacific region. Moreover, the South China Sea dispute engages most of the important regional players in the wider Indo-Pacific.

The second criticism is more pointed:

> Some countries, particularly China, could well have misgivings about seeing the region through an Indo-Pacific prism. Is the Indo-Pacific really just code for balancing against or excluding China. — Medcalf 2012

It is difficult to rule out such a viewpoint which indicates a strategic encircling of the People's Republic of China. The constitution of the major proponents (Japan, Australia and India) of the term mixed with their geographical location at three opportune junctures in the Indo-Pacific does indicate towards a tri-locking strategy against China. This also indicates, however, that the term in its current form is a geopolitical imagination. The next section focuses on the Indo-Pacific as a geopolitical imagination and the possibilities it offers to the Indian establishment.

The current Japanese prime minister in his earlier term as the prime minister of Japan, during 2007, addressed the Indian Parliament. He began with saying:

> The Pacific and the Indian Oceans are now bringing about a dynamic coupling as seas of freedom and of prosperity. A "Broader Asia" that broke away geographical boundaries is now beginning to take on a distinct form. Our two countries have the ability — and the responsibility — to ensure that it broadens yet further and to nurture and enrich these seas to become seas of clearest transparence.
>
> — Baru, The Hindu, 19 December 2012

> "Confluence of the Two Seas", the Pacific and the Indian Oceans — anticipating Hillary Clinton's idea of the "Indo-Pacific" — Mr. Abe asked the Indian Parliament if it was not time for a value-based and an interest-based relationship between India and Japan.
>
> — Baru, The Hindu, 19 December 2012

The Indo-Pacific theatre holds tremendous stakes for the US as the sole superpower as it comes to terms with the rising Chinese power in the region. An established analyst of the US Navy, Toshi Yoshihara argues for an increased US presence in the Indo-Pacific region. Accepting that the US strategy has reconciled to the Indo-Pacific "pivot", he argues for the deployment of 60 per cent of its naval strength to be allocated to the region by the year 2020 (Yoshihara 2013). The strategic, political and economic dynamism of the countries inhabiting the Indo-Pacific Rim will exert an almost gravitational pull on the US interests. This is an intellectual, policy and material reorientation of considerable significance for the US (Yoshihara 2013).

Indonesia as a "Pivot" in the Indo-Pacific

Indonesia — in particular, the island of Sumatra — and peninsular Malaysia on the opposite side of the Strait of Malacca form the heart of maritime Asia (Kaplan 2010). The Strait of Malacca is the Fulda Gap of the twenty-first century multi-polar world, the place where almost all of the shipping lanes between the Red Sea and the Sea of Japan converge at the most vital choke point of world commerce; where the spheres of naval influence of India and China meet; where the Indian Ocean joins the western Pacific (Kaplan 2010). Indonesia, besides being a major oil producer, will remain East Asia's primary supplier of natural gas for decades. The country's vast archipelagic nature, its energy resources, its ethnic diversity, predominant Muslim religion, institutional weaknesses and ultra-strategic location will make it a critical hub of world politics (Kaplan 2010).

Indonesia is located at the cusp of the Indian Ocean and Pacific Ocean, and thereby at the very centre of the "Indo-Pacific" imagination. Kaplan further presses the issue of the importance of Indonesia in the region with underlining that from the northern entrance to the Malacca Straits to the exit from the Straits is marked by the Indonesian territory, specifically the eastern coast of the island of Sumatra:

> the entry point of the Strait of Malacca, which is more than 500 miles in length and 200 miles wide here at its northern end. But it is only 11 miles across at its heavily congested southern entrance near Singapore, a place made narrower by treacherous shoals and the very volume of ship traffic, from supertankers to small tugs and fishing boats all vying for space. — Kaplan 2010

The commercial dependence on the waterway of the Malacca Straits is almost absolute for the countries located east of the Straits. The point can be substantiated further by the fact that "of the fourteen nations constituting East and South-East Asia, twelve are highly dependent on Middle Eastern oil, which mainly comes through here" (Kaplan 2010). Historically, the towns situated on the islands of Sumatra (Indonesia) and the Malaya Peninsula (Malaysia) have been hubs of international trade and commerce. The eastern end of the Indian Ocean marked by these important hubs constituted the regional arena which extended from eastern coast of Africa to the South China Sea.

Indonesia's importance in the Indo-Pacific is enhanced manifold with the realization that alternative routes, except the Malacca Straits, to the East Asia and North-East Asia also traverse through the Indonesian territory. The Sunda and Lombok straits offer alternative routes to and from the East Asia and the Pacific Ocean. The geopolitical coherence for the Indo-Pacific construct comes from the Sea Lanes of Communications (SLOCs) which criss-cross this newly-imagined space. Indonesia, geographically, is the pivot of the Indo-Pacific by being situated at the critical juncture which facilitates these SLOCs and offers a range of options for transport and communication in case of any eventuality. The devastating tsunami in 2006 is an example of such happenings in the region which are a common occurrence owing to the fact the South-East Asia as region is located in a seismically active and volcanic zone.

India and the Indo-Pacific

Indo-Pacific can be discussed as a geopolitical imagination in the Indian context as well, as the one of the main actors in the space is India. Globalization and its multifarious manifestations have expanded the ambit of the space India can influence in its neighbourhood from the IOR to the "Indo-Pacific", a term also used by C. Rajamohan in his latest work *Samudra Manthan: Sino–Indian Rivalry in the Indo-Pacific*. Rajamohan uses the term drawing analogy from oceanography and indicates that increasingly a "confluence of the two seas", i.e. the Indian Ocean and the Pacific Ocean is at the forefront of discussion in academia as well as in the statecraft, particularly that of India, Australia and Japan (Rajamohan 2013). The term in itself can be put to scrutiny as discussed above through the usage of various climatic classifications which form the backbone of climatology, on the basis of which major regionalizations of the planet are arrived at. The only explanation for the term comes from the fact that regions can be geopolitical imaginations which serve the interests of a state or a particular group of states. Indo-Pacific in this sense is a geopolitical imagination directed at China.

In this case, the rise of China and the concerns which occur due to it in the immediate region are addressed through such regionalizations. As expressed above the term is a geopolitical code for China. Though there are two variants to the Indo-Pacific which are currently being concretized through debate by strategic thinkers.

> The first system embraces *Indian Ocean-centric issues* — that is, issues that are specific to the Indian Ocean and its littoral. These include issues of economic development and human security, the environment, the seabed and fisheries management, among others. These issues are best addressed by the states with direct stakes in them, and which therefore potentially form the essential reform agenda of the current pre-eminent regional body, the Indian Ocean Rim Association for Regional Cooperation (IOR-ARC).
>
> — Rumley, Doyle and Chaturvedi 2013

They further explain the Indo-Pacific with its larger dimensions:

> The second system sees the Indian Ocean as part of an arguably wider Indo-Pacific "strategic system" that embraces the trade routes and sea lanes that cross the Indian Ocean itself but also extend past the Straits of Malacca and the Sunda and Lombok Straits into the South China Sea and north to China, Taiwan, Korea and Japan, and indeed on the west coast of North America. As trade highways, these routes are arguably the most important in the world today, and the "choke points" and contested waterways along the highway attract critical attention of the "hard security" kind. Given the range of stakeholders, this is an inclusive framework, and the issues embraced within it are played out at a high political level.
>
> — Rumley, Doyle and Chaturvedi 2013

The Indo-Pacific imagination is frequently justified as a "confluence of two seas/oceans" (Abe 2007 (Ministry of Foreign Affairs 2007); Rajamohan 2013). However, these formulations do not explain the strategic significance of the Indonesian archipelago at this confluence. The paper makes an attempt to explain the significance of the term Indo-Pacific by invoking the following facts about Indian Ocean and the trade which flows on its SLOCs. Globalization relies ultimately on shipping containers and the Indian Ocean accounts for one half of the world's container traffic. Moreover, the Indian Ocean rimland from the Middle East to the Pacific accounts for 70 per cent of the traffic of petroleum products for the entire world (Kaplan 2010).

China, whose demand for crude oil doubled between 1995 and 2005, and will double again in the coming decade or two, as it imports 7.3 million barrels of crude oil daily by 2020 — half of Saudi Arabia's planned output. More than 85 per cent of that China-bound oil will pass across the span of the Indian Ocean through the Strait of Malacca: the reason China is desperate for alternative energy routes to the Pacific, as well as overland ones into China from Central Asia, Pakistan and Burma (Myanmar). The combined appetites of China, Japan, and South Korea for Persian Gulf oil already make the Strait of Malacca home to half of world oil flows and close to a quarter of global trade (Kaplan 2010).

An Indian government document *India's Maritime Military Strategy* (*IMMS*) published in 2007 elaborates that India's maritime geography enhances its importance in the IOR through an unimpeded access to the Indian Ocean on both the eastern and western coasts and the advantageous location of island groups in the region. It is in this context that India should adopt an oceanic strategy than a coastal one (*IMSS* 2007). The document in the chapter on "Indian Ocean Region and Its Geopolitics" lists the strategic chokepoints in the region namely Strait of Hormuz, Suez Canal, Strait of Bab-el-Mandab,

Malacca Strait, Sunda Strait, Lombok Strait, Nine Degree Channel, Six Degree Channel and the Cape of Good Hope.

The list of India's maritime interests is expanded in the latest version of India's maritime strategy document of 2009 called the *Indian Maritime Doctrine* (INBR 8) and elaborate attention is provided with the classification of primary and secondary areas of interest of the Indian Navy with the inclusion of (INBR):

- The Southern Indian Ocean Region, due to our interests in Antarctica, and the friendly littoral states in the continents of Australia and Africa.
- The Red Sea and its littoral states.
- The South China Sea, other areas of west Pacific Ocean and friendly littoral countries located therein.
- Other areas of national interest based on considerations of diaspora and overseas investments (INBR 2009).

Significant here is the inclusion of the South China Sea and the west Pacific Ocean as areas of interest of the Indian Navy. It is pertinent to mention at this point that the US has been more than willing to engage with India in the IOR through joint naval exercises since 2002 named MALABAR at locations both in the Indian Ocean and in the West Pacific furthers India's geopolitical stature in the IOR space. The multilateral nature of these exercises involving Japan, Singapore and Australia does provide significant geopolitical leverage to India in the IOR space. India has been involved with other naval exercises including Brazil and South Africa (IBSAMAR 2008, 2010) off the South African coast; involving India and the United States (SALVEX 2007; HABUNAG 2008, 2010); with Japan and the United States (TRIALTEX 2007), Operational Deployment of Eastern Fleet in South-East Asia 2011 in which the Indian Navy conducted exercises with the Singapore Navy (SIMBEX 2011) in the contentious South China Sea (Indian Navy Website 2013).

Conclusion

The rise of China as a major player in the international system has evoked debates about a geopolitical shift in the international system and there has been a recalibration of various state policies around the phenomenon. This has manifested itself in the formulation of various geopolitical codes by the United States as well as the states located within Asia and its immediate neighbourhood. However, the coinage of the term Indo-Pacific can be traced back to the years of Nazi Germany in the writings of Karl Haushofer during the inter-war years. The recent usage has been that by the Japanese Prime Minister Shinzo Abe during his address to the Indian Parliament to draw common frameworks of strategy between the two states of India and Japan. The US also declared the present century is destined to be an Asian Century and therefore US efforts will be directed towards the Asia-Pacific space. The Indo-Pacific does not have a solid geographic basis but the conception could be explained through literature in critical geopolitics. From a critical geopolitics perspective it can be explained as a geopolitical imagination rooted in the particular state strategies toward other states either to counter rival strategies or to support the strategies of allies. Such imaginations are also termed as geopolitical codes. The Indo-Pacific also covers maritime disputes ranging from delimitation of boundaries to sovereignty disputes in East China Sea and South China Sea which have all the requirements to become a conflict zone. The Chinese and the Japanese claim sovereignty on the same set of islands in the East China Sea, whereas there are disputes related to clear demarcation of the Exclusive Economic Zones in the South China. In both the cases the situation is complicated further with the presence of hydrocarbon and mineral resources. It is estimated that the South China Sea is host to 70 billion barrels of oil and has the potential to become a new "Middle East". The disputing parties are Vietnam, China, the Philippines, Taiwan, Indonesia, Malaysia and Brunei in the case of South China Sea dispute whereas the East China Sea dispute involves Japan and China.

This chapter has attempted to highlight, with the use of data for trade in the region to arrive at the conclusion, that Indonesia holds a geostrategic position overlooking major transactions of trade and commerce in the region which is growing very rapidly. The term pivot signifies the geopolitical value of the Indonesian archipelago which hosts the major trade and commerce routes which run through the Indo-Pacific space. States located on either west or east of the Indonesian archipelago will in the future realize the importance of this state, geographically located at a point of substantial value in Indo-Pacific construct. The fact of location of five of the largest ten economies of the world combined with the two most populous states which are emerging powers is significant for Indonesia. These economies also are slated to be the largest consumers of energy in the near future and the energy trade will flow through the Indonesian waters. The flow of commodities will also increase as Chinese economy continues to grow at impressive rates and its "manufacturing hub" produces for the markets which are available in the region as well as globally. Indonesia owing to its archipelagic character which provides favourable SLOCs through its territorial water and through its EEZs will hold immense strategic value in deciding the longevity and formidability of the term Indo-Pacific.

References

PRIMARY SOURCES

Integrated Headquarters, Ministry of Defence (Navy), 2007, *Freedom to Use the Seas: India's Maritime Military Strategy*, New Delhi.

———, 2009, *Indian Maritime Doctrine* (INBR 8), New Delhi.

Ministry of Foreign Affairs of Japan (2007)"Confluence of the Two Seas" Speech by H.E.Mr. Shinzo Abe, Prime Minister of Japan at the

Parliament of the Republic of India, August 22, Website of the Ministry of Foreign Affairs of Japan,Available at: <http:// www.mofa.go.jp/, Accessed on 21st August, 2014

SECONDARY SOURCES

Agnew, John, 1998, *Geopolitics: Re-visioning World Politics*, London: Routledge.

———, 2012, "Is US Security Policy 'Pivoting' from the Atlantic to Asia-Pacific", *Dialogue on Globalization*, Berlin: Friedrich Ebert Stiftung.

Albert, Mathias and Paul Reuber, 2007, "Introduction: The Production of Regions in the Emerging Global Order-Perspectives on 'Strategic Regionalization'", *Geopolitics*, **12**(4): 549-54.

Baru, Sanjay, 2012, "The Importance of Shinzo Abe", *The Hindu*, 19 December.

Clinton, Hillary, 2011, "America's Pacific Century: The Future of Politics Will Be Decided in Asia, not Afghanistan or Iraq, and the United States Will Be Right at the Centre of Action", *Foreign Policy*, October.

Critchfield, Howard J., 2001, *General Climatology*, New Delhi: Prentice-Hall of India.

Feng, Zhu, 2008, "Regionalism, Multilateralism and Institution Building in East Asia" in V.R. Raghavan (ed.) *Asian Security Dynamic: US, Japan and the Rising Powers*, New Delhi: Promilla & Bibliophile South Asia, pp. 14-23.

Harvey, David, 1992, *The Condition of Postmodernity: An Enquiry into the Origins of Cultural Change*, Oxford: Wiley Blackwell.

Kaplan, Robert D., 2010, *Monsoon: The Indian Ocean and the Future of American Power*, New York: Random House.

———, 2013, *The Revenge of Geography*, New York: Random House.

Khurana, Gurpreet S., 2007, "Security of Sea Lines: Prospects for India–Japan Cooperation", *Strategic Analysis*, **31**(1): 139-53.

Neumann, Roderick P., 2010, "Political Ecology II: Theorizing Region", *Progress in Human Geography*, **34**(3): 368-74.

Medcalf, Rory, 2012, "A Term Whose Time Has Come: The Indo-Pacific", *The Diplomat*, 4 December.

Rajamohan, C., 2013, *Samudra Manthan: Sino-Indian Rivalry in the Indo-Pacific*, New Delhi: Oxford University Press.

Rumley, Dennis, Timothy Doyle and Sanjay Chaturvedi, 2013, "'Securing' the Indian Ocean: Competing Regional Security Constructions", *Indo-Pacific Governance Research Centre*, Policy Brief No. 2, Adelaide.

Sidaway, James D., 2012, "Geographies of Development: New Maps, New Visions?, *The Professional Geographer*, **64**(1): 49-62.

Spalding, Mark D., Helen E. Fox, Gerald R. Allen, Nick Davidson et al., 2007, "Marine Ecoregions of the World: A Bioregionalization of Coastal and Shelf Areas", *Bioscience*, July/August, **57**(7): 573–83.

Yoshihara, Toshi, 2013, "The US Navy's Indo–Pacific Challenge", *Journal of the Indian Ocean Region*, **9**(1): 90-103.

13

The Evolution of India–Indonesia Relations
From Ramayana to China

Nishit Kumar

Abstract

Close cultural and commercial contacts for about two millennia, close collaborations for the cause of African and Asian independence and the Non-Aligned Movement (NAM)[1] are the first things that come to mind during any discussion on relations between India and Indonesia. However, the relations between these two countries are much deeper and have deeper connotations, particularly in the twenty-first century.

This paper intends to examine the political and strategic relations between the two biggest democratic countries of the world and maritime neighbours — India and Indonesia. Tracing the history of the relationship between these two countries, beginning from ancient times, this paper posits that these two Asian regional powers cherish good relations and hence moving into a glorious phase with an

1 NAM was founded in Belgrade in 1961 but it was largely conceived by India's first Prime Minister Jawaharlal Nehru and Indonesia's first President Sukarno. While some meetings with Third World perspective were held before 1955, historians consider that the Bandung Asian–African Conference is the most immediate antecedent to the creation of NAM.

unprecedented surge of interaction in various fields including trade, investment and culture.

Viewing from the prism of Prime Minister Manmohan Singh's visit to Indonesia in October 2013, this paper attempts to picture the broader vision of the relationship. It looks into the planning, actual outcome and other engagements during the visit. It argues that there are grounds to believe that this relationship may develop into a broad-based political and security partnership.

Objectives

1. This paper endeavours to throw light on the implications of joint statement on five initiatives for strengthening the India–Indonesia strategic partnership.

2. Through the lens of the past and present, it looks into the pivotal role played by Indonesia in India's current maritime trade and regional security.

Introduction

INDIA'S quest for regional power and global supremacy leads it to crave for direct political and security role in South-East Asia. Indonesia, given its size,[2] its geographical location as a maritime neighbour and its leading role in the region, is most likely to become an indispensable factor in India's regional strategy. This article argues that Indo–Indonesia relations have the potential to eventually evolve into a broader security-based partnership. It begins with the analysis of cultural, economic and historical relations between the two countries. It examines how their democratic set-ups and Islamic populations bring the two closer. Indonesia constitutes about 13 per cent of the world's Muslim population, while Muslims in India make up 10.9 per cent of India's 1.2 plus billion population. Also, India is the world's largest

---

[2] Indonesia, largest archipelago in the world extending 5,120 km from east to west and 1,760 km from north to south. Indonesia presence in Indian Ocean and its ties with India are important to maintain regional peace.

democracy while Indonesia is the third. These factors definitely play a role in shaping up the relations between the two.

Another factor that is common and has been constant in both the countries' policy and security issues is that of the China factor. In the case of Indonesia, the Chinese claim to a gas-rich corner of Indonesia's Exclusive Economic Zone (EEZ)[3] is a constant irk; in the case of India are the border disputes with China in Arunachal Pradesh and in Aksai Chin. Given the fact that international relations in the twenty-first century are viewed more in terms of security that encompass both the military and the economic factors, Indian and Indonesian responses to these issues with China definitely factor in China's status as the largest manufacturing base in the world, and value the trade relationships with China as being important. Thus, an outright escalation of conflict is not possible, which is evident from how India and Indonesia deal with the China question. This is another aspect that is common to both India and Indonesia that needs closer study. In order to understand the current relations between India and Indonesia, it first becomes pertinent to trace the historical and political relations between the two.

Political Relations and Historical Facts

The relations between these two Asian countries are not just historic but cultural and economic as well, and these linkages have existed since time immemorial. The ties between the two date back to the times of *Ramayana*.[4] Yawadvipa (Java) finds a

---

[3] The Indonesian Exclusive Economic Zone (EEZ) is the outer strip bordering the Indonesian territorial sea as determined by the law applicable to the Indonesian waters, covering sea-bed, the subsoil thereof and the water above it with an outermost limit of 200 nautical miles, measured from the baseline of the Indonesian territorial sea.

[4] *Ramayana* is an important part of Indonesian culture, performed as *wayang kulit* (shadow puppet) and ballet.

mention in *Ramayana*, while historical records confirm trade relations between subcontinental India and the Srivijaya kingdom[5] in the fourth century. The relation continued right up to the eleventh century, when Indian traders carried Hinduism and other aspects of Indian culture including Sanskrit and the Brahmi script[6] to Indonesia. At that point in history what existed was a collection of islands ruled by kingdoms — Srivijaya, Medang, Sunda and Majapahit being some of the largest. Trade and cultural ties continued getting stronger with the arrival of traders from Gujarat and Kunnur, Kerala. Existing inscriptions in some of Indonesia's oldest kingdoms such as Yupa Kutai, Tugu of Tarumanagara and Kalinga are testimony to this long bilateral relationship.

In terms of culture's role in formulating ties between the two it can be stated that Indian epics such as *Ramayana* and *Mahabharata* play an important role in Indonesian history and culture. In theatres of the Prambanan in Java the *Ramayana* dance is performed by Javanese Muslims on full-moon nights. Similarly the Borobodur[7] and Prambanan temples of the ninth century are examples of the Buddhist influence on Indonesian culture. Similar to Indonesia's culture, Indian clothing forms of the *lungi* and *sarong* state how India has been influenced by Indonesia. Other similarities in cuisines, particularly in Kare or Curry state the cultural similarity between the two.

---

[5] Srivijaya empire was originated in Palembang on Sumatra and soon extended its influence and controlled the Strait of Malacca. It was a maritime and commercial kingdom that flourished during seventh–thirteenth centuries in Malaya archipelago.

[6] After coming into contact with Indian merchants, speakers of Javanese adapted the Pallava script, a variant of Brahmi script during fourth century.

[7] Borobudur Temple is a Buddhist temple complex located in central Java, dating from the eighth century.

The two sides also share similarities at the political front. India and Indonesia, both born in the early post-Second World War era are among the top three largest democracies in the world. In 1945-49, during the National Revolution and formation of Republic of Indonesia, India and Egypt were the earliest nations that supported and recognized Indonesian independence. India's first Prime Minister Pt. Jawaharlal Nehru and Indonesia's first president Sukarno were among the pioneers of the NAM, while the introduction of India's Look East Policy in 1991 and India becoming a partner of the Association of South-East Asian Nations (ASEAN),[8] helped New Delhi and Jakarta to revitalize ties that had been disrupted after a military rule in Indonesia between 1965-98.

Strategic Partnership in Twenty-first Century

In November 2005, Indian Prime Minister Manmohan Singh and Indonesian president Susilo Bambang Yudhoyono declared a new strategic partnership between the two countries and agreed to take the bilateral trade to US $ 10 billion by 2010, which was achieved as bilateral trade between the two stood at US $ 13.2 billion in 2010 with India's exports to Indonesia being US $ 3.3 billion against imports of US $ 10 billion, the balance of trade tilting in Indonesia's favour. The recent past has also been manifested by strengthening of defence and security co-operation. Indonesian president Susilo Bambang Yudhoyono paid a state visit to India in 2011,[9] and a wide range of bilateral agreements and MoUs were signed which

---

[8] ASEAN is an organization of ten countries, established on 8 August 1967. It includes Indonesia, Malaysia, Philippines, Singapore, Thailand, Brunei, Burma, Cambodia, Laos and Vietnam. It aims to achieve economic growth, social progress, cultural development among its members, protection of regional peace and stability.

[9] Indonesian president Susilo Bambang Yudhoyono was the chief guest of India's Republic Day celebration in 2011.

covered areas like security, economic, science and technology, media, education and cultural spheres. According to the report of the Joint Study Group on the feasibility of India–Indonesia Comprehensive Economic Co-operation Agreement, India and Indonesia are working together on Coordinated Patrols (CORPATs), anti-piracy operations and maintenance of security of sea-lanes. The two have signed an extradition treaty, a manual legal assistance treaty and working towards an agreement on transfer of sentenced persons. There is increased co-operation in countering terrorism, curbing drug trafficking and cyber crimes. The two countries are taking steps for closer collaboration at Indian Ocean Rim Association (IOR-ARC) and recently held a trilateral track II dialogue[10] on the Indian Ocean-related issues. Our modern bilateral relations can be more observed through continuous trading relations. According to Indian government data, the India–Indonesia bilateral trade amplified five times since the inking of the strategic partnership agreement and reached a historic US $ 20 billion mark in 2012-13. Indian companies have noteworthy investments in Indonesia's infrastructure, power, textiles, steel, automotive, mining, banking and Fast Moving Consumer Goods (FMCG) sectors. Even several Indonesian companies have also invested in Indian infrastructure projects. India is the largest buyer of crude palm oil from Indonesia and imports coal, minerals and pulp. India exports refined petroleum products, maize, commercial vehicles, telecommunication equipment, oil seeds, animal feed, cotton, steel products and plastics to Indonesia. Famous Indian companies in Indonesia include Tata Power, Reliance, Adani, L&T, GMR, Videocon, Punj Lloyd, Aditya Birla, Jindal Stainless Steel, ESSAR, TVS, Bajaj, BEML, Godrej, Balmer & Lawrie and SBI.

---

[10] Track II diplomacy is an informal kind of diplomacy in which academic scholars, public figures, social activists, retired civil and military officials are engaged in dialogues and it helps in conflict resolution and confidence building.

Analysing these factors, combined with the recent visit of Manmohan Singh to Indonesia and the inking of new MoUs to strengthen ties, it can be stated that a new kind of strategic relationship between the two is in the offing. During the visit, both sides also agreed for international co-operation on combating corruption between the Central Vigilance Commission (CVC) of India and Komisi Pemberantasan Korupsi (KPK) of Indonesia, which takes co-operation to new and unexplored spheres. The two have formed an Eminent Persons Group (EPG) and tasked it to make a Vision Document 2025 within a year. Both sides also shook hands on enhancing the existing co-operation and capacity building in the fields of hydrography, joint surveys and maritime domain awareness. Recognizing the common threats to national security from global terrorism and other transnational crimes, New Delhi and Jakarta resolved to significantly enhance bilateral co-operation in combating terrorism, money laundering, arms smuggling, human trafficking and cyber crime. They also agreed to enhance concrete co-operation on youth and sports affairs, and to promote relevant government agencies. Both sides signed MoUs on strategic engagements, defence and security co-operation, comprehensive economic partnership, cultural and people-to-people links, and co-operation in responding to common challenges.

The China Factor

China's intervention in Indian Ocean and the much debated strings of pearls clearly reflect a threat perception and can never be denied. In the case of Indonesia, even though it has not been that vocal as Vietnam and Philippines have been, fact remains that Chinese policies on South China Sea takes an extremely high position in the Indonesia strategic thought, and justifiably so. Looking from the perspective of recent development in India–Indonesia ties, Indonesia will play a pivotal role in India's maritime issues and to counter China's Strings of Pearls.

A common response to dealing with China's assertiveness is that of balancing,[11] wherein countries which face challenges from China directly or indirectly seek US protection. But given the fact that trade ties with China, which has become one of the most important players at the global level, disruption of ties with the country in the face of its growing assertiveness is also not an option. For countries such as India and Indonesia, which are rapidly growing economies, the more pragmatic approach lies in maintaining strategic autonomy from major powers, and to increase economic and strategic co-operation so as to contribute to the management of the increasingly global and regional situation at their own level. As tensions between the powers in the international system increase, particularly in Asian waters, both India and Indonesia need to step up their naval and maritime co-operation in more real terms and give practical shape to many agreements that have already been signed. In its attempts to consolidate its role as a security provider in the Indian Ocean and to raise its profile in the Western Pacific, India has forged strategic co-operation with several countries which include Vietnam, South Korea and Japan. While Indonesia needs to move to a more encompassing strategic bilateral relationship with India, India needs to step up its economic ties with Indonesia. The recent

---

11 In the process of balancing in international relations, states join alliances in order to prevent stronger powers from dominating them. The concept of balancing derives from the Balance of Power theory, and is the most influential strand in the realist school of thought. However, it needs to be emphasized that the theory as well as the practice suffer from several shortcomings. In the case of India and Indonesia, both are important players in the region, and form important players at the global stage. Thus joining alliances and yielding concessions are not the options that either of the two can choose.

past does indicate a brighter economic relationship between the two, but it needs to be ensured that there is no slipping back on what has been accomplished so far. More political visits from the two sides are also a necessary requisite to ensure better relations between the two. Both the countries in the twenty-first century need to intensify their political co-operation to ensure that Asian economic prospects are not endangered by renewed political conflicts in the global arena.

Conclusion

Given the fact that India and Indonesia are both important players in international relations in the twenty-first century which has moved from the traditional concepts of security to encompassing issues such as those of terrorism, piracy, drug trafficking, corruption and food security to name a few, deepening co-operation between the two is inevitable. The China factor also brings the two countries to a higher degree of similarity, and even though the "C" word is mentioned overtly, it definitely is a part of covert diplomacy of both India and Indonesia.

If both the countries can ensure mutually beneficial results out of the co-operative arrangements the two have, keeping history, culture, geography and more importantly economic and strategic factors in mind, the relation between the two countries is definitely one of the most important relations in South-East Asia, and has the potential to bring widespread benefits not just at the bilateral level but also for the domestic populations. Thus it is pertinent that one should watch out for Indo–Indonesian relations in the near future.

References

PRIMARY SOURCES

Record, Govt. of India, Ministry of Commerce and Industry, Department of Commerce, "Memorandum of Understanding Between the Ministry of Commerce and Industry of the Republic of India and the Ministry of Trade of the Republic of Indonesia on the Establishment of Binnial Trade Ministries' Forum", New Delhi, 2011.

Prime Minister's Press Release, "Joint Statement on Five Initiatives for Strengthening the India–Indonesia Strategic Partnership", 11 October 2013. Prime Minister of India: Manmohan Singh, at pmindia.nic.in/press-details.php?nodeid=1713

Record, Foreign Affairs, "India–Indonesia Maritime Boundry Agreement" (MEA, Library) XXIII (1977): 2.

Report, Govt. of India, Ministry of Commerce and Industry, Department of Commerce, "Report of the Joint Study Group on the Feasibility of India–Indonesia Comprehensive Economic Cooperation Agreement (CECA)", 15 September 2009, Department of Commerce, New Delhi.

Record, F.A., 1977, "India–Indonesia Maritime Boundry Agreement", XXIII, 2, at http://commerce.nic.in/trade/india_indo-nesia_jsg_report_2009.pdf

JOURNALS

Bhattacharya, S.S., 1981, "India–Indonesia Relations", *Strategic Analysis*, **4**(11): 520-24.

Brewster, David, 2011, "The Relationship Between India and Indonesia: An Evolving Security Partnership?", *Asian Survey*, **51**(2): 221-44.

Jha, Pankaj K., 2008, "India–Indonesia: Emerging Strategic Confluence in the Indian Ocean Region", *Strategic Analysis*, **32**(3): 439-58.

Raja Mohan, C., 2013, "A Moment for Asian Solidarity", *Indian Express*, New Delhi, 9 October 2013.

ONLINE SOURCES

Anjaiah, Veermalra, 2008, "Indonesia–India Relationship Moving into Splendid Phase: Envoy", accessed on January 2013 at http://www.thejakartapost.com/news/2008/08/15/indonesiaindia-relationship-moving-splendid-phase-envoy.html

Brewster, D., 2011, "The Relationship Between India and Indonesia an Evolving Security Partnership", *Asian Survey*, **51**: 221-44 at: http://www.jstor.org/discover/10.1525/AS.2011.51.2.221?uid=3738256&uid=2&ui d=4&sid=21102926864247

Cullum, Lee, 2010, "A Conversation with Mary Natalegawa, Ministry of Foreign Affairs, Republic of Indonesia", accessed on 25 May at:

www.cfr.org/indonesia/conversation-marty-natalegawa-audio/p22975

Devare, Ashwini, 2011, "Neighbouring Warmth Infuses Indonesia–India Relations", accessed on November 2013, at: ibnlive.in.com/news/indiaindonesia-relations-warmer-than-ever-before/202811-61.html

Encyclopaedia Britannica, "Srivijaya Empire", accessed on November 2013 at: www.britannica.com/EBchecked/topic/562024/Srivijya-empire

Guha, R., 2009, "Superpower Fantasies: India Should Seek Other Goals than Joining a Global Race", Calcutta, *The Telegraph*, 12 September, at: http://www.telegraphindia.com/1090912/jsp/opinion/story_11472930.jsp

Hargreave, Keith and Smriti Mishra, 2013, "Together, Indonesia, China and India Could Be Making a Real Difference", accessed on November 2013, at: www.thejakartaglobe.com/archive/together, indonesia, china

Mohan, A., 2013, "India and Indonesia: Twins of a Kind", New Delhi: Govt. of India, Ministry of External Affairs, 8 October, at: http://www.mea.gov.in/in-focus-article.htm?22301/India+and+Indonesia+Twins+of+a+Kind

Rana, P.B., 2013, "Five Years After the Global Crisis, the World Is no Safer", *East Asia Forum*, 15 November, at: http://www.eastasiaforum.org/2013/11/15/five-years-after-the-global-crisis-the-world-is-no-safer/

Rediff News, 2010, "How India Is Undoing China's String of Pearls", accessed on November 2013, at: http://news.rediff.com/column/2010/oct/07/column-how-india-is-undoing-chinas-string-of-pearls.htm

Sekhar, Vibhanshu, 2011, "India and Indonesia: Relationship and Beyond", 26 October 2011, accessed on February 2013 at: bargad.org/2011/10/26/india-indonesia-relationship/

Singh, Amit, 2013, "South China Sea Dispute and India", accessed on October 2013, at: maritimeindia.org/article/south-china-sea-dispute-and-media

Singh, U.B., 2007, "Major Powers and the Security of Southeast Asia", New Delhi, May, IDSA, at: http://www.idsa-india.org/an-may-07.html

Supriyanto, Atriandi Ristian, 2013, "The Unfulfilled Promise of India–Indonesia Defense Ties", accessed on November 2013, at: http://

thediplomat.com/flashpoints-blog/2013/05/31/the-unfulfilled-promise-of-indonesia-india-defense-ties/

Takenaka, H., 2012, "Indonesians 'Should Think Twice' before Going Nuclear", *The Jakarta Post*, 3 May, at: http://www.the-jakarta-post.com/news/2012/05/03/indonesians-should-think-twice-going-nuclear.html

The First Post, 2013, "India and Indonesia Strengthen Bilateral Ties, Sign Six MoUs", accessed on November 2013, at: www.thefirstpost.com/world/india-and-indoensia-strength-bilateral-ties-sign-six-mous-1167433.html

Wagner, Daniel and Daniel Jackman, 2011, "China and India's Battle for Influence in Asia", accessed on November 2013, at: http://www.huffingtonpost.com/daniel-wagner/china-and-indias-battle-f_b_833371.html

Zee News India, 2013, "India Eyes Stronger Ties with Indonesia", accessed on November 2013, at: http://zeenews.india.com/news/nation/india-eyes-stronger-ties-with-indonesia_882558.html

14

India and Indonesia as Natural Partners in the Asia-Pacific Security Architecture

Asif Shuja

INDIA's Look East Policy has been hailed as one of India's most effective and successful foreign policies in recent times. Starting in the early 1990s, this policy has earned rich economic dividends for India. The Association of South-East Asian Nations (ASEAN) serves as a linchpin of this policy and therefore Indonesia as the biggest country of ASEAN becomes truly important for India. From this perspective, and being one of the leading economies of Asia, Indonesia becomes crucial in India's foreign policy calculus from the economic point of view. However, in recent times, especially after the US pivot shift from Middle East to East Asia as announced by Obama administration in 2012, looking east for India has become imperative not only from economic point of view but also from strategic point of view.

The nature of the relationship between the current superpower of the world, the US, and the strongest contender of superpower position, China, is not yet clear. Further, it is not yet clear whether China's rise would be peaceful or otherwise. In recent times India has got increasingly closer to the US. However, India's relation with China has not been warm enough to mitigate future apprehensions. Therefore, regardless of the prospect of co-operation or conflict between the US and China, it is imperative for India to engage in the Asia-Pacific not only through regional organizations such as ASEAN and the East Asia Summit (EAS), but also bilaterally. Neither the domination of superpowers nor the superpower rivalry in the region is India's interest.

It is in this context that India has forged strategic partnership with Japan, Vietnam and South Korea. Similar is the context of India's strategic partnership with Indonesia which is becoming increasingly more important for India for evolving regional security architecture in the Asia-Pacific. The visit of India's Prime Minister Manmohan Singh to Indonesia in October 2013 and the consequent agreements between the two nations underline this fact. Accordingly, this paper argues that India and Indonesia can be seen as natural partners in the Asia-Pacific security architecture.

Defining "Security Architecture"

The term "security architecture" as a holistic concept is yet to evolve fully.

> Use of the architectural metaphor to describe forms of international co-operation and co-ordination emerged from the calls to reform international financial governance in the wake of the 1997-98 international financial crises.[1]

First applied in the economic field, the metaphor "architecture" is now increasingly used in the geopolitical domain to describe the security of a region. As in the economic field where this "metaphor conveys not just the sum of co-operative measures but also the concerted, multifaceted effort required to cope with the complex problems of international economic governance",[2] in the geopolitical domain too this idea is applied

---

1 Bisley 2007: 342-43.

2 Ibid.: 343.

to evolve a co-operative mechanism to deal with transnational security threats.

Most of the security discourses in the twentieth century essentially carried the prefix "national", causing every country to talk about its own "national security". This was motivated by the onset of a large number of nation states who got freedom from their colonial rulers. The threat of being subjugated again by the foreign powers forced these countries to focus on their national security. Since the realization of the need of national security was caused due to the real external threats, its remedy too was real, based on clearly defined deliverables. The result of such realizations gave prominence to a strong national defence system in each country. With the passage of time economic power became as important as the military power. Consequently, the nation states also indulged in enhancing their economic powers apart from continuously strengthening their respective military capabilities. Later, as the Cold War ended and globalization became the norm, nation states realized that the economic interdependence had become imminent. This caused them to think about co-operative mechanisms to ensure their financial security.

By the end of the twentieth century, the process of globalization changed the world not just in economic terms but in every sphere of peoples' lives. Consequently, if the good things of the world now know no borders, then the bad things too do not respect any borders. Such bad things are generally known by the term "non-traditional security threats" which include food security, water management, pandemics, piracy, terrorism and natural disasters. These threats do not affect one country in isolation, but their impact proliferates to all the countries of a particular region. Such non-traditional security threats have now compelled the nation states to think about regional security through collective and co-operative approaches for mitigating all kinds of external threats. Indeed, "co-operation is a defining element of comprehensive security, especially in the external sphere".[3]

If a country talks about regional security, it does not do so out of benevolence or philanthropy. Rather, such concerns are motivated by the shear need of national security. If a country realizes that it would be directly affected by a regional problem, that country, if capable enough to deal with them, would surely think about mitigating such a threat. Since such mitigation would involve trans-border activities, co-operation with the countries involved would be a natural corollary. Adding the suffix "architecture" to such a regional security mechanism simply enables the policy makers to concretize what is otherwise abstract. Thus, when we talk about "Asia-Pacific Security Architecture", we automatically think about the security-related systems and processes that are in place. A clear vision of what is already in place would be helpful in determining the missing links. If the goal is clear — which is the security of the region from external threats, both traditional and non-traditional — then it would not be difficult to conceive such a mechanism which ensures security of all constituting countries of the region.

Accordingly, "in terms of its overall impact on regional security architecture, a non-traditional security framework promotes multiple stakeholders, multi-level governance and cross-sectoral international co-operation".[4] For instance, "new institutional arrangements within the ASEAN Political and Security Community (APSC) pillar under the ARF and ADMM Plus, while ad hoc, have led to new regional configurations and responses".[5] Further, since the countries constituting a

---

3 Memorandum 3 of CSCAP.

4 Report of the 1st Meeting of the CSCAP Study Group on Regional Security Architecture, 2013, p. 2.

5 Ibid.

particular region would be directly impacted by security threats, it is pertinent for them to ensure their own security. The way sole dependence on an external security provider is not a good idea for a particular country; the same applies to a region. Also, the need of regional security does not necessarily mean that the region should be unified. For instance, the model of the European Union may not be the ideal state of regional security architecture.

Finally, the security of a region may not only be threatened by the external threats such as an eventual invasion by another country or non-traditional security threats, but it may be affected by the ill motives or overambition of a regional actor. This is particularly so in case of the Asia-Pacific region, where China's growing assertiveness is a matter of concern for all stakeholders. Under such circumstances if an outside security provider is looked at for providing security — in this case, the US — it would first look into its own interests and not those of the region. This is perhaps the most teasing question in the context of security of the Asia-Pacific region. It is feared that because of such individual ambitions, "the current regional security architecture based on co-operative security arrangement might decay into a competitive security system".[6] Current co-operative security institutions in place in the Asia-Pacific such as the ASEAN Regional Forum (ARF) and the ASEAN Defence Ministers Meeting (ADMM) Plus "which mostly focus on dialogues and trust building are unable to manage structural conflicts related to sovereignty, balance of power, and security dilemma, even though they attained measured success in functional areas such as anti-piracy, humanitarian assistance and disaster relief (HADR), pandemics, etc.".[7]

---

6 Report of the 1st Meeting of the CSCAP Study Group on Regional Security Architecture, 2013, p. 2.

7 Ibid.

The Asia-Pacific Security Architecture

The multilateral architecture that is emerging in the Asia-Pacific region today now accommodates a great variety of security structures, ranging from bilateral to multilateral arrangements, military alliances to institutional expressions of co-operative and comprehensive security.

> Asia Pacific has seen the emergence of numerous new multilateral institutions since the end of the Cold War, such as the ARF and the EAS, as well as groupings operating at the Track 1.5 level such as the Shangri-la Dialogue and, at the Track 2 level, the Council for Security Cooperation in the Asia Pacific (CSCAP).[8]

Consequently, the Asia-Pacific security terrain is now overcrowded with numerous multilateral security frameworks. Further, "the network of ASEAN-centred institutions assumed a higher profile as the US rebalances within Asia, while China enters the Indian Ocean and India reaches out towards the Pacific".[9] These geopolitical developments have made South-East Asia "the critical hinge" of the Indo-Pacific or the Asia-Pacific.[10]

Initially formed due to economic imperatives, the Asia-Pacific institutions are now increasingly considering security roles for themselves. For instance,

> ASEAN, the ARF and even the Asia-Pacific Economic Cooperation (APEC) forum, originally formed to encourage trade and investment liberalization, have been accorded a role in the campaign against terrorism.[11]

---

8 See Seng Tan and Emmers 2010: 193.

9 Report of the 1st Meeting of the CSCAP Study Group on Regional Security Architecture 2013: 4.

10 Ibid.

11 See Seng Tan and Emmers 2010: 194.

However,

> despite these developments and the presence of a growing number of overlapping structures, institutionalism in the Asia Pacific has continued to suffer from weak structural capacities that limit its ability to respond to security challenges.[12]

Consequently, in the Asia-Pacific context, it would be good for all countries of the region to think about comprehensive security architecture. Such a security mechanism could draw from the strengths of the outside entities, but should not depend on them. To be precise, China is perceived as a growing power in the region which is considered as highly nationalist and whose motives are widely doubted. There are wide scale perceptions that this situation may create regional conflicts. On the other hand, the US has announced its pivot shift to Asia, which is widely perceived to be a strategy to contain a rising China while retain its own superpower position. If this stance of the US is seen by the South-East Asian countries such as the Philippines or Vietnam, which have territorial disputes with China, as a hedge against China, then that might amount to miscalculations on their part. The only credible and effective security in a particular could be one which is primarily conceived by the constituting countries themselves.

It would serve India well to think of the Asia-Pacific security based on the involvement of constituting countries of the region. In this context Indonesia becomes the most natural ally of India in envisioning such security architecture. Simultaneously, it is also important to take a cue from the behaviour of the US in the Middle East in the context of a net security provider, both in terms of securing an individual state of the region as well as the region as a whole. A careful analysis would reveal that the individual states such as Saudi Arabia

---

[12] See Seng Tan and Emmers 2010: 194.

has been feeling betrayed while the Middle East region is largely in a state of chaos. While drawing from the strengths of the US might be a good idea, depending entirely on the superpower for the regional security may promise further instability. Until the time a credible security architecture is evolved in the region, ASEAN may be seen as playing the most dominant role in the region since

> ASEAN's assigned managerial role derives as much from its unparalleled though imperfect institutional experience as from the lack of an alternative source of leadership acceptable to all.[13]

And being the greatest player within ASEAN, Indonesia's role is important in both cases, whether we subscribe to ASEAN-centrality or not.

Designing an Effective Asia-Pacific Security Architecture

For the development of effective regional security architecture, it is important to reconcile the contending versions of the regional security. Under the current practice, a number of security processes exist in the region, each having its own modality to address a particular issue. There are also differing opinions related to the expectations concerning different types of security architecture and how best the security of the region can be managed. However, it would be a useful exercise to decipher the commonalities of the available security architectures and forge a comprehensive framework that could be acceptable to all stakeholders in the region. Streamlining of the disconnected security processes thus becomes of paramount importance which could be done by linking them together through their functional aspects.

---

13 See Seng Tan and Emmers 2010: 196.

For effective management of peace and stability it is important to define the broad contours of the required security framework. This could be done by precisely defining the specific security threats of the region. It is possible to construct a common security framework for the region by consolidating the various security processes. Such a framework would be more effective and functional than the present one of diverse and disconnected ones catering to their own specific needs. In this context, the recommendation[14] of the Council for Security Cooperation in the Asia Pacific (CSCAP) is worth noting which suggests three pillars to the security architecture:

> A leaders' forum to address global and regional issues of common interest and concern; A forum headed by foreign and defence ministers to address the security and defence agenda; and A forum headed by trade and finance ministers to address the economic and trade agenda.[15]

According to this recommendation, these "pillars (EAS + ARF + APEC) should be the model to be adopted if opportunities arise or can be created to adapt the existing processes. However, confidence in the EAS will have to rise before APEC's prime movers agree to discontinue the summit dimension of this process".[16]

The Track 2 processes support and complement the efforts of Track 1 in promoting and managing regional security. Institutions and forums such as CSCAP, ASEAN-ISIS, the Asia-Pacific Roundtable and the Shangri-la Dialogue facilitate discussions and exchanges on regional security. They also provide policy recommendations and input to the official Track 1 processes. While it is important to further enhance the contribution of Track 2 processes to regional security, it is

---

14 Report of the 1st Meeting of the CSCAP Study Group on Regional Security Architecture 2013: 4.

15 Ibid.

16 Ibid.

at the same time important to understand the limitations and weaknesses of such processes. For instance, it should be noted that each think tank, which is the primary instrument of Track 2 processes, has its own mission statement that mandates its activities. This mandate is largely deterministic in its area of reach and domain coverage. Further, the mandate of a particular think tank would also be determined by the mandate of its funding agencies. For instance, since most of the think-tanks working in the area of Asia-Pacific security lie within the ambit of ASEAN and are largely funded by this organization, their recommendation would most likely emphasize on ASEAN-centrality in most of the security frameworks. Similarly, unlike states, think-tanks are constrained to work with relatively smaller networks of similar organizations. Therefore, their recommendations would naturally be supportive of the existence of discreet and disconnected security framework.

Nevertheless, ASEAN's leadership role in the Asia-Pacific security is not without contestation. In fact, it is said[17] that Indonesia should move beyond ASEAN if it wishes to play any meaningful role in the Asia-Pacific region.

> Moreover, the singling out of Indonesia, the only South-East Asian member of the G-20, rather than ASEAN as a whole in the Australian premier's vision of an Asia-Pacific community is perhaps noteworthy, as is Indonesia's — and several other ASEAN members' — purported growing support for the idea or parts of it.[18]

India's Approach to the Asia-Pacific Security Architecture

In the past couple of decades, India has shown a persistent growth in its economy and military development. Accordingly,

---

17 See Seng Tan and Emmers 2010: 196-97.

18 Ibid.

it has been increasingly realizing its regional and global commitments. In Asia-Pacific region India has been working with China, Japan and other neighbours towards building security architecture in order to create an environment in which "India can further develop and prosper".[19] Significantly,

> India is now part of all the ASEAN-led institutions that emerged during the last decade, including the East Asia Summit and the expanded consultations among the region's defence ministers.[20]

The fact that India and ASEAN have entered into strategic partnership in the India-ASEAN Commemorative Summit in Delhi in December 2012 exemplifies that ASEAN has now recognized India's role in security and stability of the region. In the Asia-Pacific security framework, India's approach can be characterized by a deliberate aversion of seeking a leadership role in the region while at the same time being sceptical of the collective security mechanism. Simultaneously, India also prefers "an inclusive arrangement, rather than an exclusive one" and "believes that without the participation of all the great powers, no security system in the region can succeed".[21] It is indeed a remarkable achievement that India can simultaneously work with both China and Japan for the stability of the region.[22]

In the contemporary era, the Asian states are participating in bilateral as well as multilateral mechanisms to ensure their security. However, the proliferation of multilateral institutions in the Asia-Pacific clearly reflects the confusion and inadequacy of the existing institutions. In addition, mutual suspicion makes the evolution of these multilateral institutions an extremely

---

19 *The Economic Times.*

20 Raja Mohan 2013.

21 Raja Mohan 2009: 50.

22 *The Economic Times.*

complex exercise. Due to these reasons, it has become important not only to keep working on the improvement and consolidation of the existing multilateral institutions but also to continue to forge new bilateral alliances. India too realizes the limitations and inadequacies of multilateralism and seeks to mix bilateralism with multilateralism for ensuring its regional security imperatives. Consequently, India is now building strong partnerships with regional powers and its relationship with Indonesia is important in this context, which was amply illustrated by the visit of Indian prime minister to Indonesia in October 2013.

Indonesia as India's "Natural" Partner

It may be argued that the way Iran serves as India's natural partner in any foreseeable regional security architecture in the Middle East, Indonesia is India's natural partner in the Asia-Pacific security architecture. Commonalities between India and Indonesia are striking — in terms of geographic, demographic and economic size; historical linkages; democratic, religious and cultural practices; and aspirations of the people of the two countries. Even from strategic and geopolitical points of views, the two countries have great deal of commonalities. Both India and Indonesia have sophisticated military capabilities and despite their military and economic might, they have deliberately abstained from espousing regional leadership role. India as the major power in South Asia has meticulously abstained from projecting itself as a leader in the region and has practised this policy in the most important regional forum of South Asia, the South Asian Association for Regional Cooperation (SAARC). Similarly, despite being the largest and most powerful country of South-East Asia, Indonesia has abstained from espousing any leadership role in the region and has meticulously practised this policy in the most important regional forum, ASEAN.

Now that India is looking for its imminent role in Asia-Pacific and Indonesia has been increasingly recognized as the linchpin of ASEAN, it would be a natural step for the two countries to join hands. In this context, it is pertinent to mention here that there are definitely other countries in the Asia-Pacific region, such as China, Australia, Japan and South Korea which are more powerful than these two countries in many respects. Suggesting that India should forge strategic partnership with Indonesia does not mean that it should be based on the exclusion of India's relationship with these countries, or for that matter, other major powers of the world such as the US and Russia. For regional security it is possible to leverage from the relative strengths of all these powers.

Being two great democracies and economic powers of Asia, India and Indonesia can play prominent role in managing the political and security institutions of the Asia-Pacific. It is important for both the countries to ensure that the gains in economic field are not lost due to an unsecured political environment. It is high time that they work on their naval, maritime and military co-operation and implement the agreements that have already been signed.

> Nehru and Sukarno had the vision to embark upon defence co-operation, but did not have all the means to advance it to the logical conclusion. Their successors today in Delhi and Jakarta have the financial resources — they are the ninth and 16th largest economies in the world. What Delhi and Jakarta now need is the political will.[23]

In the twenty-first century, where the Asia-Pacific is witnessing a redistribution of power, India and Indonesia can co-operate together to make the region peaceful, prosperous and progressive.

---

23 Raja Mohan 2013.

It is easy to establish that of all the stakeholders in the Asia-Pacific, maximum convergence of interest is found between India and Indonesia. Still, a convincing proof of two countries being "natural" partners does not guarantee that they would "naturally" be partners. The way two brothers of the same blood need to make special efforts to remain together, extraordinary efforts would be required by India and Indonesia to stand together in the construction of a credible Asia-Pacific security architecture.

References

Bisley, Nick, 2007, "Asian Security Architectures", in Ashley J. Tellis and Michael Wills (eds.) *Strategic Asia 2007-08: Domestic Political Change and Grand Strategy*, Washington: The National Bureau of Asian Research, pp. 341-70.

Memorandum 3, Council for Security Cooperation in the Asia-Pacific (CSCAP), "The Concepts of Comprehensive Security and Cooperative Security", http://www.cscap.org/uploads/docs/Memorandums/CSCAP%20Memorandum%20No%203%20--% 20 The%20Concepts%20of%20Comp%20Sec%20and%20Coop %20Sec.pdf, accessed on 3 February 2014.

Report of the 1st Meeting of the CSCAP Study Group on Regional Security Architecture held during 3-5 September 2013 in Kuala Lumpur, Malaysia, Council for Security Cooperation in the Asia Pacific (CSCAP), http://www.cscap.org/uploads/docs/Regional-%20Sec%20-Architecture/1RSASG Report Sep 2013. pdf, accessed on 4 February 2014.

Seng Tan and Ralf Emmers, 2010, "Security Architecture and Institutionalism in the Asia Pacific", in Desmond Ball and Kwa Chong Guan (eds.) *Assessing Track 2 Diplomacy in the Asia-Pacific Region: A CSCAP Reader*, Singapore: S. Rajaratnam School of International Studies, Nanyang Technological University, pp. 191-201.

The Economic Times, 3 February 2014, "India Plans to Build Security Architecture in Asia-Pacific: National Security Advisor Shivshankar Menon," http://articles.economictimes.indiatimes.com/2014-02-03/news/46963269_1_security-architecture-fumio-kishida-sure-japan, accessed on 5 February 2014.

Raja Mohan, C., "A Moment for Asian Solidarity," *The Indian Express*, 9 October 2013, http://www.indianexpress.com/news/a-moment-for-asian-solidarity/1180113/0, accessed on 10 November 2013.

Raja Mohan, C., 2009, "India in the Emerging Asian Architecture: Prospects for Security Cooperation with ASEAN and Australia," pp. 40-57; in William T. Tow and Chin Kin Wah (eds.), *ASEAN-India-Australia: Towards Closer Engagement in a New Asia*, Singapore: Institute of Southeast Asian Studies, pp. 40-57.

15

Determinants of Outward Foreign Direct Investment

A Study of Indian Manufacturing Firms

Priya Arora

Introduction

In today's globalized world trade between countries has increased tremendously. Foreign Direct Investment (FDI) is the process whereby residents of one country (the home country) acquire ownership of assets for the purpose of controlling the production, distribution and other activities of a firm in another country (the host country). It is universally acknowledged that FDI inflows benefit the host country in many ways. According to a report by United Nations Conference on Trade and Development (UNCTAD) (1999), presence of Multinational Enterprises (MNEs) in a country increases its financial resources for development, improves its export competitiveness, generates employment, strengthens the skill base and most importantly, enhances technological capabilities through transfer, diffusion and generation. Due to these reasons inflow of FDI is important for a country, however outflow of investments from the source country to the host country is also important. OFDI is a business strategy where a domestic firm expands its operations to a foreign country either via greenfield investment, merger/acquisition and/or expansion of an existing foreign facility. In India, the policies for OFDI have been modified gradually after 1991, which has led to the increase in FDI flows from India.

The Guidelines for Indian Joint Ventures and Wholly Owned Subsidiaries Abroad, as amended in October 1992, May 1999 and July 2002, provided for automatic approval of OFDI proposals up to a certain limit that was expanded progressively from US $ 2 million in 1992 to US $ 100 million in July 2002. In January 2004, the limit was removed altogether and Indian enterprises are now permitted to invest abroad up to 100 per cent of their net worth on an automatic basis. As the government of India slowly opened the economy; liberalization along with it brought increasing competition, better technology and a vast variety of products to offer to the consumers. To survive in the ever-mounting competition and to protect their profitability, the efficient domestic firms started investing abroad to reap the benefits of foreign markets. The domestic firms have created a niche in the foreign markets which has put India on a global stage. From 2000s onwards, after seeing the benefits to the economy, the government started encouraging the domestic companies to invest abroad. Today, India is being looked upon as a major strategic partner for foreign countries. OFDI from India is increasing at a tremendous rate for the last few years. Annual FDI has jumped fiftyfold times after 2000. Self-grown Indian MNEs acquired controlling interest in overseas firms aggressively in order to spread their wings and become the global players. India is investing in many countries and Indonesia is one of them. However, these two countries have a long history. The ties between these two countries date back to the times of *Ramayana*. "Yavadvipa" (Java) is mentioned in India's earliest epic, Ramayana. India's investment in Indonesia is substantially large which dates back to the 1970s.

However, for the last few years it has been observed that in India inflow of FDI has been declining whereas outflow of investment to other countries has been increasing. The problems in attracting FDI are reflected in international comparisons of the investment climate. In the *World Bank Doing Business Report* 2012, India is ranked 132 out of 183 countries. In addition to this, according to *Global Competitive Index* (2012-13) which measures the set of institutions, policies and other factors that affect the business environment of a country published by World Economic Forum, India has been ranked 59th out of 144 countries. India's rank is poorer as compared to China (30th) and other ASEAN countries like Singapore (2nd), Malaysia (25th), Thailand (38th) and Indonesia (50th). The reasons behind India's disappointing performance and failure to attract global investment are insufficient and ill-adapted infrastructure, and institutional problems like corruption and bureaucracy. Due to these reasons many small and medium Indian enterprises particularly in the manufacturing sector are investing in countries where infrastructure is available which reduces the cost of production to a great extent.

Apart from these reasons there are several other factors that push a firm to invest in other countries. One of the major reasons is poor investment climate in home country. A study by Rao and Dhar (2011) shows that even the inflow of FDI in India has substantially declined in the manufacturing sector. "Development-oriented" FDI that could add to the existing manufacturing facilities currently formed only a small proportion of the total reported inflows. The conclusion given by them is that a major portion of the FDI flowing into India is more akin to portfolio investment and not direct investment. The share of manufacturing sector in FDI inflows declined from more than 41 per cent in 2005 to about 20 per cent in 2008. During 1990s the share was more than 60 per cent. All these reasons have contributed to the increasing share of manufacturing firms in the OFDI from India. According to RBI report on OFDI (2010), 43 per cent of OFDI has been made by manufacturing sector, 27 per cent by financial, insurance, real estate and business service, 11 per cent by wholesale, retail trade, restaurants and hotels, 7 per cent by construction and 11 per cent by other industries. Clearly, the share of manufacturing sector in OFDI is the highest.

Based on the above discussion on FDI and OFDI at global and Indian scenarios, the objective of the current study is to find out the determinants of OFDI in the manufacturing sector of India. In particular, the study seeks to answer, among the OFDI firms why do some firms invest more than others in foreign countries?

Literature Review

Review of literature available on OFDI reveals that firms from different countries have various reasons to invest in other countries. Studies by scholars like Pradhan, (2008) have shown that during 1975-90 the Indian OFDI was more concentrated in the developing countries of South-East Asia, East Asia and fewer investments were made in the developed countries. The reason behind this investment behaviour is to have a geographical proximity, ethnic and language links. Large distance and the cultural differences between the developed and developing countries were the main reasons for low investment in the Western countries. But after 1990s domestic companies changed the rules of the game and the major portion of the investment started flowing to the developed countries. UK and USA have become the top two host of OFDI from the Indian firms. According to RBI (2010) the leading destinations for India's OFDI are Singapore, Mauritius, Cyprus, the Netherlands, the United States, the British Virgin Islands and the Channel Islands. Among the different types of firms, like business group-affiliated firms and stand alone firms, have their own reasons and motives to invest in different regions of the world. In the Indian scenario, business groups have been the initiator as well as the key players of the OFDI process. According to Pradhan (2009) the two earliest Indian OFDI projects took place in 1960s when the Birla Group established a textile company in Addis Ababa, Ethiopia.

Indian firms are investing abroad to access foreign markets, production facilities and international brand names. For example, Tata Tea acquired Tetley Tea to access the Tetley brand name and market. Access to technology and knowledge has been a strategic consideration for Indian firms, for example, in 2003, Wipro acquired Nerve Wire Inc. (USA) to secure deep domain knowledge and other IT-related benefits, including access to markets. Reliance Infocomm paid money for Flag Telecom (UK) to access to the undersea cable network and connect with key regions such as Asia, Europe and North America. A number of such motives including access to foreign technology, sourcing of raw materials, aspirations for global leadership or due to institutional and policy voids in the home country Propelled such OFDIs. Firms also try to take advantage of double taxation avoidance implemented by some countries.

However reasons for Indian firms investment in Indonesia are quite different from others. As per the Government of Indonesia, FDI inflows in Indonesia for the year 2008 rose by 73 per cent and the reason behind this is the political stability and improving the outlook for South-East Asia's biggest economy. The state investment agency of Indonesia (BKPM) reported that the foreign investments came mainly into the telecommunications, pharmaceuticals, pulp and food-related sectors. Table 15.1 gives the FDI inflows into Indonesia and India from 1970 to 2007.

However, the motive for investing abroad depends on the size of the firm. Large-sized firms might have different reasons to invest in other countries as compared to small and medium firms. This has been proved by Hollenstein (2005) in his study on *Determinants of International Activities: Are SME's Different?*, which confirms John Dunning's well-known Ownership Location and Internalization (OLI) paradigm. Ownership advantages turn out to be the main drivers of internalization, irrespective of firm size and internalization strategy. However, the knowledge base on which ownership advantages of small firms rest is narrower than that of large companies. Location advantages like wages, regulatory framework and infrastructure primarily are relevant in case of small firms as compared to large firms.

Table: 15.1: FDI Inflows in Indonesia and India from 1970 to 2007
(US $ Million)

Year	*Indonesia*	*India*	*Year*	*Indonesia*	*India*
1971	299.07	4.766	1990	109.30	236.69
1972	253.52	17.79	1991	148.20	75.53
1973	581.00	37.91	1992	177.70	276.51
1974	182.12	56.97	1993	200.40	550.37
1975	1,292.06	–10.32	1994	210.90	973.27
1976	747.59	7.706	1995	436.00	2,143.62
1977	235.00	–36.06	1996	619.40	2,326.05
1978	417.71	18.09	1997	467.70	3,577.33
1979	226.00	48.57	1998	240.80	2,643.69
1980	300.09	79.16	1999	1,865.62	2,168.59
1981	133.00	91.92	2000	134.00	3,548.21
1982	225.00	72.08	2001	–297.79	5,471.94
1983	292.00	5.64	2002	145.08	5,620.04
1984	222.00	19.24	2003	–596.62	4,322.74
1985	310.00	106.09	2004	1,896.08	5,771.29
1986	258.00	117.73	2005	8,336.25	6,676.52
1987	385.00	212.32	2006	5,579.69	19,962.00
1988	576.00	91.25	2007	6,928.00	22,950.00
1989	682.00	252.10			

Source: World Development Indicator, the World Bank Group, 2008.

Determinants of OFDI of Indian Manufacturing Sector

ANALYTICAL FRAMEWORK AND HYPOTHESIS

OFDI behaviour and determinants of Indian enterprises have been studied by Lall (1983, 1986) and Pradhan (2004). These studies have found out firm-specific characteristics that resulted in an increase in OFDI from India before and after 1991 which Pradhan described as the first and second wave of OFDI from India. Before 1991 only firm size and capital intensity were the most important factors that determined FDI outflows from India. However after 1991 many variables like age, size, in house R&D, export intensity, managerial skills, labour productivity and policy liberalization were found to have an increasing effect on OFDI from India. Large firms were likely to do more outward investment than small and medium enterprises. Firms that exported more have higher chances of investing in other countries since they have a better knowledge about the market and the institutional structure of the country. Liberalization process and the policy changes also played a major role in reframing the situation of OFDI in Indian scenario.

According to the OLI framework given by Dunning in 1980, a firm invests abroad in response to three types of advantages, mainly ownership, location and internalization. A firm has ownership advantage if it has specific knowledge of capital or intangible assets in the form of human capital, technology, patents, brand name, goodwill, etc. and can be exploited through exports, market transfers or FDI. However internalization advantages depend on the transaction cost. If the internalization advantages are large and substantial then FDI is the preferred mode otherwise licensing of the intangible asset to third parties is adopted by firms (Siddharthan 2009). If there exists ownership and internalization advantages, then the firms take the next decision of location choice. Location choice by a firm depends on the objective of FDI by the domestic enterprise. The different types of investments are resource-seeking investment, market-seeking investment, strategy-seeking investments, support-seeking investments and efficiency-seeking investments.

- *Resource-seeking investments* are those in which the firm in home country establishes access to basic material like raw materials or other input factors.
- *Market-seeking investments* are made to enter an existing market or establish a new market.
- *Strategy-seeking investments* are those when an MNC acquires other existing firms or assets through strategic operations.
- *Efficiency-seeking investments* are made when location needs favour production outside the home country and the host country has better economic and social infrastructure like transportation and power supply that reduces the cost of production and makes it more profitable to produce the good/commodity in the host country.

It is argued that the recent increase in OFDI by Indian manufacturing firms could be mainly due to efficiency-seeking investments. Small and medium firms are investing in other countries due to poor investment and manufacturing climate in India compared to certain other countries. There are various factors like government policies, governance indicators, institutions, infrastructure which influence the decisions of a firm on how and where to invest. However, institution and infrastructure are the main bottlenecks that prevent the growth of manufacturing sector in India. Inadequate power supply, transportation, corruption and tax regulations are some of the major barriers restricting domestic investments and make it more profitable to produce in other countries, particularly the

ASEAN countries. If domestic firms are investing abroad then it can also affect foreign firms investment decision in India.

Earlier studies on the determinants of OFDI by Indian firms (Siddharthan 2009; Kumar 2007; Pradhan 2004) have identified the following determinants:

- *Age of the firm* — It is calculated by subtracting the incorporation year of the firm from the current year. Higher age explains its business maturity leads to stronger linkages and increase in sources. Accumulated production experience is a source of considerable learning and absorption of know-how. These advantages can be valuable for overseas investments especially in relatively mature and standardized industries, if not in more skill- or knowledge-intensive ones (Kumar 2007).
- *Size* — This is a proxy to the sales of the firm. According to previous studies large firms are more likely to venture abroad than small and medium firms. However, if small and medium enterprises are also investing abroad, then the reason behind this could be poor investment climate in the home country.
- *Research and development* — It is expected that firms which spend more on R&D should positively affect their decision to indulge in OFDI. Further R&D efforts by a firm are also required for absorption and adaptation of knowledge imported from abroad. It also enables a firm to develop its own assets that give the firm a monopolistic advantage in the foreign location and hence increases OFDI.
- *Profit after tax* — Profitability of a firm determines the chances of a firm to expand its business and serve markets for its products in other locations. More profitable firms are more likely to invest in other countries than less profitable firms. However, if less

profitable enterprises are also investing abroad, then the reason for this behaviour could be that the cost of production is high in home country as compared to the host country.

- *Export intensity and import intensity* — These can be positively or negatively related to OFDI depending on the nature of OFDI. For example, if the nature of OFDI is replicating home country production abroad, then exports will be negative and imports positive. If the nature of OFDI is to acquire overseas company in same line of business and the acquiring firm wants to access the marketing and distribution channel of the acquired entity, OFDI will increase export of final product from home country. It has been observed that in the manufacturing sector, OFDI more than offsets the substitution of final product's export from India leading to a positive relation between OFDI and exports (Pradhan 2010).

DATA AND METHODOLOGY

The data for analysis has been taken from RBI, which gave the total amount invested by firms in other countries. The time period of my study is from 2008 to 2010. This period also witnessed a global slowdown in the world economy, due to the recession of 2008. The firm-level data for analysis has been taken from Prowess, which is a database of the financial performance of Indian companies and also provides data on foreign equity and exports of companies providing us with a measure of outward FDI. There are around 11,000 manufacturing firms in India, but for this particular analysis data coverage is from 2008-10 resulting in 277 firms to be analysed. It is an unbalanced panel data with 88, 89 and 100 companies investing abroad in the year 2008, 2009 and 2010, respectively. Since the data set is a panel data, the advantage of using panel data is that it controls the effects of missing or unobserved information. Our data has the problem of hetroskedasticity, which has been detected by using Breusch Pagan Test. Hence robust estimates are being used. To choose between fixed effect and random effect, Hausman Test is conducted and fixed effect results are chosen on the basis of this test.

Trends and Pattern of OFDI

MEAN OFDI OF FIRMS

Table 15.2 shows the number of firms which have invested in a particular range in the present study. For example, 85 per cent of the firms have invested less than US $ 50 million out of which 166 firms have invested an amount less than US $ 2 million. However the highest amount invested is US $ 3,136.81 million by Tata Motors and the lowest amount invested is US $ 0.0104 million by Bajaj Hindustan. So, we can say that large numbers of firms are making smaller investments while only few firms are investing huge amounts abroad.

Table 15.2: Mean OFDI of Firms

OFDI (US $ Millions)	*No of Firms*	*Mean*	*Percentage of Firms*
0 –50	236.00	26.50	85.19
50–100	19.00	71.95	6.85
100–150	7.00	123.22	2.52
150–200	3.00	174.23	1.08
200–250	3.00	229.21	1.08
250–300	1.00	259.85	0.36
300–350	1.00	314.56	0.36
350–400	1.00	361.40	0.36
1,050–1,100	1.00	1,065.72	0.36
1,450–1,500	1.00	1,451.30	0.36
2,000–2,050	1.00	2,222.05	0.36
3,000–3,050	1.00	3,136.81	0.36

Source: RBI database.

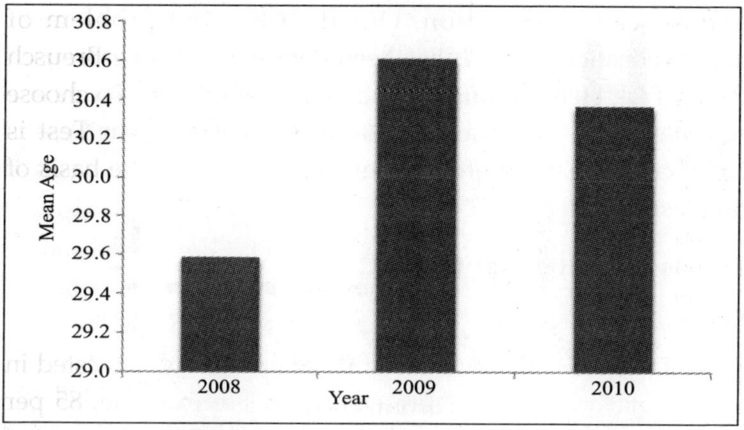

Source: Prowess Database

fig. 15.1: Distribution of age of firms

YEAR-WISE MEAN AGE OF FIRMS

Figure 15.1 represents the year-wise mean age of firms. The mean age of firms indulging in OFDI in 2008, 2009 and 2010 is 29.58, 30.60 and 30.36 years, respectively. So mostly in all the years mean age of firms is around 30 years.

NUMBER OF FIRMS AND THE MEAN OFDI OCCURRING IN DIFFERENT INTERVALS OF OFDI INVESTMENT

Figure 15.2 represents the number of firms investing in a particular range on the primary axis and their mean OFDI on the secondary axis. The mean OFDI of 85 per cent of the firms investing in the range of US $ 0–50 million is US $ 26.50 million.

COUNTRY-WISE OFDI

Here we have taken only few ASEAN countries *fig*. 15.3. So the highest investment is made in Thailand.

INDUSTRY-WISE INVESTMENT PATTERN

Figure 15.4 represents the industry-wise investments by firms in the manufacturing sector. Major investor is the pharmaceutical sector (NIC-21); around 28 per cent of firms

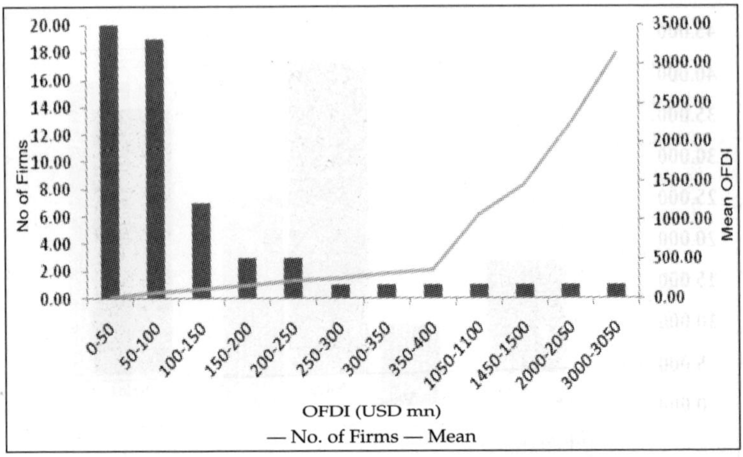

Source: Prowess Database.

fig. 15.2: Numbers of firms vs. mean OFDI

in the dataset are from pharmaceutical industry, 12 per cent of firms are in the manufacturing of chemical and chemical products (NIC-20), 4.5 per cent are in the manufacturing of basic iron and steel (NIC-29) and 3.8 per cent from general purpose machinery (NIC-28).

MEAN AGE AND MEAN SIZE
OF DIFFERENT INDUSTRIES

Transport industry has the highest mean age and mean size, although there are very few firms from this industry in our dataset. The investment rate in this sector is high due to the involvement of big players like Tata Motors, investing the largest amount in other countries (Table 15.3).

Interpreting the Results

RESULTS

The dependent variable is the ratio of OFDI amount by a firm to the sales of the firm. Therefore.

$$\mathbf{OFDI/Sales = X_{it}B + u_{it}}$$

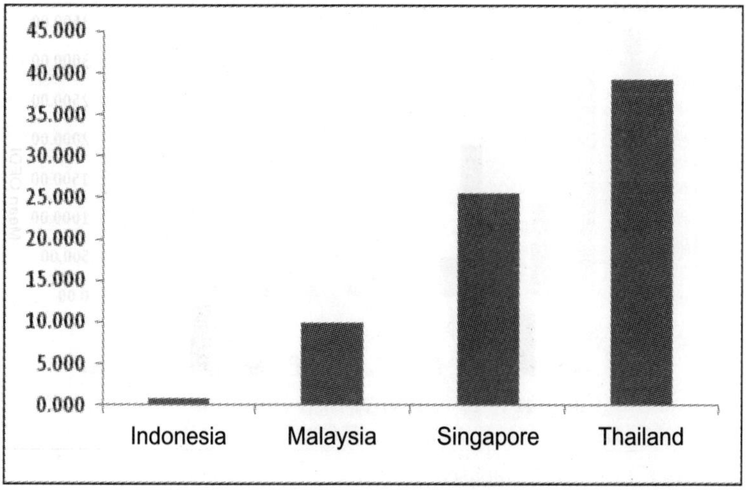

Source: Prowess Database

fig 15.3: Investment in ASEAN countries

where X_{it} is a vector of determinants that affect OFDI/sales explaining the ith firm's overseas investment decision in the tth time period. The firm-level heterogeneity can be studied by taking into account various explanatory variables and the fixed effect results obtained are given in Table 15.4.

Table 15.4 represents the value of coefficient and the values in the bracket represent the *p*-value of the variable. The results obtained in this study are not similar to the expected results and are in contrast with the results of previous studies.

The variable Age is not significant and Age 2^2 is significant, implying that mainly the SMEs are investing abroad. R&D is negatively related to OFDI, which cannot be true according to the literature review. R&D-intensive firms should be investing more abroad. However, this is not significant in our study.

The variable Exports, capturing the export intensity of a firm in the present study is negatively related to OFDI. According to the Product Cycle Theory of Vernon (1966),

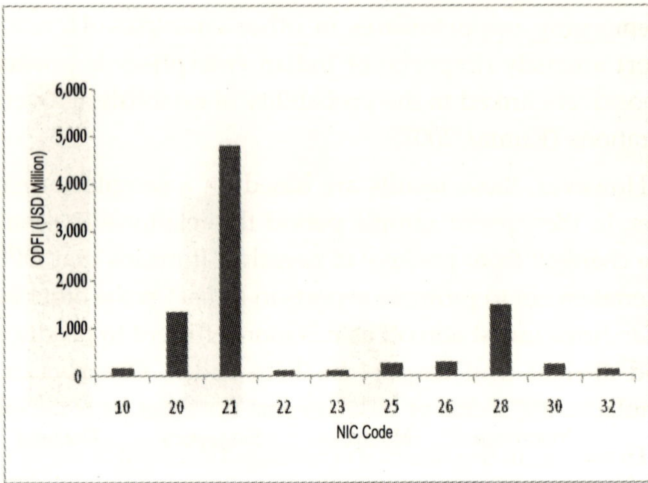

Source: Prowess Database.

fig. 15.4: Industry-wise OFDI distribution

overseas investment is postulated to follow the initial exploration of overseas markets through exporting. It has been argued that the recent boom of overseas investment by developing country enterprises has been motivated by the need to support exporting with a local presence (Kumar, 1998). Exporting activity enhances the international competitiveness of the enterprise and may also provide valuable information

Table 15.3: Industry-wise Mean Age and Mean Size

Industry	*Industry Code*	*Mean Age (years)*	*Mean Size (Log Sales, Rs. million)*
Pharmaceutical	21	28.76	8.940
Chemical products	20	33.59	9.020
Transport	29	63.00	11.980
Food products	10	38.20	9.610
General machinery	28	34.65	8.980
Basic iron and steel	24	24.84	24.840
Jewellry	32	21.20	9.105

Source: Prowess Database.

on emerging opportunities in other countries. Hence, the export intensity (Exports) of Indian enterprises is posited to be positively linked to the probability of establishing overseas operations (Kumar 2007).

However, these results are based on a sample for earlier years. In the current sample period the relationship seems to have changed from positive to negative. It means that OFDI is undertaken not to promote exports in India. On the other hand, Indian firms invest abroad as it is more efficient to produce the good abroad and import back to India. Clearly, in the manufacturing sector of India, export does not increase OFDI.

However, in this study it is not significant but if we increase the database and include data for more years, then the significance levels can change.

Imports, representing the import intensity of a firm, is positively related to OFDI in the manufacturing sector, which means that firms are importing back the goods to India produced in other countries, probably producing in their own

Table 15.4: Fixed Effect Results

Independent Variable	*Coefficient*
Age	-0.0013 (0.209)
Age²	0.00023* (0.092)
R&D	-0.062 (0.115)
Profit after tax	0.0049 (0.435)
Exports	-0.0023 (0.659)
Imports	0.0132* (0.083)
Size	-0.0018** (0.029)
Foreign spending on travelling	0.226** (0.010)
Constant	0.035 (0.027)
R square	0.099

* Significant at 10 per cent, ** Significant at 5 per cent, and

*** Significant at 1 per cent

subsidiaries located in other countries and importing back those goods in India.

Size, representing the sales of a firm, is also negatively related to OFDI intensity which shows that in the manufacturing sector of India even the small- and medium-sized firms are investing abroad. Firms of all sizes are exploring options outside to get access to advantages offered by other countries. It is not just Tatas, Birlas or Ambanis anymore.

Foreign spending on travelling is positively related to OFDI which means that firms are spending more and more on travelling abroad, business trips to these countries due to investment purpose are also an indicator of increasing outflows from the country.

Capturing the effect of profit after tax on OFDI decision taken by a firm is positively related to OFDI which means that profitable firms are investing abroad.

Conclusion

This study analyses the changing trends and patterns of OFDI intensity by the Indian manufacturing firms. Large firms are no longer the only investors abroad, small and medium enterprises of India are indulging in OFDI in a big way than before. OFDI and exports do not have a positive relation any more. The relation between these two variables has turned from positive to negative due to problems in India's infrastructure. However, the import intensity of the firms indulged in OFDI is very high. This relation of imports and exports with OFDI is in line with the OLI paradigm. Since the results of the present study are based on a time period of 2008-10 and the same period coincided with the recession of 2008, which is a period of contraction and low growth. Still the OFDI from India is significantly high during these years of global slowdown of economic activities and import intensity of India remains very high.

The key lesson emerging from the above analysis is that it is more efficient to manufacture goods in the host country because of high quality physical infrastructure like transportation, telecommunication and electricity which are extremely important for competent production of goods. OFDI in manufacturing sector has become a serious issue because of infrastructural problems in India. It has become cheaper for firms to produce outside India and import rather than manufacturing in india. This is because of poor physical and institutional infrastructure in India which acts as a push factor for OFDI among small and medium firms. In addition to this the investment climate that can be explained by the performance of individual states in terms of investment and growth in India has deteriorated. Institutional and physical infrastructure appears to be the most important constraint, as it is particularly binding in states that show low levels of domestic investment and Gross Domestic Product (GDP) growth. Appropriate institutional infrastructure like absence of corruption, quick legal dispute settlement and rule of law are very important for improving the business investment climate in a country. The larger firms can set up electricity generation plants, which increases the cost of production, because they can afford to bear this cost but small and medium firms cannot do this, so they are opting to produce outside. So, the conclusion is that small and medium enterprises in the manufacturing sector are producing abroad and importing the goods to India.

References

Azam, M., and L. Lukman, n.d., "Determinants of Foreign Direct Investment in India, Indonesia and Pakistan", *Journal of Managerial Sciences*, vol. 4, pp. 35-36.

Baskaran, S. Arockia, L.J. Charlaas, 2012, "A Study of the Outward FDI from India", *Zenith International Journal of Business Economics and Management Research*, **2**: 5.

Bhaumik, S.K., N. Driffield, and S. Pal, 2009, "Does Ownership Structure of Emerging Market Firms Affect Their Outward FDI?: The Case of Indian Automotive and Pharmaceutical Sectors", *Journal of International Business Studies*, vol. 41, pp. 439-50.

Hattari, R., and S. Rajan, 2010, "India as a Source of Outward Foreign Direct Investment", *Oxford Development Studies*, vol. 29, pp. 502-07.

Hollenstein, 2005, "Determinants of International Activities: Are SMEs Different?", *Small Business Economics*, vol. 24, pp. 431-50.

Moosa, Imad A., 2002, *Foreign Direct Investment: Theory, Evidence and Practice*, Palgrave Macmillan.

Kumar, N., 1998, *Globalization, Foreign Direct Investment and Technology Transfers*, Routledge.

———, 2007, "Emerging TNCs: Trends, Patterns and Determinants of Outward FDI by Indian Enterprise", *Transnational Corporations*, **26**: 2-20.

Lall, S., ed., 1983, *The New Multinationals: The Spread of Third World Enterprises*, New York: John Wiley & Sons.

Lall, R.B., 1986, *Multinationals from the Third World: Indian Firms Investing Abroad*, Delhi: Oxford University.

Mittal, Parul and Sandeep Aggarwal, 2012, "Analysis of FDI Outflows and Inflows in India", *Zenith International Journal of Business Economics and Management Research*, **2**: 213.

Pradhan, J.P., 2004, "The Determinants of Outward Foreign Direct Investment: A Firm Level Analysis of Indian Manufacturing", *Oxford Development Studies*, **32**: 622-36.

———, 2007, *Indian Multinationals in the World Economy, Implications for Development*, Academic Foundation.

———, 2008, "The Evolution of Indian Foreign Direct Investment", *Journal of Institute for Studies in Industrial Development*, Chapters 2, 3, 4, pp. 9-71.

———, Changing Trends and Patterns", *Int. J. Technology and Globalisation*, pp. 70-76.

———, 2009, "Emerging Multinationals from India and China: Origin, Impetus and Growth", Sardar Patel Institute of Economic and & Social Research, paper no. 18210, p. 3.

———, 2010, "Group Affiliation and Location of Indian Firm's Foreign Acquisition", *Munich Personal RePEc Archive*, paper no. 24018, pp. 2-5.

Pradhan, J.P., N. Singh, 2008, "Technological Efforts and Global Operations: Indian Auto Component Firms", *Munich Personal RePEc Archive*, **23**: 45-48.

Rao, K.C., and B., Dhar, 2011, "India's FDI Inflows Trends and Concepts", RBI/2013-14/11 Master Circular no. 11/2013-14 (updated as on 7 February 2014).

Reserve Bank of India, 2010, *A Study of the Outward FDI from India.*

Siddharthan, N., 2009, *Foreign Direct Investment: Main Determinants*, Forum for General Knowledge Sharing and Madras School of Economics, pp. 3-22.

Subramaniam, R., C. Sachdeva, and S. Morris, 2010, "FDI Outflows from India: An Estimation of the Underlying Economics, Policies and Their Impact", *IIMA*, 96, pp. 6-8.

Vernon, R., 1966, "International Investment and International Trade in Product Cycle: The Case of US Firms", *Quarterly Journal of Economics*, vol. 80, pp. 190-207.

16

India and Indonesia in the Emerging Indo-Pacific Security Dynamics

Rahul Mishra

Backdrop

HISTORICAL accounts, both oral and written, testify that India's ties with Indonesia have been more than two millennia old. India's influence on religion, culture, art and architecture of Indonesia and the rest of South-East Asian region has been remarkable. Cultural interactions have formed the bedrock of this connection. Moreover, in the past two decades, cultural aspects of the relationship have been complemented by robust co-operation in defence and economic domains. This is not only true in the context of India's interaction with Indonesia but with the other countries of the region including Singapore and Vietnam as well. However, India's relations with Indonesia have attracted attention and been of interest, mainly to scholars of international relations. A number of reasons can be cited to substantiate that. India's geographical proximity with Indonesia adds substance to the importance of India's relations with the biggest archipelagic nation in the world. Though, Indonesia is not connected with India through land boundary, the two countries are maritime neighbours. From the southernmost tip of Indian territory, i.e. from the Andaman and Nicobar islands chain of India, northernmost part of Indonesia is only about 80 miles away. This makes India and

Indonesia important stakeholders in each other's maritime security calculus. Indonesia's significance has increased manifold since setting up of India's Andaman and Nicobar Joint Command in 2001. It may be mentioned that the Andaman and Nicobar is a tri-service command of the Indian armed forces, based at Port Blair.

Furthermore, both India and Indonesia are biggest in terms of size and economic prowess in their respective regions. In fact, both India and Indonesia can be termed as "first among equals" in South Asian and the South-East Asian regions, respectively. What adds value to the critical importance of India–Indonesia relations is that both the countries have emerged as two of the most important countries in the twenty-first-century Asia. According to the media reports, India–Indonesia bilateral trade is expected to grow to US $ 45 billion by 2015 from US $ 20 billion in 2012.[1] By 2020, India could become the biggest investor in Indonesia surpassing China. In 2012, Indonesia's exports to India stood at US $ 11 billion, primarily based on natural resources such as coal, crude palm oil, rubber, furniture and wood. India exports refined petroleum products, wheat, rice, sugar and steel to Indonesia.[2] Anthony Reid has lauded Indonesia as the "third Asian giant", after China and India. Clearly, remarkable economic performance, domestic stability and rising international profile of Indonesia make it one of the most promising Asian countries that have the potential to become a prominent regional leader. Indonesia's strategic location positions it to dominate the key international waterways linking the Indian and the Pacific waters. This includes the Lombok, Makassar,

[1] Andi M. Ghalib, "India-Indonesia trade to touch $45 billion by 2015", *The Economic Times*, 15 June 2012, http://articles.economictimes.indiatimes.com/2012-06-15/news/32254649_1_andi-m-ghalib-indonesia-crude-palm-oil (accessed on 7 February 2014).

[2] Ibid.

Sunda and more importantly — the Malacca Straits. This makes Indonesia a key role player in the emerging security dynamics of the Indo-Pacific region.

Historical Background

The legacy of India–Indonesia relations is rich and deserves appreciation. Apart from the historical linkages, modern era interconnections also bind the two countries together. This is evident from the fact that India took the initiative to convene pan-Asian conferences such as the Asian Relations Conference (1947) and the Conference on Indonesia (1949).[3] Indonesia has figured as one of the key important countries for India's foreign policymakers since the freedom movement days. Under the visionary leadership of India's first Prime Minister, Jawaharlal Nehru, India strived to work towards Asian solidarity. Colonialism brought India and Indonesia under British and Dutch rule, respectively. This also led to a period of disconnect, which continued until the rise of the Indian freedom movement when Indian leaders began to take active interest in the South-East Asian affairs. For instance, Nehru organized and celebrated "South-East Asia Day" at Lucknow on 24 October 1945, and expressed solidarity with Indonesia.[4] The relationship got a fillip when many Asian countries became independent, with Nehru playing a key role in developing Asian solidarity. The Asian Relations Conference (1947), the Conference on Indonesia (1949) and the Bandung Conference (1955) served as important milestones on the path of Asian solidarity. In these conferences, India played a predominant role.[5] Appreciating the efforts taken by the Indian leaders and

---

3 Kripa Sridharan, *The ASEAN Region in India's Foreign Policy*, Singapore: Dartmouth, 1996, p. 24.

4 Saroj Pathak, *India and Southeast Asia: A Study of Indian Perspective and Policy Since 1962*, Delhi: Atma Ram & Sons, 1990, pp. 42-43.

5 Ibid., p. 55.

people of India, Indonesia duly acknowledged India's role in putting pressure on the colonial masters. Mutual empathy and support, to a very large extent, shaped India–Indonesia ties in the early years of their independence.

After Indonesia became independent in 1949, the bilateral relations between the two were significantly enhanced. The partnership was built on the platform of non-alignment, Panchsheel (Five Principles of Peaceful Co-existence) and anti-colonialism. India was also aware that South-East Asia, more than any other region, would be more receptive to India's overtures for closer relations especially because of the centuries-old contacts and cultural affinity between these two regions.[6] Issues such as the Suez crisis and Southeast Asia Treaty Organization (SEATO) witnessed the common perspectives India and Indonesia held on international affairs. In 1951, Indonesia's President Sukarno was invited as the Republic Day guest of India. During the same year, in 1951, India and Indonesia signed a treaty for bilateral co-operation. As part of its endeavour to co-operate closely with countries of the South-East Asian region, India established defence links with Indonesia and other South-East Asian countries. Most prominent among them was "India's active assistance in the creation of the armed forces in Indonesia after its independence. The Indian navy held its first-ever joint naval exercises outside the Commonwealth with the Indonesian navy in July 1960."[7] In the initial years, the relationship did gather the momentum, but mutual apathy crept in during the Cold War years due to numerous reasons. Clash of personality between Nehru and Sukarno led to frictions between India and Indonesia at the politico–diplomatic levels. India–Indonesia

---

6 G.V.C. Naidu, *The Indian Navy and Southeast Asia*, New Delhi: Knowledge World & IDSA, 2000, p. 150.

7 Ibid., p. 151.

relations went on a downward spiral due to the China factor, Indonesia's support to Pakistan, as well differences that arose between Nehru and Sukarno.

India's decision to recognize the Malaysian federation and subsequently support the Malaysian claim for United Nations Security Council (UNSC) seat in 1964 was at loggerheads with Indonesian interests. The difference of perception between India and Indonesia on the 1962 India–China War further soured the relationship. The 1965 India–Pakistan War, persistent differences on China, and during the Bandung Conference, and issues relating to non-alignment leadership further drifted them apart. Evidently, India's ties with Indonesia reached its lowest ebb during the 1965 India–Pakistan War. The Indonesian stance under Sukarno during the 1965 War in support of Pakistan (he even reportedly threatened to launch an attack on the Indian islands of Andaman and Nicobar), the creation of a Jakarta–Peking–Hanoi "anti-imperialist" axis during Sukarno's "guided democracy" period (1959-65), and his *Konfrontasi* policy toward the creation of Malaysian federation aroused suspicions in New Delhi about Indonesia's intentions.[8] For years following the 1960s, there wasn't much interaction. It was only during the Suharto era that India–Indonesia relations began to improve. Later, during former prime minister of India, Rajiv Gandhi's visit to Indonesia in 1986, the India–Indonesia relations were restored to normalcy. However, in the subsequent years, both the countries neglected the relationship, until India's Look East Policy opened India up towards the South-East Asian region and subsequently the East Asian and Indo-Pacific region. India has done much in terms of implementing the Look East Policy, and some steps have been taken on the diplomatic interactions and exchanges front with Indonesia as well, both before and after 1992.

8 G.V.C. Naidu, 2000, p. 152.

India's Look East Policy and India–Indonesia Strategic Engagement

The end of the Cold War along with the onset of globalization changed geopolitical and geo-economic realities of the Asian region and the world. Apparently, India's Look East Policy was one of the repercussions of the end of the Cold War. Look East Policy was an attempt on the part of India to build robust ties with countries of the South-East Asian region as also those falling in wider Indo-Pacific region. Over the years, India engaged the countries of the region both at bilateral and multilateral levels. India's entry into the ASEAN Regional Forum (ARF), East Asia Summit (EAS), ASEAN Defence Ministers Meeting (ADMM) Plus and signing of strategic partnership agreement with ASEAN further strengthened India's engagement with the countries of the South-East Asian region and their flagship organization — ASEAN.

Apart from being proactive on politico–diplomatic and economic front in terms of engaging countries of the region, India attempted to engage its eastern neighbours on military and strategic aspects also. At the military front, the Indian Navy made a major policy change in its approach, and came out of "self-imposed isolation and started interacting with a number of other navies in the Indian Ocean littoral and outside in a variety of ways".[9] "This came about in the form of joint naval exercises, visits to foreign ports by Indian ships, hosting of foreign ships by Indian ports, bilateral naval assistance, co-operation in disaster relief, training of naval personnel from other countries, etc. Interestingly, the first navy with which India held joint naval exercises was the Indonesian navy, off Surabaya, in 1989."[10]

---

9 G.V.C. Naidu, 2000, p. 97.

10 Ibid.

With the initiation of the Look East Policy in 1992, apart from working towards the realization of shared vision for economic growth and development and addressing common concerns relating to pressing regional issues, India and Indonesia share a common perspective on strategic issues such as defence and maritime security across the Bay of Bengal and the Andaman Sea. This is manifested by co-operation at various levels. India and Indonesia have been conducting joint maritime patrol exercises, disaster management operations, and regular exchange of officials for defence training purposes.[11] The Indian and Indonesian navies work together on naval patrols and transnational crime prevention exercises.[12] Since 1995, India has been holding naval exercises with Indonesia and other South-East Asian countries. Indonesia, Malaysia, Singapore and Thailand have also been participating in "MILAN", the biennial gathering of navies hosted by India.[13] Since then, they have held intermittent bilateral discussions on counter-terrorism and intelligence sharing.[14]

INDINDOCORPAT, the co-ordinated patrol of the international maritime boundary line by Indian and the Indonesian navies, is held twice every year. The INDINDOCORPAT, "so far has had both navies dispatch two

---

11 For details, see Rahul Mishra, "India-Thailand Relations in East Asian Security Dynamics", in S.D. Muni and Vivek Chadha (eds) *Asian Strategic Review*, New Delhi: Pentagon Press, pp. 164-82.

12 Ibid.

13 Praful Kumar Singh, "Multi-nation Exercise Milan Concludes Successfully in Andaman", *Thaindian News*, 8 February 2010, at http://www.thaindian.com/newsportal/india-news/multi-nation-exercise-milan-concludes-successfully-in-andaman_100316958.html (accessed on 5 October 2012).

14 Bilveer Singh, "Southeast Asia-India Defence Relations in the Changing Regional Security Landscape", IDSA Monograph No. 4, New Delhi, 2011, p. 33.

ships each for joint patrol of the seas against piracy, armed robbery, poaching, illegal immigration, drug trafficking and human trafficking.[15] According to the media reports, the Commander-in-Chief of the joint Andaman Nicobar Command is likely to declare the maiden India–Indonesia joint exercise open. The first ever India–Indonesia joint naval exercise will take place between March and April 2014 on the heels of a multilateral maritime exercise *Komodo* hosted by the Indonesian Navy at Batam.[16] The decision to go for joint naval exercise clearly demonstrates the rising confidence of both New Delhi and Jakarta in their bilateral relationship. It is interesting to note that two decades ago, it was Indonesia, which had serious apprehensions against Indian Navy and India's hegemonic designs in the Indian Ocean. There has indeed been a steady increase in the mutual trust between two countries, which led them to enhance their bilateral defence ties in the post-Cold War years. The years 2001 (co-operation in defence), 2002 (first biannual patrol), 2005 (strategic partnership) and 2007 Joint Commission Meeting (JCM) of Finance Ministers (FMs) and the visit of the Indonesian President, Susilo Bambang Yudhoyono (2011) are a few watershed years in terms of India–Indonesia relations in the past few years. Indian Prime Minister, Manmohan Singh's 2013 visit to Indonesia gave further fillip to India's strategic partnership with Indonesia which took a concrete shape with the signing of the "Joint Declaration on Establishing a Strategic Partnership" in 2005 during the state visit of President Susilo Bambang Yudhoyono.[17]

---

15 "India-Indonesia Coordinated Patrol Graduates into Joint Naval Exercise", *The Hindu*, 6 February 2014.

16 Ibid.

17 Ministry of External Affairs, "India-Indonesia Relations", http://mea.gov.in/Portal/ForeignRelation/India-Indonesia_Relations.pdf (accessed on 25 December 2013).

Emerging Strategic Dynamics of the Indo-Pacific: The US Rebalancing towards Asia

Since its inception, the US pivot to Asia or rebalancing towards Asia strategy, has been lauded as a remarkable shift in the American approach towards the Indo-Pacific region and deeper engagement with its security dynamics.[18] In November 2011, during his visits to Australia and Indonesia, the US President Barack Obama spoke at length about the American "Pivot" — later rechristened as "Rebalancing" towards Asia, and declared, "The United States is a Pacific power, and we are here to stay".[19]

A closer look at the US Rebalancing towards Asia strategy and consequent Chinese responses is giving "an East Asian twist to what is increasingly referred to as the 'New Great Game'".[20] The reasons for calling the emerging dynamics the "New Great Game" are simple. In the past few years, Indo-Pacific in general and South-East Asia in particular have emerged as the new global geo-political centre of gravity with a re-shift of politico–diplomatic, military, institutional and economic focus on countries of the region and their intra-regional politics. Just like the term Indo-Pacific, which attempts to hyphenate the Indian and the Pacific Oceans and their evolving politico-security, demographic and economic

---

18 For a detailed analysis of Southeast Asian response to the US Rebalancing towards Asia, see, Rahul Mishra, "The US Rebalancing Strategy: Responses from Southeast Asia", in S.D. Muni and Vivek Chadha (eds.) *Asian Strategic Review 2014 US Pivot and Asian Security*, New Delhi: Pentagon Press, pp. 149-75.

19 "Barack Obama Says Asia-Pacific Is 'Top US Priority'", BBC News, 17 November 2011, at http://www.bbc.co.uk/news/world-asia-15715446 (accessed on 26 December 2013).

20 Yang Razali Kassim, "The New Great Game: ASEAN's Balancing Act?", *RSIS Commentaries*, 17 January 2012, at http://www.rsis.edu.sg/publications/Perspective/RSIS0142012.pdf (accessed on 17 January 2012).

dynamics, the term New Great Game has also come into vogue, and generated a new set of intense and increasingly nuanced debates on the likely future of global and regional politics. Evidently, the Pivot or Rebalancing towards Asia encompasses "initiatives across all elements of American power".[21] Moreover, it attempts to make inroads into every aspect of regional dynamics. At the politico–diplomatic level, both, Obama administration I and II have been proactive in the South-East Asian region. Since he has assumed his duties as the president of the US, Obama has paid a substantial amount of attention to the region. For instance, there have been dozens of high-profile visits by top leaders of the Obama administration including Barack Obama, former Secretary of State Hillary Clinton, Secretary of State John Kerry and former Secretary of Defence Leon Panetta to the region.

Strengthening ties with Vietnam, stepping up defence co-operation with the Philippines, reinvigorating relations with Thailand and swift reconciliation with the Thein Sein government of Myanmar have been main components of the politico–diplomatic aspect of the Rebalancing strategy in South-East Asia. On the military aspect, apart from a shift in terms of focus of the US Naval Forces, it involves new troop deployments to Australia, new naval deployments to Singapore, and new areas for military co-operation with the Philippines.[22] Intensified military co-ordination with Japan, and South Korea and bridging gaps with Indonesia and Vietnam are also part of the military aspect of the American Rebalancing strategy in South-East Asia and beyond. The US

---

21 Abraham M. Denmark et al., "Regional Perspectives on US Strategic Rebalancing", *Asia Policy*, 15 January 2013, p. 2.

22 Mark E. Manyin et al., "Pivot to the Pacific? The Obama Administration's 'Rebalancing' Toward Asia", Congressional Research Service, at https://www.fas.org/sgp/crs/natsec/R42448.pdf (accessed on 26 September 2013).

desire to become the torchbearer of Trans-Pacific Partnership (TPP) and signing Free Trade Agreement (FTA) with South Korea encompass the economic dimension of the US Rebalancing towards Asia. America's proactive participation in the Shangri-La Dialogue, Association of South-East Asian Nations (ASEAN) Defence Ministers (ADMM) Plus and the EAS constitute the institutional dimension of America's Rebalancing strategy. Clearly, the East-Asian region in general and South-East Asia in particular lie at the core of the US Rebalancing towards Asia strategy.[23]

Of all the South-East countries, Indonesia holds an important place in the US foreign policy manoeuvres. By virtue of being centrally located in the ASEAN region with the largest geographic size and economic prowess, Indonesia figures prominently in the emerging geostrategic dynamics of the region. As mentioned in the foregoing paragraphs, remarkably consistent economic growth and political stability in recent years coupled with impressive domestic situation and successful diplomacy substantiate Indonesia's position as "first among equals" in the ASEAN. Today, Indonesia not only holds a key position in ASEAN, Indian Ocean Rim Association (IORA) and Indian Ocean Naval Symposium (IONS) but also keeps cordial relations with major stakeholders of the region including China, India and the US. To say that it is a common friend of China, India and the US won't be an overstatement in any way. Keeping a fine balance in relations with both China and the US is one of Indonesia's remarkable achievements. Moreover, over the years, it has tried to take some responsibility for the upkeep of ASEAN by playing a proactive role during the Preah Vihar crisis and 2012 ASEAN Summit.

---

23 Mark E. Manyin et al., "Pivot to the Pacific? The Obama Administration's 'Rebalancing' Toward Asia", Congressional Research Service, at https://www.fas.org/sgp/crs/natsec/R42448.pdf (accessed on 26 September 2013).

Comprehending the rising complexities of the region, Indonesia has devised the concept of "dynamic equilibrium" with regard to its engagement with the major stakeholders of the region. Through promotion of mutual and peaceful co-operation, it seeks to minimize superpower rivalry in the region in order to enhance regional security and stability. Moreover, Indonesia's own geographical vulnerabilities have motivated it to strive and contribute towards regional peace, which sufficiently explains its stand on maintaining ASEAN centrality and supporting moves for regional co-operation. For instance, Indonesia has been supportive of China's cordial relations with the ASEAN, despite not being at good terms with China till 1998. However, like many other countries of South-East Asia, Indonesia is mindful of the pitfalls of an increasingly assertive China, which has prompted Jakarta to encourage the US Rebalancing towards Asia; but only the calibrated and non-threatening aspects so that the Rebalancing does not lead to the creeping in of classical security dilemma in South-East Asia. Given that the US Rebalancing towards Asia is crucial for Indonesia for enhancing regional stability and peace, it favours a benign presence of the US and other major powers.

While one may argue that Indonesia's stance on Rebalancing is critically important, its role will largely depend on factors including the China–US relations, China's relations with ASEAN, Japan and India as also on Indonesia's politico–military and economic prowess in the coming years.

Enhancing Regional Security:
Role of India, Indonesia and Australia

For centuries, Indian Ocean has functioned as a bridge connecting littoral countries of the region. Trade linkages and cultural affinities have only strengthened over time through maritime interactions among the countries falling on the margins of the Indian Ocean. In the twenty-first century, these inter-linkages have strengthened owing to greater interdependence among the littoral countries on economic, political and non-traditional fronts.

Being maritime neighbours, India, Indonesia and Australia are closely linked with each other. India's relationship with both Indonesia and Australia has strengthened over the years, which is manifested through strategic partnerships India has signed recently with these two nations. Indonesia–Australia ties have also warmed up over the years, as both of them have realised the importance of each other.

Considering the importance of ensuring a safe and prosperous Indian Ocean region, IORA and IONS have been established, in which these three countries played a crucial role as founder members. IORA and IONS have provided member countries with a platform to engage in consultations in dealing with regional maritime threats and challenges. Nevertheless, numerous issues demand attention of India, Indonesia and Australia — the three major stakeholders of the region. In that regard, it has been felt that trilateral discussion would enable greater mutual understanding among these countries.

In the regional context, it is vital for Australia, India and Indonesia to work closely on issues of mutual benefit and concern that include promoting regional trade and co-operation, safety of Sea Lines of Communication, combating transnational crime, piracy and drug trafficking. This becomes all the more important due to the fact that Australia, India and Indonesia are the biggest countries in terms of their economy and geographical size in Australasia, South Asia and South Indo-Pacific region, respectively. Additionally, these countries are the rapidly emerging powers in Asia and share the common objective of realizing a peaceful Asia. China's unprecedented rise and increasingly aggressive posture in the region have emerged as both a challenge and an opportunity for them. Interestingly, while Australia has traditionally been a US ally, both India and Indonesia are becoming diplomatically and strategically closer to the US, which offers them another commonality.

Conclusion

Like India, Indonesia too follows a foreign policy based on the principles of non-alignment and free of fears or favours. Nevertheless, over the years, a remarkable shift has been witnessed in the Indonesian foreign policy. From Sukarno era's anti-Western approach and Suharto's new order government's moderate stand, Indonesia is now comfortable with the US and the West, while not being excessively sceptical of China. In retrospect, China has always loomed large in Indonesian foreign policy calculus. The Chinese designs to "engineer" coups in Indonesia in the mid-1960s led to ethnic riots in Indonesia in which several Chinese people were killed. It took Indonesian leadership and the common populace several decades to get the incident pass them. The year 1998 once again witnessed massive riots against Chinese Indonesians. Nevertheless, Indonesian fears of China subsided over a period of time, and gradually Indonesian policy makers realized that geostrategic compulsions do not allow both Indonesia and China to overlook each other. Being the biggest country in terms of geographical and economic size, Indonesia has always been looked up to.

In the context of India as well, Indonesia's foreign policy has been altered several times. The bilateral relations have witnessed phases of bonhomie to acquaintances and they are now again back to friendship. To say that Indonesia is now more for a balanced foreign policy won't be a wrong assertion. One may argue that geography has played a much more crucial role than most of the countries around in shaping Indonesia's foreign policy. Such an argument is more relevant vis-à-vis India–Indonesia relations. Indonesia is playing an important role in fulfilling India's energy needs as well as agricultural needs. India imports coal and palm oil from Indonesia. Additionally, several Indian companies are engaged in mining activities in Indonesia.

In the present context, India is strengthening its Look East Policy. Indonesia, being the largest country in ASEAN, should be a natural focus for India. Both are emerging economies sharing common economic problems and opportunities. In the recent years, thanks to high-level exchanges, a broad institutional framework of co-operation has been set up to deepen the strategic partnership between the two countries. Both the countries are adjusting to the rise of China. While both are seeking engagement with China, China's unprecedented rise has posed new challenges for India as well as Indonesia.

While there is already a framework of co-operation between India and Indonesia, the focus should be on improving, monitoring and implementation. India needs to ensure that its engagement with Indonesia is stepped up and upgraded to match that of other countries like China and the US with Indonesia. In that regard, an annual strategic and economic dialogue at the level of the foreign ministers of the two countries should be set up. The JCM mechanism could be upgraded to the strategic dialogue level. This will help bring cohesiveness to the various dialogue processes that have been envisaged. India and Indonesia's decision to hold joint naval exercises puts the strategic and security dimension of the relationship up by several notches. Such steps could attain more value if an institutional mechanism for defence co-operation and a dialogue at defence minister level is institutionalized. Joint defence production and collaboration in R&D could further add value to the relationship between India and Indonesia — Asia's two emerging economic and military giants.

17

Leadership from Below

Indonesia in a Twenty-first-Century South-East Asia

Ruth Rhea Khan

THE Association of South-East Asian Nations (ASEAN) has emerged as the geopolitical and geo-economic reference point for South-East Asia today. The formation of ASEAN on 8 August 1967 by the founding fathers, the foreign ministers of Indonesia, Malaysia, Singapore, Thailand and the Philippines set in place an inter-governmental organization that would gradually become synonymous with the region itself having provided to it a platform, a collective voice and a common world-view.

The backdrop to the formation of the ASEAN was an uncertain environment in South-East Asia with Indonesia's belief that the creation of the Federation of Malaysia by the British was a continuation of colonial rule and hence made several attempts to prevent its creation out of former British colonies. Combined with this were fears of the Chinese supporting communist insurgencies in many parts of South-East Asia. Consequently, the non-communist governments of the region came together to form an organization whose "aims and purposes were about co-operation in the economic, social, cultural, technical, educational and other fields, and in the promotion of regional peace and stability through abiding respect for justice and the rule of law and adherence to the principles of the United Nations Charter."[1]

Within the ten member ASEAN, Indonesia occupies a central role by virtue of being one of the founding members, the largest country in South-East Asia and also because it is the most populous Muslim-majority nation in the world. Besides the historic and geographic leadership, Indonesia stands tall as a developing country boasting a vibrant pluralist democracy in the twenty-first century. It is a young democracy that is making its transition to being a stable, mature democracy through the conduct of its periodic, free and fair elections and is home to a robust civil society that allows media and press freedoms.

Indonesia has proved its resilience having overthrown three decades of dictatorship marked by greed and corruption, survived the worst of the Asian Financial Crisis of 1997-98 and also the global financial meltdown of 2007-08. The sustained economic growth rate of 6 per cent (and above since 2010) Gross Domestic Product (GDP) has been a remarkable achievement considering the fact that the country has experienced two major economic setbacks within the span of a single decade.[2] Indonesia has shown remarkable ability to withstand and resurface during the very challenging phases of the Bali bombings, the tsunami of 2004, the haze from land and forest fires, and has endured separatist pressures that threatened to tear apart its societal fabric. Its unique geostrategic nearness to vital Sea Lanes of Communication — Malacca, Sunda and Lombok straits — has further consolidated its position and it is poised to play a crucial role in the

1 "ASEAN History" [Online: web], (accessed on 14 November 2013) URL: http://www.asean.org/asean/about-asean/history.

2 "The World Bank Data GDP Growth" [Online: web], (accessed on 17 November 2013) URL: http://data.worldbank.org/indicator/NY.GDP.MKTP.KD.ZG.

emerging dynamics of the Indo-Pacific maritime power configuration.

A Natural Leader

Indonesia has historically played a leading role in its articulation of a global foreign policy that strove to accommodate plurality by being inclusive and integrative. During the time of Sukarno, the desire for independence from the Dutch and later the Japanese led to the formulation of the idea of Pancasila (1 June 1945) which became the state's doctrine — nationalism, internationalism, representative democracy, social justice and theism.[3] Later this was enshrined in the constitution of the newly-independent nation.

Another major milestone in its leadership would be co-hosting the Bandung Conference of Afro-Asian Nations (1955) where participants from twenty-nine countries representing more than half of the world's population were present and discussed issues that were relevant to newly-independent countries that had been under colonial rule. Issues that were at the forefront of the deliberations were decolonization, human rights and self-determination, cultural co-operation, economic development, world peace and condemning the superpower politics of the erstwhile USSR and the US. This later led to the formation of the Non-Aligned Movement (1961) where Sukarno along with Gamal Abdel Nasser of Egypt, Kwame Nkrumah of Ghana, Jawaharlal Nehru of India and Josip Broz Tito of Yugoslavia played a crucial role in carving out a foreign policy stance that maintained equidistance from the Cold War politics of the USSR and the US.

Further, the formation of the ASEAN (1967) where Indonesia was one of the founding members substantiates the

---

3 "The Sukarno Years: Birth of the Republic of Indonesia" [Online: web], (accessed on 12 November 2013) URL: http://www.sukarnoyears.com/120sukarno.htm.

fact that as a country it has articulated a dynamic, pragmatic foreign policy that has responded to the needs of the political environment. During the signing of the Bangkok Declaration, Indonesian foreign minister Adam Malik went on to describe Indonesia's vision of a South-East Asia developing into "a region which can stand on its own feet, strong enough to defend itself against any negative influence from outside the region". Such a vision, he stressed, was not wishful thinking, if the countries of the region effectively co-operated with each other, considering their combined natural resources and manpower. He referred to differences of outlook among the member countries, but those differences, he said, would be overcome through a maximum of goodwill and understanding, faith and realism. Hard work, patience and perseverance, he added, would also be necessary.[4]

The importance of Bali in consolidating the centrality of the ASEAN can hardly be overstated. The signing of the 1976 Declaration of ASEAN Concord by Soeharto reveals that in the very formative years of the organization, the political leadership of Indonesia was committed to "improvement of ASEAN machinery to strengthen political co-operation" among the member states.[5] The idea of the ASEAN community which owes its origins to the Bali Concord II (2003) stated that it would comprise three pillars, namely political and security co-operation, economic co-operation, and socio-cultural co-operation. It reaffirmed:

---

4 "The Founding of ASEAN" [Online: web], (accessed on 17 November 2013) URL: http://www.aseansec.org/the-founding-of-asean/

5 "The Declaration of ASEAN Concord", Bali, Indonesia, 24 February, 1976 [Online: web], (accessed on 17 November 2013) URL: http://www.asean.org/news/item/declaration-of-asean-concord-indonesia-24 february, 1976.

> ASEAN is a concert of South-East Asian nations, bonded together in partnership in dynamic development and in a community of caring societies, committed to upholding cultural diversity and social harmony.[6]

The latest in the ASEAN Summit meetings in Bali (2011) led to the vision of the ASEAN community in the Global Community of Nations, known as the Bali Concord III which envisages the organization's commitment to take an increasing role in addressing global challenges.[7] Further the need to enhance the role of ASEAN in the global community of nations was stressed during Indonesia's chairmanship of the ASEAN in 2011.

Likewise, the Bali Democracy Forum (2008) was initiated by Indonesia and envisioned to promote regional and international co-operation in the field of democracy, an inclusive approach that would bring together democracies and aspiring democracies to work towards creating and emulating good and transparent governance. In the same year, Indonesia ratified the ASEAN Charter bestowing upon it a legal personality that would support the development of democracy and uphold human rights. At the ceremony to mark the coming into force of the ASEAN Charter, President Yudhoyono mentioned that with the Charter in force, "we will be able to fashion a regional architecture that will enhance our collective and individual national resilience".[8] Secretary General Dr Surin Pitsuwan mentioned that the Charter being fully ratified by

---

6 "Declaration of ASEAN Concord II" (Bali Concord II) [Online: web], (accessed on 11 November 2013) URL: http://www.asean.org/news/asean-statement-communiques/item/declaration-of-asean-concord-ii-bali-concord-ii-3.

7 "Concept Paper of the Bali Concord III Plan of Action 2012-2022" [Online: web], (accessed on 17 November 2013) URL: http://www.mfa.go.th/asean/contents/files/asean-media-center-20121203-175458-360878.pdf.

8 Statement by H.E. Dr. Susilo Bambang Yudhoyono, President of Republic of Indonesia at the Ceremony to Mark the Entry Into →

all ten members would enable ASEAN to be "a rules-based, people-oriented and more integrated entity. After the formal entry into force of the Charter, our community-building will shift to a higher gear with full steam forward".[9] Indonesia has also established the Institute of Peace and Democracy at the University of Udayana in Bali.

Thus, Indonesia has always been at the forefront in projecting ASEAN centrality and ensuring that the organization responds to the needs of the changing political, economic and security milieu, reinvents itself to deal with the newer realities and also contributes to the developments regionally and globally. Indonesia has exercised its regional leadership under the ASEAN umbrella by pushing forward the agenda of the whole rather than trying to stand out individually.

Indonesia and the US Rebalancing Strategy

The US was among the first nations to extend diplomatic recognition and established relations with independent Indonesia after the Netherlands recognized its independence in 1949. During the Cold War, US foreign policy had viewed Indonesia through the prism of the threat of communist influence in South-East Asia. After the Cold War, the focus shifted to the excesses committed by the Indonesian army known as TNI in Papua, Aceh East Timor, etc. However, after the 9/11 attacks on America, counter-terrorism co-operation have brought the two closer because Indonesia has also been a victim of several terrorist attacks.

→ Force of the ASEAN Charter, 15 December 2008 [Online: web], (accessed on 18 November 2013) URL: http://www.asean.org/news/item/statement-by-he-dr-susilo-bambang-yudhoyono-president-of-republic-of-indonesia-at-the-ceremony-to-mark-the-entry-into-force-of-the-asean-charter

9 "ASEAN Embarks on New Era : Asean Charter Fully Ratified" [Online: web], (accessed on 25 November 2013) URL: http://www.aseanhrmech.org/news/asean-charter-fully-ratified.html

Relations between the two have been steadily improving especially with the Bush Administration working at restoring military-to-military ties after 9/11. President Megawati Sukarnoputri was the first leader to visit the US after the attack and expressed Indonesia's support to the global war on terror. In the years after the attacks on the US, Indonesia has been targeted on several occasions by high-profile terrorist attacks. Notable among them would include the Bali bombings of 2002, bombing of the Marriot Hotel in Jakarta in 2003, the Australian embassy bombing in 2004, bombing against Western hotels in Jakarta and the plot to assassinate President Yudhoyono. This has strengthened the bilateral resolve to counter this menace regionally and globally.

The US decision to pump in aid and relief during the aftermath of the 2004 Indian Ocean tsunami that devastated large parts of Indonesia was viewed favourably in Indonesia and in the region. It helped in establishing a reservoir of goodwill that had been missing so far and consolidated the humanitarian leadership role of the US as a "force for good" in South East Asia.

In 2005, restrictions based on the Leahy Amendment were relaxed and International Military Education and Training (IMET), Foreign Military Sales (FMS) and Foreign Military Financing (FMF) to Indonesia were resumed.[10] The US support to Detachment 88, an elite counter-terrorism unit, has also helped in nailing down terrorists from the Jemaah Islamiya,

---

10 The Leahy Law states, "None of the funds made available by this Act may be used to support any training program involving a unit of the security forces of a foreign country if the Secretary of Defense has received credible information from the Department of State that the unit has committed a gross violation of human rights, unless all necessary corrective steps have been taken." — DOD Appropriations Act for FY 2012 (Div. A, P.L. 112-74), Sec. 8058. This is in context of the human rights violations of the Indonesian military in Aceh and East Timor.

remaining members from the Noordin Top faction, various jihadists training at the terrorist camps in Aceh, Dulmatin (key mastermind of the 2002 Bali bombings) and also the assassin planning to target President Yudhoyono in 2010.[11] The US has also provided assistance to Indonesia's new Defence University and has assisted in the procurement of C-130 Hercules transport aircrafts with the assurance that it would not be used against rebels in its troubled provinces.[12]

The election of US President Obama was seen as a welcome development in Indonesia where he spent a large part of his childhood. His *Indonesia bagian dari didi saya* speech to students at the University of Indonesia was greeted with a rousing applause as he recollected his memories of growing up in Indonesia.[13] Another development in their relationship was US Defense Secretary Robert Gates announcing in July 2010 that the US government would resume measured and gradual programme of security co-operation with Kopassus.[14] This

---

11 Jemaah Islamiah (JI) meaning Islamic group is a pan-Southeast Asia terrorist group whose initial aims in the 1990s was the creation of an Islamic state encompassing Southeast Asia that would include Singapore, Indonesia, Malaysia, Brunei, southern Thailand and southern Philippines. Noordin Top led a JI splinter group that was behind the 2009 bombings of hotels in Jakarta. See R. Gunaratna, (ed.), 2003, *Terrorism in the Asia-Pacific: Threat and Response*, Singapore: Eastern Universities Press; Z. Abuza, 2003, *Militant Islam in Southeast Asia: Crucible of Terror*, Boulder, Colorado: Lynne Rienner Publishers.

12 Bruce Vaughn, 2011, "Indonesia: Domestic Politics, Strategic Dynamics, and U.S. Interests", 31 January 2011, RL32394, Congressional Research Service.

13 *Indonesia bagian dari didi saya* is translated as Indonesia is a part of me.

14 Voice of America, 2010, US Restores Ties With Notorious Indonesian Military Unit, 21 July 2010 [Online: web], (accessed on 18 November 2013) URL: http://www.voanews.com/content/us-restores-ties-with-notorious-indonesian-military-unit/166068.html

move was thought to be hasty because several Kopassus members charged with human rights violations were yet to be prosecuted. However, this incremental approach has been viewed in some quarters as an incentive by Washington for Indonesia's counter-terrorism co-operation.

With Indonesia, the US has also been making sustained efforts in rectifying the anti-Islam image that its foreign policy has come to be associated with due to its policies in the Middle East. Even though, Indonesia has its share of misgivings over the conduct of US foreign policy with respect to its support to Israel and also with its wars on Iraq and Afghanistan, it has acted as a moderate voice in the Islamic world. Islam in Indonesia has been of a syncretic nature that has been richly influenced by earlier animistic, Buddhist and Hindu traditions. In this regard the US has more ground to cover in improving its relationship with the Muslim populations of the world.

Another notable achievement of the Obama Administration would be the signing of the Comprehensive Partnership Agreement with Indonesia that has not only strengthened but also elevated their bilateral ties furthering co-operation on trade and investment, food security, science and technology, educational exchanges and military co-operation.[15] This Agreement would refocus US attention to a long-term commitment to their bilateral relationship which would also add substance to US renewed interest in the developments taking place in the region.

The US Rebalancing strategy (2011) towards Asia involves downsizing its commitment to the Middle East and Afghanistan and intensifying its engagement with the Asia-Pacific. This involves closer co-operation with ASEAN thus

---

15 U.S. Department of State, Comprehensive Partnership United States-Indonesia Comprehensive Partnership, 8 October 2013 [Online: web], (accessed on 18 November 2013) URL: http://www.state.gov/r/pa/prs/ps/2013/10/215196.htm.

raising the organization's profile regionally and globally. With Indonesia too, the US engagement would receive a fillip covering a wide spectrum of issues ranging from increased trade and investment, securing sea lanes, disaster preparedness and energy security. However, the pronounced military component of the strategy with the deployment of 2,500 troops to Darwin has not been viewed positively in several Indonesian circles as Darwin is close to Indonesia's troubled province of Papua. They cite Washington's support to regional rebels in the 1950s when the excuse of protection of its oil companies in Sumatra was used as a pretext for intervention.[16] Similarly, the much publicized US Rebalancing strategy to Asia has led to a perception among Chinese hardliners that the US return has been triggered by the immense growth of China's influence in the region.

Notwithstanding the military component of the strategy with its increased naval presence and deployment of troops, the strategic and diplomatic commitment that been stressed by the US government can hardly be ignored. The US government has made itself explicit in mentioning that the rebalance is not containment against China.[17] Prominent US policy experts who have held senior governmental positions have reiterated this view.[18] Likewise, Wanandi mentions that

---

16 Dewi Fortuna Anwar, 2013, An Indonesian Perspective on the U.S. Rebalancing Effort toward Asia, Commentary, National Bureau of Asian Research, 26 February 2013, Washington D.C.

17 Remarks by Tom Donilon, 11 March 2013, "The United States and the Asia-Pacific in 2013 [Online: web], (accessed on 18 November 2013) URL: http://www.whitehouse.gov/the-press-office/2013/03/11/remarks-tom-donilon-national-security-advisory-president-united-states-a.

18 In a Brookings Institute panel discussion on *U.S. Strategy in Asia* (2012), Kenneth Lieberthal mentions that the U.S. is not against China. Jeffrey Bader in *Understanding the U.S. Pivot to Asia* 2012 mentions that the rebalancing is not a blueprint for containment of China.

ASEAN and Indonesia have an interest to have the relationship between the two great powers conflict- or confrontation-free.[19] Strategic competition between the two is inevitable but a power tussle in the region would spell doom for Indonesia as well as ASEAN for whom the stakes are higher as it would slow down the pace of economic integration and disrupt the peace and stability in the region.

Leadership from Below

The ASEAN having completed forty years of its existence is a successful regional organization by all standards. Indonesian foreign minister Ali Alatas had remarked:

> When ASEAN was born, there were a good number of sceptics who would not believe that, given the wide divergences of view among the ASEAN countries, the differences in the political and economic systems of its founding members, it would ever succeed in this endeavour at regional co-operation. Well, ASEAN proved all its critics wrong and it is now a vibrant reality, an Association recognized not only in its own region but also in the world at large as one of the most successful regional co-operative schemes.[20]

The economic dynamism of the ASEAN region has led to the active involvement of extra-regional powers like the US, China, Japan, South Korea, India, Australia, New Zealand, Japan, Russia, Canada, EU and the UN. The region is economically attractive because of the large market having a population of more than 620 million people and a $ 1.8 trillion dollar GDP.

---

19 Jusuf Wanandi, 2011, "Strategic Developments in East Asia: The East Asian Summit" [Online: web], (accessed on 18 November 2013) URL: http://www.eastwestcenter.org/sites/all/modules/filemanager/files/PECC_20_GM/Wanandi.EAS.pdf.

20 "The Future of ASEAN" [Online: web], (accessed on 18 November 2013) URL: http://www.asean.org/news/item/the-future-of-asean

ASEAN Free Trade Agreements (FTAs) with Korea, China, Australia, New Zealand and India, the Comprehensive Economic Partnerships with East Asia comprising the ASEAN and the Plus Six countries of China, Japan, South Korea, India, Australia and New Zealand reveal that the trade and investment potential of the region is attracting the attention of these countries. Besides this, the US–ASEAN Trade and Investment Framework Agreement (TIFA) and the Trans-Pacific Partnership (TPP) that has four ASEAN signatories (Brunei, Malaysia, Singapore, Vietnam) have led the US to seize the economic opportunities and step up the pace of economic engagements in the ASEAN region.

Its original membership has expanded to include Vietnam (1993), Laos and Myanmar (1997) and Cambodia (1999), and the ASEAN has spearheaded the growth of several organizations that have roped in key extra regional powers to stay involved in and contribute to the developments in the region. Mention worthy in this regard is the institutional mechanisms of the ASEAN Regional Forum (ARF), ASEAN Plus Three (APT), East Asia Summit (EAS), the ASEAN Defence Ministers Meeting Plus (ADMM+) that have enabled the ASEAN member states to deepen their economic and security engagement with influential powers like the US, China, Japan, South Korea, India, Australia, New Zealand, EU and Russia in South-East Asia.

ASEAN countries have been at peace with each other since the Vietnam War of the 1970s. Notwithstanding the disagreements that arise occasionally, there has been no major war among the members and the organization has thrived for over four-and-a-half decades. This has elevated the global standing of the organization as it has successfully steered itself together as a cohesive unit in international affairs.

Indonesia has constantly made efforts to keep the organization united and further has to play a critical role in furthering the cause of ASEAN leadership by preventing the development of unhealthy competition between the US and China from snowballing into a crisis. A case in point would be the fears regarding the Regional Comprehensive Economic Partnership (RCEP) and TPP trade negotiations that are underway in the region. This intensifying economic competition between the US and China that confronts ASEAN has to be handled deftly to prevent some members of the ASEAN from having to choose sides. Any ASEAN-led mechanism, that works towards integrating and advancing the economic potential of the region, has to have solid Indonesian backing.

Similarly, the simmering tensions in the South China Sea dispute have led Indonesia to take up the role of an impartial mediator in the dispute. Hawkish statements by the Chinese over the South China Sea have raised concerns in ASEAN countries about the agressiveness of China to enforce its sovereignty and jurisdictional claims with the use of force. This led to a corresponding US response that it has interests in free and open navigation in the troubled South China Sea as a substantial portion of its trade passes through these waters. Indonesia, as a non-claimant, has been pushing forward a regional framework to resolve rival claims. Indonesian Foreign Minister Marty Natalegawa while highlighting the role that ASEAN can play mentions:

> Perhaps ASEAN, as the least objectionable party to East Asia, can be the initiator for a . . . groundbreaking, perception-changing, paradigm-shifting outlook in the rest of East Asia.[21]

---

[21] Dan Washburn, 2013, "Natalegawa: Indonesia Wants to 'Facilitate Conversation' on Tense South China Sea", *Asia Society*, 19 September 2013 [Online: web], (accessed on 18 November 2013) URL: http://asiasociety.org/new-york/natalegawa-indonesia-wants-facilitate-conversation-tense-south-china-sea

Indonesia recognizes the pre-eminence of the ASEAN in the economic and political developments in the region. It acknowledges that no initiative or institutional mechanism that does not have the ASEAN in the driver's seat will be able to have an impact in the Indo-Pacific security order. Indonesia would not want to see the ASEAN region becoming a battleground for the display of great power jostling as Indonesia and the fellow member states would bear the repercussions and aftermath of such an eventuality, the fears of which have and are being deliberated both in policy-making as well as academic circles. Indonesia would stand to gain individually as a country as well as a member of the ASEAN if both China and the US refrain from using the region as a strategic space for confrontation. When there are multiple major big powers competing for space, small and medium countries stand to gain by seeking benefits from all sides. However, asymmetric power distribution would escalate tension if the weaker would feel the compulsion to overturn the status quo and seek out a larger role.

Here lies a historic opportunity for Indonesia to enable both the US and China to contribute towards the growth and prosperity of the region. Rizal Sukma writes:

> Leaning to one side is not an option. Indonesia needs and wants both the US and China as friends and partners, and would not want to see the superpowers become rivals, competing for influence in its neighbourhood.[22]

Indonesia must provide leadership from below, by working under the aegis of the ASEAN encouraging the building of norms and consensus, peaceful settlement of disputes and in

---

22 Rizal Sukma, "Indonesia and the Emerging Sino-US Rivalry in Southeast Asia" [Online: web], (accessed on 18 November 2013) URL: http://www.lse.ac.uk/IDEAS/publications/reports/pdf/SR015/SR015-SEAsia-Sukma-.pdf.

being an agent that spearheads the development of the region and promotes the well-being of over 600 million people. Indonesia has the potential to propel the ASEAN into the twenty-first century by reinforcing the organization's credibility and unity regionally and on the global stage.

Conclusion

Indonesia as an ASEAN member has drawn negative attention due to its internal politics that is characterized by poverty, inequality and corruption, poor human rights record, religious intolerance, charges of environmental degradation and damage (haze, illegal logging, poaching of endangered species of Sumatran tiger, rhino, orangutan), etc. It has been doubted whether Indonesia can play a leadership role in the Asian century.[23] Wihardja mentions that if Indonesia is to contribute to the Asian century, it must first put its own house in order. And to assume a potential leadership role in the region and globally, Indonesia needs to develop its political institutions, secure an "ocean-focused" development strategy that complements its status as an archipelagic nation, become a real champion of regional and global co-operation, and create a well-educated and competitive workforce and labour market. Accepting these observations, one also has to bear in mind that these are the challenges that a young democracy faces and also the periodic convulsions of a country that has experienced leadership transition within a short frame of time.

In spite of these realities, Indonesia can and must unceasingly work to improve the domestic situation, play a larger role through the mechanism of the ASEAN in bridging

---

23 Maria Monica Wihardja, 2013, "Can Indonesia play a leadership role in the Asian century?", 3 September 2013 [Online: web], (accessed on 18 November 2013) URL: http://www.eastasiaforum.org/2013/09/03/can-indonesia-play-a-leadership-role-in-the-asian-century/

the gap in a two-tiered ASEAN (Lower Mekong initiative to boost economic assistance to weaker ASEAN countries) and contribute to reducing the lopsided economic development between maritime and mainland South-East Asia. Indonesia is suitable to provide leadership to the ASEAN as it has been conducting its foreign policy in an independent and pragmatic manner since its emergence as a post-colonial state. The presidential and parliamentary elections of 2004 and 2009 had been largely fair and free according to international observers and Yudhoyono's leadership has been appreciated regionally and globally as he has acknowledged ASEAN centrality as a prerequisite for the peace and prosperity of the region. Further, Indonesia's leadership — economically and diplomatically — will provide the required ballast to ASEAN's centrality in the emerging security and economic institutional architecture of the region.

18

India–Indonesia Relationship
Maritime Security

Sudhir Singh

INDIA and Indonesia are perhaps among few countries that have been interconnected through many channels since millennia. After the Second World War, both countries emerged in the landscape of Asia Pacific. Cold War was at its peak and both were intended to explore a middle path through Bandung Conference of Asian–African (1955) and founders of Non-Aligned Movement (NAM). NAM was intended to adopt a middle path between the prevailing rivalries of capitalist bloc led by the US and the communist bloc led by USSR. India's first Prime Minister, Jawaharlal Nehru was the first world leader to condemn Dutch Police Action against Indonesia during 1947-1948. Nehru stated:

> No European country has any business to set its Army in Asia against our people. When it does so, the spirit of New Asia will not tolerate such things.[1]

In recognition of India's role in Indonesia conferred the highest title of "Pahlawan Indonesia (Hero of Indonesia) to Jawaharlal Nehru and Biju Patnaik, who took great risk in flying a plane

1 L.P. Singh, 1967, "Dynamics of Indian-Indonesian Relations", *Asian Survey*, September 7(9): 656.

to Jogyakarta, the then republican capital to rescue Sukarno and another independence figure, Sultan Sjahrir.[2] In 1950, Indonesia's first President Sukarno called upon the people of Indonesia and India to "intensify the cordial relations" that had existed between both the countries "for more than 1,000 years".[3] In this spirit the Treaty of Friendship was inked between both countries in March 1951 which proclaimed "a perpetual peace and unalterable friendship between the two countries".[4]

In Indonesia, Indian arts and cultural legacy remains all-too-obviously evident in ancient architecture, literatures, dances and music, cuisines, language vocabularies, etc. In the military realm too, Indian influence is somewhat traceable. For example, the Javanese method of warfare has some resemblances to *chakra-byuha*, a battle formation in the Indian classical text of *Mahabharata*. Ancient Indonesia also adopted India's *mandala* concept, which is based upon the centre–periphery relationship as a method of socio-political governance.[5] Indonesia's two great ancient kingdoms of Srivijaya and Majapahit exerted a *mandala* control over its tributaries, where the court's control was largely diffused, nuanced, and gradually diminished along the peripheries.

There was some baggage of history too. Indonesia extended a strategic silence during 1962 Sino–Indian War and extended all-around support to Pakistan during 1965 Indo–

---

2 Baladas Ghoshal, 2011, "Indonesia in India's Look East Policy", *IDSA Issue Brief*, 20 January, p. 15.

3 Lok-Sabha Secretariat, 1959, *Foreign Policy of India, Text of Documents 1947-59*, New Delhi, 54.

4 *Treaty of Friendship between India and the Republic of Indonesia*, 3 March 1951.

5 Paul Michel Munoz, 2006, *Early Kingdoms of the Indonesian Archipelago and the Malay Peninsula*, Singapore: Editions Didier Millet.

Pak War.[6] India also supported Malaysia in its confrontation with Indonesia.

The convergences started to overlap divergences in post-Cold War scenario. Indonesia also emerged a central state to ensure the objectives of Look East Policy launched by Prime Minister Narasimha Rao in 1992 to maximize Indian national interests in South-East Asia. In 2011 China superseded Japan as largest trade partner of Indonesia. China–Indonesia relations are cordial, but the irritants of trust deficits are there including the South China Sea issue. Indonesia has also emerged as an oil importing country since last many years. Containment of terror, piracy and maritime security has remained an issue of concerns for both India and Indonesia being the littoral countries of the Indian Ocean.

Despite their shared historical and cultural affinities, the bilateral relationship between India and Indonesia is perhaps the least explored, researched and developed among all the bilateral relations both countries have forged in.

Both are maritime neighbours. This is particularly so in the field of defence, being both neighbours with only 80 nautical miles distance between Indonesia's westernmost province of Aceh and India's southernmost Indira Point in the Great Nicobar Island. Both countries have large Muslim populations and share common democratic values. These factors should be both ingredients and incentives to warrant closer defence co-operation. Why then do they seem embroiled in mutual neglect?[7]

---

6 Mohammad Ayoob, 1990, *India and Southeast Asia: Indian Perceptions and Policies*, London: Routledge, pp. 10-11.

7 C. Raja Mohan, 2011, "India and Indonesia: A New Strategic Partnership?", *RSIS Commentary*, no. 10, 1 February, p. 1, http://www.rsis.edu.sg/publications/Perspective/RSIS0102011.pdf (accessed on 10 November 2012).

Being the world's largest archipelagic nation, the sea has a special place in Indonesia's strategic world-view. The archipelago lies at a maritime "crossroad location" (*posisi silang*) between the Indian and Pacific oceans, and serving as a bridge between the Eurasian landmass and Australian continent.[8] It is transited by four of the world's strategic maritime choke points, namely the Malacca, Sunda, Lombok, and Makassar straits, thus making it a pivotal state for global shipping. Complemented by the rich natural resources like oil, gas and coal, Indonesia is a swing state for major powers to court, not least, for India.

This stood in contrast to the archipelago's ancient history which is arguably closely related to India. Archaeological and historical evidences show that maritime South-East Asia has been closely interconnected with the Indian subcontinent, although the South-East Asian legacy is equally influenced by local flavour. On the other hand, Jakarta welcomes the re-invigoration of bilateral defence relationship as stipulated in its 182-page long 2008 Defence White Paper.[9] With a bilateral defence co-operation agreement on 11 January 2001 and which got ratified in December 2007, Jakarta sought to engage New Delhi in defence dialogues, co-ordinated patrols in the Andaman Sea, defence personnel exchanges and defence industry. Compared to defence co-operation with other countries, however, the agreement was somewhat slow in implementation — it even took seven years to ratify. Co-operation with China, for example, only required five years

---

[8] Evan Laksmana, 2011, "The Enduring Strategic Trinity; Explaning Indonesia's Geopolitical Artitetcure", *Journal of Indian Ocean Region*, **1**(1): 96-98.

[9] Indonesia's Department of Defence, *Buku Putih Pertahanan Indonesia 2008* [Indonesia's Defence White Paper 2008], Jakarta: Departemen Pertahanan Republik Indonesia, 2008, pp. 148-49.

for Jakarta to start a joint naval missile development, as well as maritime surveillance systems with Beijing, after both countries signed a Strategic Partnership Agreement in 2005.

The overthrowing of Suharto government in 1998 was a major turning point in Indonesia's history. It brought many transformative changes in Indonesia. This created ripples on the non-geographical distances between Indonesia and India. Gravitationally, Indonesia and India are much strong economically now than before as evident from the increased bilateral trade volume and value, which made them more diplomatically assertive on the global stage. In 2010–11, bilateral total trade volume increased almost 38 per cent to US $ 16 billion. Indonesia's Ambassador to India said that by 2015, the volume is expected to reach US $ 45 billion, and by 2020, India could be Indonesia's largest foreign investor.[10] In terms of Gross Domestic Product (GDP), both countries are among the twenty largest in the world under the so-called economic grouping of Group of Twenty (G-20).

Indonesia agreed to establish a Strategic Partnership with India in November 2005. India too has looked into South-East Asia through its Look East Policy to promote economic co-operation, in addition to developing its soft power through cultural and academic exchanges.[11]

The Indonesian president visited India in January 2011 and inked many agreements. The Defence Co-operation Agreement signed in January 2001 was a significant milestone in bilateral relations. Not only did it mark a re-establishment of defence co-operation started fifty years ago, but also signalled Jakarta's

---

10 Andi M. Ghalib "India-Indonesia Trade to touch $45 billion by 2015", *The Economic Times*, 15 June 2012, http://articles.economictimes.indiatimes.com/2012-06-15/news/32254649_1_andi-m-ghalib-indonesia-crude-palmoil (accessed on 12 November, 2012).

11 Baladas Ghoshal, "Indonesia in India's Look East Policy", no. 2.

positive perceptions on New Delhi. The Agreement stipulated the establishment of a Joint Defence Co-operation Committee (JDCC) to study and identify various possible fields of defence co-operation. For Jakarta, this means it has a major partner to co-operate with on its Indian Ocean frontier.

But the much significant arena of bilateral co-operation is maritime security. Both countries are emerging economies and lot of stakes in ensuring safety in free lane sea communication.

Indonesia is an emerging economic and strategic power. Its major objectives likes keeping Asia multi-polar converge with India. This has given a new twist to bilateral relations of both countries. Long back, great Indian strategic thinker, Kautilya had stated that convergences of interests are shaping the contours of foreign policy. During last one decade it has achieved remarkable growth on economic front. Having overcome the crisis of the late 1990s, when it required aid from the International Monetary Fund (IMF), and the anemic growth of the early 2000s, Indonesia is positively buoyant now, with annual growth rates hovering above 6 per cent from 2010 to 2012.[12]

For Asian solidarity, Nehru and Sukarno were the founding fathers. It was consolidated through Bandung in 1955. They along with three other great personalities of Ghana, Egypt and Yugoslavia, formed The Non-Aligned Movement (NAM) together. But it unfortunately was not duly translated into the realms of bilateral relations. Treaty of friendship was signed in March 1951, which opened the door for active defence co-operation. This was followed by three agreements in the 1950s for intensive exchanges for military co-operation. Nehru extended support to Indonesia's counter-insurgency

---

[12] Paige Johnson Tan, 2013, "Yudhoyono's Legacy; Between Politics & Principle," *Current History* , September, p. 234.

campaign at home, and the two held their first naval exercises in 1960. Till the advent of Look East Policy in 1992 bilateral relations between these two big countries of Asia remained routine. Many bilateral treaties in the realm of defence co-operation were made but unfortunately their compliance was not adequate.

Maritime security must be the key of future relationship between both countries. India and Indonesia are the 9th and 16th largest economies of the globe, respectively. Their over 80 per cent trade is sea borne. It needs to be duly protected. Since last one decade this co-operation is going on well but due to changing demands it needs overhauling. Political will is required to fulfil these essential requirements. It will provide a win–win situation for both the countries. In 2012 India's trade with ASEAN was US $ 80 billion which is slated to touch US $ 200 billion by 2022. For the realization of this target and wider necessity of Indian foreign policy, India–Indonesia bonhomie is utmost required. Indonesia–India trade is increasing sharply. The fact that India has become Indonesia's second largest coal-export destination after China is significant. In 2010 12, total volume of coal-export doubled from 40 to 70 million tons.[13] Economic interdependence should deliver strategic ramifications given both countries are also Indian Ocean littoral neighbours. The two countries, along with Australia, could establish a trilateral strategic dialogue on issues of common concern to complement the Indian Ocean Rim Association for Regional Co-operation (IOR-ARC). Sea lanes security must be the focal agenda of these dialogue processes due to growing importance of energy as the driver of sustainable growth.

The growing dissent among ASEAN countries against China on South China Sea issue and China's assertiveness has

---

13 "India and Indonesia Aim to Double Trade", *BBC News*, 25 January 2011.

reminded ASEAN countries of the incidents of 1960s and 1970s. They wanted multi-polarity in this crucial region and do not want to accept Chinese hegemony. The South China Sea is in the middle of the maritime stretch running from the Eastern Indian Ocean to the Western Pacific. Indian politician and strategists, as well as American and Australian figures have started using the term Indo-Pacific in the past few years for these adjacent waters.[14] For India, the South China Sea region gains salience in terms of its trade with the Asia-Pacific region. Nearly 55 per cent of India's trade transits through the straits of Malacca choke points to and from the South China Sea. India has already expanded its Look East Policy with its emerging presence in the South China Sea. According to Raja Mohan, one of the seminal contemporary strategic thinkers:

> New Delhi's "Look East" policy was acquired a distinct naval dimension, then, between the Indian Ocean and the Pacific are beginning to blur. . . . With a growing economy and expanding naval capabilities, India is more self-assured in the way it thinks about the ocean spaces around it. India is now looking beyond Strait of Malacca to include the South China Sea in its national security calculus.[15]

Indonesia's leading role in South-East Asia, together with its geographical position as the gatekeeper between the Indian and Pacific oceans, might make it indispensable regional partners for India. A broad-based defence co-operation between both countries could transform India's role in South-East Asia. Deepening of relationship with Indonesia will be strengthening India's posture on South China Sea because Indonesia is also one disputant country against China over

---

[14] Scott, 2012, "The Indo-Pacific New Regional Formulations and New Maritime Frameworks for US-India Strategic Convergences", *Asia-Pacific Review*, **19**(2): November 85-109.

[15] Raja Mohan, 2011, "India and Australia: Maritime Partners in the Indo-Pacific", *Asialink Essays*, November **3**(7): 2-3.

South China Sea. Indonesia is a big country within ASEAN region and intends to keep the region as multiple entities, therefore it is in its interest to ensure Indian presence in the region.

The US dominates the globe as a unipolar power. The US is also encouraging India to assume a greater role in the South-East Asian balance of power, including developing its defence relationships with US allies and friends in the region. Washington is also actively promoting the idea of Indo-Pacific as a single security region, which justifies India playing a greater defence and political role in East Asia/Pacific. In longer terms this includes potentially assuming a direct security role in the Malacca Strait and the South China Sea. The US hopes that India might become an important political partner in East Asia, which can help bolster its efforts to tamper with China's raising strategic aspirations.

China is willing to covert its new-found economic autonomy into military power particularly in the domain of Navy. The deepening trust deficit between the US and China, and Japan and China in one hand, and between ASEAN countries and China on the other hand on the issue of South China and East China Sea has further deteriorated the situation. The US has already declared its Pivot Asia policies and hell bent to contain China from capturing its space on the larger canvass of Asia-Pacific. It has also rung the alarm bell among ASEAN countries particularly on their stakes in South China Sea.

Meanwhile, India and Indonesia have stepped up their maritime co-operation to garner maximum benefits from this situation. The Indonesian and Indian navies conduct co-ordinated maritime patrols on their common maritime border on a regular basis. Jakarta perceives the establishment of a Joint Command at Port Blair in the Andaman islands in a positive light, as it could contribute to greater monitoring of the northern approaches to the Malacca Strait, providing prompt assistance when needed, as well as to increase bilateral co-operative activities, like joint exercises and patrols with the Indonesian Naval Western Fleet Command. The INDINDOCORPAT, for example, has seen Indonesian navy warship visiting Port Blair more often and the Indian Navy has reciprocated by visiting Indonesia's local naval command centres in Sabang and Belawan in northern Sumatra. Indonesia also participates in India led multilateral naval exercises such as MILAN and SAREX exercises, and the Indian Ocean Naval Symposium (IONS). In the aftermath of 2004 tsunami, Jakarta highly appreciated Indian Navy's "Operation Gambhir" in January 2005 to send food and medicinal supplies to Indonesia through its hospital ship INS Nirupak and a corvette INS Khukri.[16] Recently, India offered Indonesia the establishment of a formal maritime domain information-sharing arrangement between the two navies.[17] Such an arrangement could improve awareness along their shared maritime boundaries in the Andaman Sea and Indian Ocean. More bilateral co-operation is required in this arena. It will fulfil the interests of both the countries.

Conclusion

During 1960s South-East Asia perceived India as a natural strategic partner and a potential security guarantor, consistent with its principles of non-alignment. But India refused to participate in any such proposed security arrangements.[18] It

---

16 Vibhanshu Sekhar, 2007, "India-Indonesia Relations; An Overview", *IPCS Special Report*, New Delhi, no. 38, March.

17 Sitanshu Kar, 2012, "India and Indonesia Agree to Significantly Step Up Defense Cooperation", *Press Information Bureau of India*, 16 October.

18 Ajay Kumar Das, 2013, "Soft & Hard Power in India's Strategy Toward Southeast Asia", *India Review*, **12**(3): 151.

was Nehru's obsession with idealism, which proved detrimental for Indian interests. With the Look East Policy, India has corrected those blunders and has established strong relationship with South-East Asian countries in general and with Indonesia in particular.

India is a member of all important forums of South-East and East Asia. ASEAN–India annual summits are also working well. Trade is growing at par with the expectations. The December 2012 New Delhi India–ASEAN summit is an important step in this direction. India must be proactive in this significant region for both economic and strategic reasons. It was expressed very nicely in an editorial of *Jakarta Times:*

> The evolving geo-strategic framework inexorably impels countries in South-East Asia to accept China and India as major regional powers. In the first case, it is necessary consequence of the former. . . . Beijing has also shown an unequaled zest in its economic diplomacy with the Association of South-East Asian Nations (ASEAN). Delhi on the other hand has been a late bloomer. . . . ASEAN wants India's presence as much as India needs to be active in the region. . . . ASEAN makes available a strategic framework and regulated forum which India can bluntly interact with economic powers Japan and South Korea along with fellow regional power China. This is an opportunity in which Delhi must not be hesitant. It cannot afford to miss the boat again.[19]

India's relationship with Indonesia through not adequately developed may be a key factor to its strategic role in South-East Asia in coming years.[20] New Delhi has long perceived Indonesia, the dominant state in the archipelagic South-East Asia, as being a linchpin of any strategy to constrain Chinese

[19] "Is India Ready to be a part of Southeast Asia Again?", Editorial, *Jakarta Post,* 18 June 2007.

[20] Dvid Brewstar, 2011, "The Evolving Security Relationship between India and Indonesia", *Asian Survey,* March/April, **51**(2): 221-44.

influence in South-East Asia.[21] Indonesia is by far the largest state in South-East Asia and is regarded as *primus inter pares* in ASEAN. It represents a big market for Indian exports as well as major supplier of resources due to the changing profile of Indian development. A close relationship with Indonesia would enhance India's role in the region as well as helping India to develop its own relationship across South-East Asia. Indonesia's historical concern about China also makes it potentially important partner in balancing China's economic, political and strategic influence in East Asia. As Kautilya has stressed that foreign policy is shaped by the convergences of interests, fortunately, India and Indonesia have convergences on gamut of issues. Therefore, they must enhance their maritime co-operation. It has not only the potential to transform the bilateral relations between India and Indonesia but it has also a big potential to add new fillip for the success of India's Look East Policy in a transformative manner. The development of a broad-based relationship with Indonesia would require a major political, economic and security commitment by New Delhi that has so far not been adequate. Deepening maritime co-operation could be a game changer for the overall security and economic relationship with Indonesia in particular and rest South-East Asia in general. Needless to say those deepening joint maritime security efforts will also contain piracy and will ensure the safety on the Sea Lanes of Communication.

---

21 C. Raja Mohan, 2011, "India and Indonesia: A New Strategic Partnership?", *RSIS Commentary*, no. 10, 1 February, p. 36, http://www.rsis.edu.sg/publications/Perspective/RSIS0102011.pdf (accessed on 10 November 2012).

19

India–Indonesia Science and Technological Collaboration
Prospects

Son Kuswadi
Gautam Kumar Jha

Introduction

SINCE its inception as a nation state India stressed on solving its basic needs and problems by emphasizing on the higher education of science and technology. It had to come over with numerous challenges, i.e. to feed one of the largest populations in the world, to counter aggressive neighbourhood, i.e. China and Pakistan, and also emerge at par with the developed countries in the world. Jawaharlal Nehru, the first prime minister of India (1947-64) initiated various reforms in higher education, science and technology. Having closer ties with the Soviet Union initially, it realized the dreams of producing state-of-the-art technologies which fulfilled the needs of the mass.

The foundations of Indian Institute of Technology (IIT), Indian Space Research Organization (ISRO), Bhabha Atomic Research Centre (BARC), and All India Institute of Medical Sciences (AIIMS), were few examples of Nehru's progressive thinking.

Historical evidences show that India was a hub for higher education for the overseas scholars. It had already discovered the concept of gravity and atom during the second or sixth century BCE (as per the two sources) by Maharishi Kanada.[1] Panini, the Sanskrit grammarian and mathematician from ancient India (fourth century BCE), whose work on grammar the *Ashtadhyayi* is one of the earliest known grammars of Sanskrit to be used in the modern-day computer science.[2] Thus, India only needed the right platform and apt infrastructure to launch itself.

There are scores of fields in the science and technologies where India can collaborate with Indonesia for various positive developments. Geographical and cultural proximity makes the atmosphere conducive for both the countries to collaborate each other. With Indian investment in Indonesia surpassing US $ 20 billion mostly in the field of power, automotive, and cooking oil, the two countries' target of US $ 25 billion bilateral trade by 2015 does not seem to be a far-fetched objective seeing the increase in the trade volume during 2007-08–2010-11 (Table 19.1).[3]

Table 19: 1 Trade Volume between India and Indonesia during 2007-11[4]

Year	Trade volume $ in million	% of Growth
2007-08	19,421	2.95
2008-09	30,751	58.34
2009-10	41,009	33.36
2010-11	45,136	10.06

1 http://en.wikipedia.org/wiki/Kanada accessed on 27 June 2014, Delhi.

2 file:///C:/Users/USER/Downloads/parulrrst2011-9091-25181-1-PB.pdf accessed on 27th June 2014, Delhi.

3 http://www.bbc.co.uk/news/world-asia-pacific-12274815 Accessed on 28 June 2014, Delhi.

4 http://dgciskol.nic.in/annualreport/book_3e.pdf accessed on 5 July 2014, Delhi.

The recent space activities have placed India among the peer group of few countries in the world and the same has immensely inspired Indonesia. In near future the Indonesian government can take advantage of the present cordial relations with India in exchanging the know-how in space technology.[5]

The Mangalayana, the Indian Mars orbiter which was launched into earth's orbit in November 2013 by ISRO has been travelling at a speed of 1.55 km per second and expected to reach the Mars orbit on 24 September 2014,[6] is still in current news and the whole world is waiting to see the "mission complete day". The significant aspect in the entire process of launching of the Mangalayana is its cost. The world was surprised to know the cost of the entire project — US $ 76 million — which is incredibly cheaper as compared to a Hollywood space science fiction movie *Gravity* which costed US $ 100 million.[7] These successes led ISRO to commercialize the technologies and they have recently launched five foreign satellites onboard the Polar Satellite Launch Vehicle (PSLV-C23) in June this year.[8, 9]

---

5 K.S. Jayaraman, "Fully Domestic Indian Rocket Launches Geo Satellite", *SpaceNews*, 5 January 2014 http://www.spacenews.com/article/launch-report/38925fully-domestic-indian-rocket-launches-geo-satellite, accesed on 17 June 2014.

6 Mars Orbiter Mission, Wikipedia http://en.wikipedia.org/wiki/Mars_Orbiter_Mission, accesed on 17 June 2014.

7 Gravity movie budget: US $ 100 million. Indian Mars Mission: US $ 72.9 million, *Volcan Post*, http://vulcanpost.com/4263/gravity-movie-budget-us100-million-indian-mars-mission-us72-9-million/ accessed on 17 June 2014.

8 http://timesofindia.indiatimes.com/city/bangalore/Isro-to-launch-5-foreign-satellites-on-June-30/articleshow/36911712.cms accessed on 6 June 2014, Delhi.

9 T.E. Narasimhan, "ISRO to launch 5 satellites for Antrix this Month", *Business Standard*, 17 June 2014 http://www.business-standard.com/article/current-affairs/isro-to-launch-5-satellites-for-antrix-this-month-114061300487_1.html , accessed on 17 June 2014.

As technologies are being improved in India, there has been rapid advancements in automobile, engineering, pharmaceutical, health care, media, entertainment and telecommunication sectors as well. Media and Entertainment (ME) industry, especially Indian film industry, has already established its strong global foot. According to the Ministry of Information & Broadcasting (MIB), this sector is estimated to have generated about US $ 17.8 billion in revenue in 2010, which is projected to grow at 19 per cent per annum to reach US $ 25.2 billion in 2012.[10]

Indian government declared 2010-20 as the "Decade of Innovations", which prompted the whole world being optimistic towards India's future. As per *Economic Times Report*, multinational companies present in India have set up more than 750 R&D centres across the country for the last twenty years with added advantage of vast talent pool of young professionals from the top science and technology institutions.[11] Moreover, India is a highly attractive destination for the investors due to competitiveness in the labour cost and inexpensive manufacturing capabilities.

The 2014 election was fought on the core issue of progress and development. India still faces challenges such as poverty, corruption and poor infrastructure, despite it being globally acclaimed for rapid economic growth in the last decade.[12]

There is a great need of potential strategic partnership between India and Indonesia. India equipped with achievements in science and technologies and Indonesia having

---

10 http://www.ey.com/Publication/vwLUAssets/Entertainment_economy_of_India/$FILE/Indias-Entertainment-Economy_Oct_%202011_.pdf accessed on 25 July 2014.

11 "Innovation in India: Opportunities and Challenges", ASSOCHAM, 2013, http://www.assocham.org/publications/genpub/php, accessed on 27 July 2014.

12 J. Dreze, A. Sen, "An Uncertain Glory: India and Its Contradiction", Penguin, 2013.

abundant natural resources can come together for the welfare of mankind.[13]

Collaboration Achieved

AGREEMENTS IN THE PAST

Indonesia and India signed an MoU on 29 December 1955 that envisaged many programmes and consequently the signed agreements were realized. One of the such programmes, MTech degree programme in Water Resources Management for Indonesian engineers at the University of Roorkee (now IIT Roorkee) was immediately started. Indian scientist and engineers visited Indonesia for several co-operation and research programmes related to agriculture, family planning, illiteracy eradication, etc.

The co-operation was then extended to science and technology field, by establishing the India–Indonesia Joint Committee on Scientific and Technical Cooperation co-chaired by the Secretary of the Department of Science and Technology, Government of India and the Secretary, Ministry of State for Research and Technology, Government of Indonesia in February 1982 in Jakarta.

SPACE TECHNOLOGY

On 7 December 2000, an agreement reached by co-chairman of the Joint Committee in the area of co-operation and modalities for implementation of various activities in science and technology. An MoU regarding research and technology

---

[13] The prime minister of India and the president of Indonesia expressed satisfaction at the steady growth of political, security, economic, science and technology and cultural exchanges between the two countries, see the Joint Statement of both leaders during the State Visit of President of the Republic of Indonesia Dr Susilo Bambang Yudhoyono during 24-26 January 2011 and as the chief guest on the occasion of India's Republic Day on 26 January 2011.

was signed by Muhammad A.S. Hikam, Minister of State for Research and Technology of Indonesia and Ajit Kumar Panja, Minister of State for External Affairs of India. The MoU then renewed and signed by Suharna Surapranata, Minister of State for Research and Technology of Government of Indonesia and T. Ramasami, Secretary, Department of Science and Technology, Government of India, during President S. Bambang Yudhoyono's state visit on 25 January 2011.

Based on the MoU, several collaborations were implemented such as space technology co-operation between National Institute of Aeronautics and Space (LAPAN), Indonesia and the ISRO. Both the agencies signed an MoU in 2002, and accordingly ISRO built Telemetry, Tracking and Command (TTC) Station in Biak (West Papua, Indonesia). LAPAN also launched its LAPAN TUBSAT nano satellite using PSLV launcher of ISRO in 2008. Another LAPAN satellite such as LAPAN A2 and LAPAN-Orari are already in pipeline to be launched. Nano satellite that jointly built by six Indonesian universities/institutions under INSPIRE Project will also be launched by ISRO launcher.[14] A remote sensing data reception from IRS satellite will jointly be developed at the Prepare Ground Station, Indonesia.

fig. 19.1: Ambassador visits ISRO headquarters in Bengaluru

[14] Meeting between INSPIRE Project team of Indonesia and ISRO was held on 28 December 2012 at ISRO headquarters in Bengaluru, to finalize the planning of nano satellite launching.

fig. 19.2: Annual governing board meeting of CSSTEAP

Centre for Space Science and Technology Education in Asia and the Pacific (CSSTEAP) was established in 1995 as a multilateral collaboration among Asia-Pacific nations in the field of space, science and education, which was hosted by India having the LAPAN chairman as one of Governing Board. Several Indonesian engineers pursued their research and studied at the centre through the Indian Institute of Remote Sensing (IIRS) at Dehradun, Space Application Centre (SAC) at Ahmedabad and Physical Research Laboratory (PRL) at Ahmedabad.[15]

INFORMATION & COMMUNICATION TECHNOLOGY (ICT)

India is well known for its achievements in the field of ICT. It began to evolve in the 1980s, with few small companies offering application and maintenance services to client overseas and gradually it turned to be the primary driver of growth in Indian economy for the last two decades. The sector's contribution to the country's GDP was around 6.4 per cent in 2010-11. It added 240,000 new jobs in the same year, taking total number of employees to 2.54 million. The IT industry grew by 19 per cent to the tune of US $ 76 billion.

As stated above, the key success of IT industry in India is because of the abundant skilled human resource, adept in technical knowledge. Therefore, it is invaluable if we can collaborate in this sector, i.e. IT education.

15 CSSTEAP, http://cssteap.org accessed on 23 June 2014.

One of the institutes in the field of IT is the International Institute of Information Technology (IIIT), Bengaluru, located in Electronic City which is financed and supported by the state government and leading IT companies like Cisco, HP and Microsoft. IIIT offers only post-graduate and doctorate degrees. The high quality of research enables students to get exposed to the real-time problems of the IT industry which further help the IT companies when they recruit such experienced scholars. When we visited the IIIT in November 2012, its director offered us that they would support ten Indonesian students a year in order to develop a real-time and robust software. We needed such a team that these students would be trained to handle a real-time project and after returning to Indonesia, they would work together to develop the IT industry there.

DEFENCE INDUSTRY

The nature of Indian defence equipment is about 30 per cent indigenous production and they are willing to increase up to 70 per cent in the long-term interest of their defence need.[16]

India's defence industry has been growing substantially recently. Growth of domestic demand is steadily increasing due to governmental policy. The Narendra Modi administration, as part of its national strategy for local defence production, is likely to give a major boost to hi-tech and high value-added defence export through incentives in the upcoming Foreign Trade Policy (FTP) for 2014-19.[17] India's defence export during 2010-12 were just US $ 183 million.

The BJP manifesto with focus on job and asset creation, besides increasing private sector participation in the sector

---

16 A.P.J. Abdul Kalam and Y.S. Rajan, *India 2020: A Vision for the New Millenium*, New Delhi: Penguin Books India, 1998, p. 192.

17 Narendra Modi government flexes arms, pushes for high-value export, 100 per cent FDI in defence, *The Indian Express*, New Delhi, 31 May 2014.

and strengthening the Defence Research and Development Organization (DRDO) is implemented, it is bound to take Indian economy further.

India as a new entry in the defence industry needs trusted partners who are open minded in collaboration not only in the production side but also in R&D. For example, Skanda Aerospace, Hyderabad, was established seventeen years before with a total investment of US $ 100 million for making integrated defence system. Their focus is on manufacturing defence system as well as refurbishment of defence systems. They are very keen to establish joint venture in Indonesia, including R&D facilities to develop a new defence system. Also, they are willing to transfer their technology on designing new device as well as re-engineering component. Meanwhile, Indonesia also has plenty of defence industries such as PT PINDAD, PT Dahana, PT PAL, and IPTN and they are looking appropriate partners abroad to work closely.

AGRICULTURE

Concerns related to food security will remain a global issue for the next fifty years and beyond. Meanwhile a climate change is a crucial factor to determine food security in many regions in India.[18] A rapid growth of population is a significant factor in developing agriculture to meet the increasing demand, necessitating innovation in this sector. With 1.2 billion of population, India has to ensure food for its people.

Government spent was increased in the Union Budget 2013-14 to US $ 4.98 billion. Meanwhile private sector also played an important role. For example "The White Revolution" initiated by Dr V. Kurien makes India as one of the largest

---

[18] P.S. Brahmanand et al., "Challenges to food security in India", *Current Science*, **104**(7), 10 April 2013: 842-46.

milk producers by establishing a national milk grid.[19] Another example of success story is the one which called as "precision farming" that focused on utilizing resources optimally to improve the quality and quantity of crops, while lowering the cost of production.

The use of ICT in agriculture in rural area is also intensified. For example, "AGRIWATCH" employs rural service providers, providing location-specific information to farmers including supply and demand trends and technical expert's advice related to cultivation, etc.

By considering the history of Indian government to maintain its food security, it is important for Indonesia to study India's achievement in innovations while maintaining the ecosystem with the help of technology in agriculture and implement the same accordingly.

ENGINEERING

According to a study conducted by NASSCOM and Booz Allen Hamilton, India accounted for about 28 per cent of all available engineering service outsourcing talent in low-cost countries.[20] Expenditure on engineering services, which totalled US $ 750 billion in 2004, is projected to reach US $ 1.1 trillion by 2020. According to *Dataquest* research, of the total engineering R&D service revenues in 2009, third party Indian service providers — including HCL Tech, TCS and Wipro — contributed 58 per cent, captive engineering services unit accounted for 40 per cent, while non-Indian IT players captured the remaining 2 per cent. Automotive, telecom and aerospace are the major verticals currently spending heavily on outsourcing engineering services.

---

19 Innovation in India: Opportunities and Challenges, ASSOCHAM, 2013.

20 The Best of India in Services, India Brand Equity Foundation (IBEF), p. 18.

Based on the above figure, first, it is invaluable for Indonesia to do benchmarking on how India could supply qualified manpower for its engineering services.[21] Second, Indonesia should carefully select Indian partners to be involved in its industries like aircraft, telecommunications, automobile to boost the production and to lower the production cost. Third, to invite Indian partners to collaborate in setting up R&D centres in Indonesia with local counterparts.

Conclusion

Indonesia–India relationship in science and technology has already taken a strong leap. Further collaboration in the sectors like space science, defence, agriculture and engineering can yield promising results.

There are many steps needed to bring the collaboration into a meaningful result. It must be started by a strong policy commitment from both countries' leaders, followed by firm and realistic co-operation, mutually advantageous.

21 Under PMO, India set up skill council for several sectors, including IT, telecommunication, automotive to provide a massive training and certification for youngsters to meet the market demand.